The Dilemma of Prison Reform

The Dilemma of Prison Reform

Thomas O. Murton

Department of Criminal Justice Studies
University of Minnesota

Holt, Rinehart and Winston
New York

Library of Congress Cataloging in Publication Data

Murton, Tom.
   The dilemma of prison reform.

    1. Prisons—United States. 2. Corrections—United States. I. Title.
HV9471.M87   365'.7'0973   75-25788
ISBN 0-03-013076-X

Copyright © 1976 by Holt, Rinehart and Winston

All rights reserved.

Printed in the United States of America
6 7 8 9   059   4 3 2

*In memory of the late Joseph D. Lohman,
whose personal experiences regarding
the cyclical nature of political reform movements
inspired my interest in prison reform
and resulted in this work.*

In 1933, when the Communists were imprisoned, I did not lift my voice. I did not say to my congregation, "Be on your guard. There is something wrong happening here." And when the feeble-minded were murdered, I said to myself, "Am I to be the guardian of the feeble-minded?" I could not even claim that I was ignorant of the persecution of the Jews, but I did nothing. I only started speaking out when the faith of the Church was persecuted. For this neglect I am greatly to blame. I have sinned.

— Pastor Martin Niemoller
(Nazi Germany)

Contents

Preface		xi
Prologue		xvii
Chapter 1	The Evolution of Penology in the United States	1
	Punitive Sanctions	2
	Banishment	
	Corporal Punishment	
	Capital Punishment	
	The Deterrent Effect of Capital Punishment	
	The Origins and Evolution of Penal Institutions	5
	The Prison	
	National Prison Association	
	The Reformatory	
	Prison Labor Systems in America	
	Penal Reform	14
	Early Reform Efforts	
	Modern Reform Efforts	
	General Description of the Penal System Today	18
	Crime Trends	
	Jails	
	Felony Institutions	
	Ratio of Prisoners to General Population	
	Prisoner Characteristics	
	Summary	24
Chapter 2	Prisons in America: Conditions after 100 Years of "Reform"	29
	Oregon	30
	California	31
	Kansas	33
	Arkansas	35
	Indiana	38
	Ohio	40
	Florida	44
	New York	46
	The Attica Atrocity	48
Chapter 3	The Traditional Prison Model	53
	The Dogma of Penology	54
	Dealing with the Dogma	56
	The Reality of Rehabilitation	60

	The Traditional Prison Model in Practice	65
	The Fiction of Prison Control	
	The Case of Harold A. Porter	
	The Case of Edward F. Roberts	
	The Medical Model: The "Treatment" Game	
	Confrontation Is the Norm	
Chapter 4	The Facade of Reform	77
	After the "Disturbance": Initial Reforms	78
	Methods of Reform	79
	The "Blue Ribbon Committee"	
	The Consultant	
	The Recommendations	
	Pseudo-Reform	86
	The Reality is a Facade	
	Tokenism	
	Fraud	
	Consequences of the Facade	92
Chapter 5	Anatomy of Reform Efforts	97
	Abdication of Leadership	99
	The Correctional Administrator	
	Bureaucratization	101
	No Room for Dissidents	
	Conformity of Thought	
	An Answer Without a Question	
Chapter 6	Functional Roles in Prison Reform	111
	Internal Roles	112
	The Neophyte	
	The Careerist	
	The Warrior	
	The Therapist	
	The Curator	
	The Diplomat	
	Summary	
	External Roles	120
	The Oracle	
	The Prophet	
	The Prostitute	
	Characterizations	123
	The Clark Kent Syndrome	125
	Summary	125

Chapter 7	The Spiral Nature of Reform Movements	131
	The Alaska Division of Corrections	133
	The Alaska Jail System	
	The Youth and Adult Authority	
	The Effects of Compromise	
	The Results of Reform Efforts	
	The Arkansas Department of Correction	146
	The Decadent Past	
	Reform Efforts	
	Regression of Reform	
	The Cycle of Hopelessness	
	The Spiral of Reform: A Theory	160
Chapter 8	The Substance of Real Reform	163
	Assumptions	165
	Postulates	169
	Philosophy	171
	Characteristics	173
	Methodology	175
	Ramifications	179
	The Gradualism Theory	180
	The Impact of Real Reform	185
	The Official Reformer	
	The Staff	
	The Inmates	
	The Real Reformer	
	The System	
Chapter 9	Participatory Government: An Alternative Prison Managerial Model	189
	A New Prison Community	191
	Inmate Guards	
	Participatory Management	194
	Alexander Maconochie (1787–1860)	
	Thomas Mott Osborne (1859–1926)	
	Howard B. Gill (born 1889)	
	Thomas O. Murton (born 1928)	
	Summary	220
Chapter 10	An Alternative Correctional Regime	227
	Personnel	229
	Organizational Structure	232
	An Alternative Correctional System	233
	The Village	
	Programs	

Chapter 11	Reformation or Revolution?	249
	The Penologists	250
	The Professionals	252
	The Professional Association	258
	The Scholars	266
	The Courts	270
	Summary	276
Epilogue:	Reflections on Reform	281

Preface

One might reasonably ask, "Why study the prison?" Most penologists would respond with statistics indicating that 95 percent of prison inmates ultimately return to the street. The more astute observer would avow that *all* inmates except those who die in the prison system will return one day to the free society. Self-preservation would dictate that concern for oneself should inspire the citizen to take a personal interest in reforming the prison.

Furthermore, perhaps one should examine the quandary in which the penologists find themselves in attempting to implement the various mandates imposed on the prison administrator. The warden is charged with the responsibility of concurrently instituting the philosophies of punishment, deterrence, retribution, incapacitation, and rehabilitation. But there may be an even more basic reason to become informed about the prison: if one wishes to study a culture and to understand it, attention should be focused on the manner in which that society deals with its deviants.

> *The prison is the American society in microcosm.*

Examination of the prison provides a unique opportunity to study, observe, and analyze the manipulation and exploitation of man, as well as the harshness, bitterness, and underlying greed that motivate both staff and inmates in the prison community. If for no other reason, the prison should be scrutinized as a cultural phenomenon in order to examine the coarseness of human relationships without the facade of respectability that so often masks our freeworld relationships and blocks comprehension of human behavior.

Anyone who has had much contact with the field of penology, either in person or through the literature, becomes convinced that the general mode of "reform" is a long journey consisting of gradual improvements of the existing system. He becomes equally impressed with the fact that even after nearly a two-century quest for prison reform, it thus far has not been achieved. Real reform emerges from time to time only to be suppressed. The student of penology will note brief references to real reform islands along the journey. After a mutiny, the prison ship may anchor temporarily in the harbor of real reform until control is reestablished. But then the traditional prison ship will cast off and set sail for the *mirage* of real reform on the horizon.

Reform of penal practices has often appeared to follow the motto "Do something, even if it proves to be wrong." Penal measures have evolved through banishment, exile, death, corporal punishment, and institutionalization. Man eventually devised a variety of brutal techniques in an effort to suppress crime, but these have served only to escalate the war between the keepers and the kept.

The evolution of the penal system in the United States has really been a story of one alternative after another. Corporal punishment rose as a pragmatic alternative to hanging. The prison was created as an alternative to corporal punishment. To compensate for the defects of the prison, the reformatory was erected with goals of teaching, training, and curing the offender. Yet eventually it too became another prison in appearance and practice. And still other alternatives were sought.

Noninstitutional treatment in the form of probation and parole became more sophisticated. The minimum-custody camp came into existence. A host of other "correctional" fads have been tried with no more demonstrated success in halting criminality than their forerunners. Nonetheless halfway houses, reception and diagnostic centers, prerelease centers, and, more recently, community correctional centers have been heralded as reforms.

Juxtaposed on this morass of institutions has been a multitude of "programs" of varying ideology, quality, and effectiveness in aiding "rehabilitation." For our juvenile offenders, a system parallel to the adult prison system has been developed. We have changed the words describing prisons and criminals over the decades, but a rose by any other name still has thorns.

Unfortunately, these penological fads have dissipated energies, diffused the attack on criminality, confused legislators, deluded the public, and primarily have served to create more positions for staff while providing minimal improvement in goods and services for inmates. According to the American Correctional Association, over 95 percent of all corrections budgets in the United States in 1970 were allocated for those considerations having directly to do with custody of prisoners. Only the remaining 5 percent was directed toward "treatment" programs.

If past experience is the best indicator of future patterns, then an examination of the antecedents of events could establish causal relationships. Once identified, obstacles to reform of systems can be overcome; or so one would conjecture. But it often appears that a study of history only reveals that man is apparently destined to act out the drama of life as if he were plowing new ground.

The question of whether prisons should exist or not is a moot point. Although a strong argument can be made by the abolitionists that the "walls should come down," prisons *do* exist and are likely to continue for the foreseeable future. In fact, for some criminal offenders there probably always will be a need for secure detention. Until the walls do come down (if ever), it appears productive for reformers to set forth an analysis of the present system and to offer some alternative modes of management.

In attempting to explain what this book is all about, it might be productive to say what it is *not*. It is not offered as a comparative study of penology. Its purpose is to answer the question: Why has prison reform not been attained after at least one hundred years of sincere efforts by generally well-meaning, experienced individuals? A secondary purpose is to provide some insight into the cyclical nature of reform movements in general and to explain why they do not achieve their objectives.

The method chosen to answer the research question is historical. The focus is on identifying the real problems. As suggested by the title, the two dimensions of the investigation are the substance of reform and the dilemmas in trying to achieve it. The history of penology is traced to provide a basis for examining contemporary prison conditions. The traditional prison management model with its facade of reform and the resultant role models for staff are contrasted with the substance of real reform. The cyclical nature of reform movements based on two case studies of real reform efforts is postulated in a theory of reform.

Analysis of the system as it is and a synthesis of successful efforts at participatory management lead to suggestions for an alternative correctional structure. A cautionary note is added lest the real reformers place hope in the traditional reform agents outside the prison system, such as the courts, the professional association, and the academicians. The book concludes with some reflections on reform.

The primary sources of material for this treatise are *The Freeworld Times*, contemporary literature, and the author's personal experiences. *The Freeworld Times* was a national prison reform newspaper published by The Murton Foundation for Criminal Justice, Inc., between 1972 and 1974. The contributors—including penologists, inmates, practitioners, scholars, and laymen—probably have provided the best description of contemporary conditions and issues related to prisons and their reform.

Current research from a variety of sources is included to support conclusions drawn in the book. These evaluations are drawn from criminology, psychology, and sociology. In addition, wardens, penologists, and authorities in other fields are quoted to allow the system to define itself.

Finally, some of the author's experiences are included with the acknowledged hazard that they will appear to be self-serving. The Alaska and Arkansas experiences are relevant, and it is perhaps unfortunate that there are not other examples to demonstrate the point being made. The fact that the author was a participant in these movements is not important; the reader's attention is focused on the activities and the implications they have for reform movements. The editorial device of attempting to disguise the obvious by using the third person was deemed less than honest, so this material is presented as a first-person description.

Many individuals have contributed both to the substantive content of this book and to shaping the author's conclusions about the nature of reform, conclusions that have been formulated over the past 20 years. These unknown soldiers of reform include countless prison officials, officers, inmates, and, most importantly, the author's formidable critics who have unintentionally forced a refinement and reevaluation of his notions about real reform.

In addition to Joe Lohman, to whom this book is dedicated, special acknowledgment is given to Dr. Richard Korn for his incisive criticism of the manuscript. His assistance has been valuable in crystallizing the author's thinking, but it should not be construed as his endorsement of either the analysis or conclusions. In concise terms, these conclusions state that real reform is not a function of more money, more staff, more programs, or more studies. There must be other factors that affect reform movements. It seems that reform, or lack thereof, is a function of organizational structures, techniques of problem solving, moral courage, integrity, and vision.

What is needed at this time, after a century of "prison reform," is basic research and penologists with the courage to challenge the sacred, but unproven, tenets of penology. The entire philosophy of corrections must be reevaluated. Attention should be focused on the prison, for therein lies the greatest need and possibly the greatest potential for revolution. Contrary to popular opinion, we do have some evidence of what will work.

In essence, this book is a critique of reform movements in general. The theoretical implications for strategies of change apply to a range of disciplines beyond criminology. The book's significance depends on its application by those would-be reformers who have the courage to "dream of things that never were and ask 'Why not?' "

Tom Murton

Prologue

The Orbital Nature of Prison Reform Movements
OR
Why We Can't Get There from Here

In order to get an idea of the nature of reform efforts in the United States, envision a planetary model that is composed of Planet Earth (the present location of the prison), a rocket ship (representing the prison itself), and the Planet Real Reform (the destination of the prison).

Certain hazards are inherent in the operation of the prison rocket ship if it is kept standing on the launching pad. The captain most certainly will tire of plotting and replotting the course while waiting for the countdown signaling the movement toward Real Reform. The crew (staff) will become restive and complain of the monotony of checking and rechecking the systems to reconfirm that the vessel is ready. The prisoner-passengers will pass the time by reading periodic information bulletins issued by Mission Control extolling the virtues of the destination and the in-flight activities designed to entertain them en route. Unfortunately, the rocket ship has been on the launching pad for ages, and the hazards are almost impossible to avoid.

During a guided tour through the ship, a visitor comments that the ship is firmly bolted to the pad; some of the passengers overhear this comment and question if they have mistakenly boarded the wrong vessel. Cabin attendants attempt to allay these fears by directing the passengers' attention to the reflection of the rocket engines through the windows. But eventually it becomes apparent that the rosy glow reflected on the cabin ceiling is caused by a multi-colored spotlight beamed through the cabin windows by Mission Control. Later, an inquisitive passenger enters the engine compartment only to discover that the thunderous roar of the "engines" is created by an amplified Muzak sound track from a previously aborted launching.

The passengers reexamine their tickets and discover that the destination is "Nowhere" instead of "Real Reform." Angry over the fraud and deception, they attack the crew, seize the captain as hostage, and demand to be taken "Somewhere." If the Mission

Controller cannot or will not issue the necessary orders to rectify the situation, he may be run off by the spectators who paid admission to see an actual launch.

A new Mission Controller is then chosen to direct the destiny of the entire space reform program. He promptly appoints concerned spectators as a Blue Ribbon Committee to determine why the launching was not accomplished. While the committee is examining the site, the Mission Controller submits an emergency request for funds to build a new vessel instead of removing the bolts that anchor the current ship to the pad. These two tactics provide sufficient time for him to conduct his own investigation and attend to more pressing problems relating to the air conditioning in the control center.

An expert consultant (someone from out of town) is chosen to assist in the inquiry. He examines the prison vessel, suggests methods of preparing it for the voyage, and charts a course toward reform. When the investigations are completed, the reports rendered, and the decisions made, resources are marshaled with much ceremony to demonstrate a sincere effort to launch the ship.

The first investment is in concrete and steel to build a new launching pad in a remote area where it will not contaminate the surrounding freeworld people. But the spectators are not willing to finance or await the construction of a new rocket ship; instead, they suggest renovation of the old, rusty hulk with a coat of paint so "we can forge ahead toward Planet Real Reform."

A new captain who has commanded many other rocket ships is selected. Although most of the applicants for the position could honestly boast of never having lost a ship in space, they neglected to inform the Mission Controller that the principal reason for this unblemished record is that they have rarely gotten one off the pad. Reform of most prisons has never even been attempted; cosmetic changes may nonetheless have created that impression. While the majority of prison ships remain on the pad of traditionalism, those which have tried some type of reform may actually succeed in getting off the launching pad. The correlation between the skills involved in keeping a rusting hulk intact on the launching site and those required to guide one in an actual voyage is never questioned—except by the passengers, whose complaints are not heard since they are quarantined and held incommunicado for the duration of the journey.

With great pomp and ceremony, the prison reform rocket ship is readied for dispatch. A new captain and crew come aboard to take the same old passengers to the supposed destination of Real Reform. Assurances are made that all ties that inhibit movement away from the site have been severed. The passengers accept the word of the captain with some caution. After all, they have seen other captains enter and leave the command module, and none has ever told them the truth or succeeded in taking them anywhere except to a safe orbit.

Security passes to the actual launch site are issued to members of the press who are present to record the details of this historic event. A new open-press policy is heralded as a major innovation. Few take the time to realize that if the launch is successful, the rocket will be literally "out of sight" thereafter and thus inaccessible to the media.

In a spectacular display, the rocket gradually rises from the pad, follows the predetermined path toward Real Reform (or so it appears to the crowd), and quickly disappears into a fog created especially for the occasion by seeding the storm clouds with the sodium iodide of reform rhetoric.

The rocket fumes dissipate, speeches are concluded, the applause subsides, and the reformer-spectators amble toward the exits, secure in the belief that at last the prison problems have been solved and real reform will be achieved. A lone figure remains after the crowd has dispersed. He seeks out the officials at the control center to ask, "Isn't this just another form of exile?" (There always seem to be some dissidents who don't really understand the master plan and always cause trouble by criticizing the sincere men who have served faithfully as commanders of other prison rocket ships.)

The Mission Controller responds, "We are sending them to outer space for training to become better citizens when they return to Earth. What? No, it doesn't seem inconsistent to me. It's obviously too dangerous to train them here, and they need the structured environment of a space ship so they can concentrate on their deficiencies." The logic of the prophet's discourse is lost in the roar of the rocket's engines as they propel the ship relentlessly toward "reform."

The camera crews linger to grind away as the rocket disappears, suspecting that this may be the last time they will be able to view the prison ship up close unless it should fail to achieve orbit and fall back to Earth in disaster.

Mission Control announces after a short time that orbit has been achieved. The ship has attained reform. The masses cheer because the prison problem has been removed from the community; the economy has improved as a result of the funds expended in creating a new launching pad from which other ships will be sent forth; and additional personnel have been employed to service the control center and serve as crews for later flights. The Mission Controller takes pride in reciting the amount of money invested in this project, the difficulties that were overcome, and the great distance traveled. The fact that the ship is moving but never really going anywhere is disturbing neither to the captain nor to the crew.[1] They regard reform as a place in orbit, not a destination.

The chief of state points with pride to the orbiting vessel as an accomplishment. It can be observed, *at a distance*, at each circuit of the Earth. Assurances are given that reform is taking place within the ship, although newsmen are unable to assess personally what is going on because the reform effort has taken it further from their view. The administrators point out that really safe shuttle craft between Earth and the rocket ship have not yet been devised and that the journey is full of peril for visitors.

The media must rely on reports from the captain of the rocket ship concerning conditions within. Periodic bulletins are issued to avert or dissipate political storms as necessary. Efforts to establish direct communication with the passengers are of no avail. As the captain explains, the passengers do not understand the functioning of the ship or guidance systems—and, besides, they cannot be trusted to operate radio equipment. Thus, they are not given communication privileges because their distorted views of the flight might cast doubts on the success of the mission and would be bad for the crew's morale.

The captain is pleased with the responsibility he has to command the refurbished vessel, which is at least going *somewhere*. He dutifully checks off points on the ground as he passes over them—again, and again, and again. The fact that his route is circuitous and that he will never really reach a destination poses no problems for him. After all, his sealed orders, opened once he had reached orbit, came as no surprise. He had been privately briefed both at the time of his appointment and before departure that the purpose of the mission was to achieve orbit—not to venture into the outer space toward Real Reform.

The facade of reform is achieved with orbit, and the captain is content with his lot. His quarters are better in this remodeled ship, he has a cleaner view of the world, and he no longer has to suffer, with the inmates, the smog that engulfs the control complex. And he shall remain in command as long as he keeps the ship in orbit.

---

[1] Crew members who challenge the correctness of the heading will voluntarily transfer to another ship or be ejected from the prison reform rocket.

The captain entertains the infrequent penological pilgrims who visit the prison ship by displaying flow charts, diagrams, and statistical tables to prove that reform has been achieved. The only negative note is sounded by the captain when he announces that if money were not so hard to get, he could hire more crew members who would do more of something which would enable the craft to achieve a more stable orbit. The pilgrims travel back to Earth and report that the reform voyage is a smashing success and that the passengers are being readied to return to Earth.

Boredom is interrupted occasionally when the passengers complain that there has been no change in their condition. They point out that although the vessel is brighter and cleaner and there are lots of leisure activities, they are not being prepared to return to Earth but are becoming more remote from it all the time.

Life on the pad was primitive but uncomplicated. Some passengers had been assigned the task of repairing the ship; others bailed out the rain that seeped in. The choice was simple: one could either patch or bail; failure to do one or the other would result in irreparable damage—either to the ship or the passenger.

In space, it is not quite clear what must be done to survive in this strange environment. Also, individual reentry back into the Earth's atmosphere entails certain hazards. It is far more complicated to journey from the space craft to a specific objective on Earth than from the rocket on the launching pad to the security fence surrounding the complex.

There appear to be as many mutinies on the reform ship as there were in the derelict ship on the pad. The only difference is that the public is not as likely to become aware of the routine disturbances because of the ship's remoteness. But eventually a disturbance occurs that seriously jeopardizes the path of reform.

Traditional techniques of suppression are applied (because the captain knows of no other approaches to problem solving), and the uprising is smothered. On at least one occasion, the captain requires reinforcements from Earth.

The only real danger to Mission Control is if the captain should become dissatisfied with the lack of a goal and decide to change orbit. This restlessness can usually be detected by the transmissions sent back to control asking permission to accelerate and lessen the risk of a decaying orbit. At this point, the captain is reminded that he must depend on Mission Control for resupply missions; if this support is withdrawn, he cannot survive in outer space. To his critics, the captain replies: "If I'm not allowed to function as the captain, I can't really take the ship anywhere. I must be *in* the ship if I am going to continue the direction toward reform. By moving slowly, I can increase speed gradually until I achieve escape velocity and *then* I can move directly toward the planet of Real Reform."

He ignores the fact that similar vessels have been orbiting Earth for nearly two centuries—and none of them has ever gotten away from the gravitational pull of Earth interests. All he may achieve is a higher orbit that will increase the distance of travel but will fall short of breaking loose from Earth control.

The flight log reflects the number of orbits that will be recounted as achievements by Mission Control. But one day passengers realize that they are not being taken to their promised destination and claim that once again they have been cheated of reform. The fraud is exposed aboard the ship. The passengers demand either to be taken to the original objective or to be transferred to another vessel destined for Real Reform. The captain is in a dilemma because he lacks the authority for the latter and is not willing to risk the former, for he knows that it is professionally suicidal to change the mission.

This inevitable conflict results in a clash of such proportions that it becomes visible from Earth. Mission Control is embarrassed because the vessel is not responding to its programmed instructions, and the situation portends disaster. In addition to the danger that the ship will be destroyed, Control Central itself may be wiped out. News of rebellion is communicated to Earth by released passengers or by major explosions on the ship that cannot be concealed from the Earth-bound viewer. If the rebellion cannot be put down during that portion of the orbit on the dark side of the planet, it will become apparent to ground observers as it passes overhead in the next orbit.

When it is revealed that a small fleet of reform vessels is circling endlessly overhead and has never traveled anywhere, another Mission Controller is chosen to provide direction toward Real Reform. He selects a captain to gain control of the vessel and he agrees to continue to support the mission toward its destination. He rejects the present orbit and mission of the vessel and commissions the reformer-captain to take the prison ship toward the planet of Real Reform.

The reformer demands, and is granted, authority to select his own crew and to operate independently from ground control. He realizes that the traditional orbit has become comfortable to the crew and that they will resist any effort to change the direction of the vessel because they fear the unknown.

Freedom from remote control and reliance on manual control is essential if the meteorites opposing reform are to be avoided while the rocket is changing orbit. Sometimes, of course, ground control support will be required when the orbits of other derelict prison reform ships come into a collision course with the reform ship.

The real reformer cautiously slips into the pilot's seat of the command module, recognizing that the passengers are actually running the ship (a fact that was consistently denied by his predecessor). Since there is a lack of impetus from the ground for reaching new orbits, he sets about getting the passengers to help him toward the destination of Real Reform. The passengers discover that boarding the prison ship did not strip them of their native talents and abilities. Some contribute to official management of the vessel and, in many cases, perform better than the crew.

The directional system is locked onto the planet of Real Reform, and it is collectively agreed that this will be the destination. Even for the apathetic passengers, a destination *anywhere* is an improvement over the endless monotony of the merry-go-round of past reform efforts. By setting a common goal, the captain mobilizes the resources of the passengers through the simple device of offering them the chance to escape from the treadmill of tradition. Of course, he is resisted by some passengers as he attempts to reach escape velocity. There are those who have been allowed to exploit the other passengers during the routine orbits; for one thing, rackets have emerged in food service. By a parasitic existence, many passengers have been able to live better aboard ship than on Earth.

Those who attempt to retard movement out of orbit are transferred to other vessels in the fleet that have no desire to leave the comfortable orbit of tradition, or even the launching pad.

Excess baggage is cast overboard, restrictive ties to other vessels are cut, and the new crew of staff and inmates combine their efforts to change the direction of the ship.

The pilot knows that escaping Earth's gravitational pull depends on both thrust and speed. If the prison ship is to escape from the larger systems of Earth Control, it must have the thrust of innovation, executed swiftly before ground observers detect a change in course. The initial changes are internal as the captain attempts to gain control of the vessel.

The press is brought aboard. To gain long-range support, both the captain and the Mission Controller have agreed to inform the public of changes. Initially it is necessary to expose the conditions aboard ship in order to convince some skeptics that there is a real need for change. Cries of "It won't work" are neutralized by demonstrating that "it has worked" over the months of orbit when the critics did not realize that changes had been taking place. What was considered experimental has thus become a working part of the reform movement.

The additional speed and thrust succeed in achieving a higher orbit. But as the ship moves farther from Earth, there is an increasing risk of collision with asteroids in the path of the reform route. These bodies drift aimlessly without any destination or purpose, and their number and size makes travel difficult. But the pilot knows he cannot deviate from the trajectory toward Real Reform or the vessel may be diverted to wandering endlessly in the abyss of outer space, or be tangentially deflected to an interminable orbit around a dead planet. When a collision course appears on the scene, the captain calls on promised support from Mission Control to deflect the obstacle from his path.

A problem of another nature crops up, however. Many officials who have a vested interest in maintaining the status quo for other components of the government are having second thoughts. Control suggests that a new path around the obstacle—rather than trying to deflect it—would be the most congenial solution to the confrontation. The real reformer argues that he "cannot get there from here" if he changes course. A secondary objective, a lesser planet, is then suggested as a compromise solution to reform, but the captain knows he will lose the support of both his passengers and crew and fall back into the former orbit if he goes along with this compromise. He is painfully aware that he cannot achieve real reform without removing some obstacles. The real reformer chooses to risk official censure and rely on the skill of his crew and his strategy to avoid the obstacles. With the known risks, the passengers once again choose to attempt the original destination.

Utilizing the impetus of speed and the thrust of innovation, the captain succeeds in avoiding obstacles in spite of the Controller's refusal to help. He is also subjected to pressures from other celestial reform bodies that have reported sightings of, and some abrasive confrontations with, the real reform prison ship.

Even after official support is withdrawn, the momentum continues through inertia. The captain is determined to take the ship to Real Reform and apparently has the power to do so. But just as escape velocity is about to be achieved, the Mission Controller expresses serious reservations about the direction of the reform movement.

He reasons, "If I am no longer Mission Controller, I cannot direct any ship toward Planet Real Reform. Therefore, I must control orbiting and minimize conflicts. We should be satisfied with attaining a higher orbit that compares favorably with previous administrations.

The prison reform ship may not achieve reform, but it will have traveled farther and higher than previous efforts."

He communicates his fears to the pilot, who argues that the ship will either move toward reform or away from it. Neither the pilot nor the passengers are willing to be cheated again by settling for a secondary planet or just a higher orbit. They argue that the best way for the ground controller to remain in power is to fulfill his promise of attaining Real Reform.

The farther the real reformer moves from Earth, the more erratic the transmissions become. He must rely on information relayed through an intermediary in a space station who may misunderstand or improperly translate the communication.

A dichotomy of missions becomes evident as the flight progresses. The Mission Controller seeks to rally his forces to assure his reelection, and these plans do not include Real Reform. He now sees that there is danger to him in the journey to that planet because there are times when he must control the ship from the ground for his own purposes. Therefore, the captain must continue to pilot his vessel toward reform without support.

Having successfully avoided all hazards, having changed the very nature of the ship, as well as its direction, the real reformer is finally confronted by the one obstacle he cannot overcome—the Mission Controller, who has devised an ingenious plan to prevent the ship from reaching Planet Real Reform.

The plan is really simple; the Controller curses himself for not having used it sooner. If you do not approve of the direction the reform movement is taking, then instead of relying on natural obstacles to thwart the trip, simply remove the captain and thus abort the mission.

The Mission Controller removes the rebellious crew, transfers passengers who assisted in the reform movement to other ships, and sends another captain to take control of the helm. Although the inertia of the reform journey carries the ship farther out into space, it is successfully deflected from the original path. Thrust is exerted quickly to redirect the vessel into a safer orbit around the Earth. Innovations are stopped. Passengers are returned to their seats. The prison ship, having survived the trauma of real reform efforts, eventually settles into a new orbit. Some of the accoutrements of the journey toward Real Reform are retained because they are useful in appeasing Earth observers.

Conclusion

The lineal difference between the two orbits will determine the net gain (or loss) in movement of the prison toward real reform.

There appears to be no way to move from one orbit to another without traveling the former one until sufficient speed is attained to raise the reform ship to a higher orbit. The new orbit, and eventual escape from the Earth's pull, depends on a spiral movement outward from Earth.

Thus far, the infrequent probes into the outer space of real reform by intrepid captains have resulted primarily in their being grounded—which is cited by their critics as evidence that "it didn't work." But one must look beyond the personal tragedies of the real reformers and realize that they were fired not because they were failing but because they were succeeding.

And nothing is more frightening to the traditionalist than the success of a "heretical" notion.

The prognosis for success of the reform journey is good only as long as the main objective remains in sight. It may be, of course, that the Planet Real Reform is farther away than it looks. Or it may be that what appears to be real reform is a mirage or an illusion and thus is unattainable. It may be necessary to become a time traveler or to enter some other dimension in order to circumvent the impediments to reaching real reform.

Another possibility is that the Planet of Real Reform does not exist. What we perceive as such may, in fact, be a reflection of our own planet on a gigantic mirror across the solar system. Perhaps Planet Earth *is* Planet Real Reform, and the difficulty in reaching it is not a question of technical skills but rather a failure in our perception of the essence of real reform.

The flight plans of former voyages have been preserved and are available to all pilots. Yet they gather dust in a storeroom of the space center while research teams look in vain for a long-lasting preservative paint for the old ship.

1

The Evolution of Penology in the United States

> Oftentimes have I heard you speak of one who commits a wrong as though he were not one of you, but a stranger unto you and an intruder upon your world.
> But I say that even as the holy and righteous cannot rise beyond the highest which is in you,
> So the wicked and weak cannot fall lower than the lowest which is in you also.
> And as a single leaf turns not yellow but with the silent knowledge of the whole tree,
> So the wrongdoer cannot do wrong without the hidden will of you all.
>
> ....
>
> You cannot separate the just from the unjust and the good from the wicked;
> For they stand together before the face of the sun even as the black thread and the white thread are woven together.
> —Kahlil Gibran[1]

Punishment for criminal offenses has taken many forms since the beginning of recorded history, and what have been identified as the crimes warranting punishment have varied. In primitive societies people were punished for social revenge, to placate the gods, and to protect society.

In some early societies public and private crimes were differentiated. Some of the major areas of public crimes—such as endogamy (marrying within the same clan) and incest (marrying within the same family)—were considered taboo. Witchcraft, treason, and cowardice were also considered public crimes. Private crimes con-

---

[1] Kahlil Gibran, *The Prophet* (New York: Alfred A. Knopf, 1923), pp. 49, 50.

sisted of murder, adultery, theft, slander, and assault. In some societies there was also a third category consisting of offenses against the family; the offender was punished by tribal action and the defendant killed and perhaps eaten.

Other methods of retaliation were humiliation, corporal and capital punishment, banishment, and outlawry. Clan punishment usually was expressed in the form of a blood feud; a perpetual vendetta between two tribes or clans that sometimes continued until there was no one left. Any injury to a member of the clan was viewed as a collective injury that brought about collective retaliation. In this context, criminal acts were restricted to one's own clan, since crimes committed against another clan were not considered punishable by the defendant's own clan.

A cause-and-effect relationship was assumed for every "evil" occurrence. If the crops failed or someone was accidentally injured, it was believed to have been brought about by the gods in retaliation for some wrongful act by a member of the tribe or clan. In many instances, sacrifice of babies or other members of the clan was required. The most common punishments were death, exile, or compensation in some form. The Mosaic Law, cited in the Bible and usually referred to as the "eye for eye, tooth for tooth" doctrine, is commonly misinterpreted as an overly harsh criminal sanction. However, the intent of this doctrine was to limit the punishment of a defendant to the extent of the injury inflicted on the victim. Prior to the rendering of the Mosaic Law, the Hebrew custom was to punish the offender by doing to him a greater harm than he himself had originally perpetrated.

In ancient Israel, as early as 2000 B.C., six Cities of Refuge were established. A defendant who was accused of committing a crime that was punishable by the blood feud could escape to one of these towns, where he would be safe as long as he remained within the confines of the city. After the establishment of the organized church and houses of worship, the sanctuary provided by the Cities of Refuge was extended to the church edifice.[2]

Punitive Sanctions

The blood feud was replaced in England in the thirteenth century through the mechanism of "maintaining the king's peace." Although the philosophy of vengeance was retained, deterrence of others became an added purpose.

---

[2] This practice is not uncommon today in many countries, for there are laws prohibiting the police from seizing an offender within the confines of a church.

In more progressive societies, a wide variety of methods—such as trial by ordeal, trial by battle or combat, torture, and compurgation—were later used to determine guilt or innocence. Compurgation was a system by which the accused was allowed to bring witnesses who would take an oath and swear to facts relevant to his case. On the basis of this testimony, he was either acquitted or convicted.

Later, compensation of one type or another was instituted. In the American Indian culture, for example, victims were given a number of blankets in restitution for injury. A sliding scale of values was established, with a standard number of blankets specified for compensation in each case. Coin of the realm, tools of trade, or other articles of value to the tribe were also used as forms of compensation.

Banishment

The transportation or deportation of prisoners from a state has ancient origins. Banishment almost inevitably resulted in death, since the individual was sent into the forest or desert without weapons or means of survival.

By the end of the sixteenth century, the use of the galley with its prisoner oarsmen was ended because of the change to more effective sailing warships. Also, with increased crime, England was forced to develop an alternative that could provide a service for the state as well as solve the detention problems for the growing number of state prisoners.

Deportation to America commenced in 1597 for the purpose of "ridding England of criminals" and was an alternative to hanging from 1678 forward. As a labor force for the colonies, these prisoners were not incarcerated on arrival, but worked for the Crown under the supervision of the governor of the commonwealth. They were free to live as other persons, generally, but could return to England only under the pain of death. From 1717 until the Revolution of 1776, they were considered bond servants and, in essence, slaves to the state or to the master placed over them.

With the American Revolution, the transportation of prisoners to America was interrupted, and a backlog of prisoners accumulated in England. Having no workable alternative at that time, some of the hulks of the British fleet anchored in the harbors were used as detention facilities for these prisoners; they became, in other words, floating jails.

Soon after the discovery of Australia by Captain John Cook in 1770, it became apparent that Australia could be used to relieve the growing prisoner problems. Thus a colony was founded by convicts at Botany Bay in 1787, and over 135,000 British convicts (40 percent of whom died en route) were transported to Australia between 1787 and 1875. A penal colony was established on Van Diemen's Land (Tasmania) in 1803.

Other colonizing nations also used transportation to solve the problem of their rising criminal population. France established penal colonies in French Guiana in 1854; Portugal, as early as 1414, deported prisoners to North Africa; Spain, in 1497, transported prisoners to Hispaniola; Italy deported prisoners to Sicily; Holland[3] used the Dutch East Indies; and Denmark deported prisoners to Greenland.

Transportation or banishment from the dominant society has been frequently used, the primary function being the elimination of the deviants. Except in Australia, no effort was made to reform the convict.

In the United States as late as the end of the nineteenth century, it was proposed that Alaska be formed as a penal colony for prisoners of the United States. This proposal was seriously discussed by both congressmen and public-spirited citizens:

> *Two important points would be secured by establishing a penal colony in Alaska or elsewhere; first, society would rid itself, by a natural and proper method, of the human beasts who prey upon it, and threaten its security. It would say to the burglar, the robber, the confirmed thief—"You are no longer worthy to live among us; go into exile"—And, secondly, we should provide a future and open a career in a new land to such of the convicts as choose to reform and live honest lives.*
>
> *With children's aid societies to rescue the young from vice and crime, and deport our homeless children to the Western prairies, and with penal servitude in distant Alaska, for the convicted criminal, we might hope to really and considerably decrease our criminal population.*[4]

Corporal Punishment

Corporal punishment was in general use from biblical times until the close of the nineteenth century and is still used in many countries. As recently as the late 1960s, Arkansas, Louisiana, and

---

[3] During the latter part of the eighteenth century, imprisonment was authorized in lieu of transportation.

[4] Charles Nordhoff, "What Shall We Do With Scroggs?" *Harper's New Monthly Magazine*, vol. 47 (1873): 44.

Mississippi legally whipped prisoners on a regular basis. Branding was another method of corporal punishment common to England as well as America, where it was authorized by New Jersey statutes in 1668 and 1675. Maryland also used branding, as did Massachusetts State Prison as late as 1829.

Mutilation was used in England to enforce the Forest Laws of 1016. It was also used by King Henry I as a punishment for counterfeiting. It was even used in Rhode Island for the same crime, and for other crimes in Massachusetts. Other paraphernalia of corporal punishment included the ducking stool, leg chains, and collars.

Capital Punishment

Capital punishment has been a practice for deterring crime since antiquity. Methods have included stoning, flaying, impaling, burning, crucifixion, drowning, poisoning, and beheading. Other methods have been throwing offenders from cliffs, using the wheel, starvation, burning in oil, and burying alive. As the criminal law developed in postcolonial America, hanging became the accepted method because of the legal tradition brought from England. Hanging gained wide use in frontier communities, as demonstrated by vigilante law. California uses the cyanide gas chamber and Utah the firing squad, but the most common method of capital punishment in the United States is electrocution, which was introduced in Auburn Prison in New York in 1890.

The Deterrent Effect of Capital Punishment

One of the most abiding and popular myths is that if criminal offenders are executed it will deter others from committing capital crimes. Table 1-1 shows the comparative homicide rates per 100,000 population of the ten states leading in the use of capital punishment.

As will be noted, seven of the top ten states that use capital punishment also have the highest homicide rates. The fact that Georgia, for example, ranks second in number of executions per 100,000 and third in homicides would tend to refute the contention of capital punishment advocates that the death penalty serves as a deterrent to homicide. In fact, a strong (but erroneous) argument could be made that the result of higher execution rates is actually an *increase* in the homicide rates. But as with other myths, this one dies hard and the empirical evidence is of little value in swaying beliefs.

The Origins and Evolution of Penal Institutions

Imprisonment was illegal under Roman law. Emperor Justinian proclaimed in A.D. 533 that "prison ought to be used for detention

TABLE 1-1. COMPARATIVE HOMICIDE RATES PER 100,000 POPULATION OF THE TEN LEADING STATES IN USE OF CAPITAL PUNISHMENTS

State	Executions*	Rank	Homicides*	Rank
Nevada	9.3	1	8.8	9
Georgia	9.2	2	12.0	3
Mississippi	6.6	3	10.0	7
Arkansas	6.6	4	8.5	11
So. Carolina	6.5	5	13.3	1
No. Carolina	5.7	6	10.1	6
Alabama	4.0	7	12.9	2
Louisiana	4.0	7	8.7	10
Kentucky	3.4	8	6.7	17
Delaware	3.0	9	6.7	17

*1960 was chosen as the base year because there was no moratorium on executions at that time.

only, but not for punishment." Imprisonment as punishment, as opposed to detention, is a relatively new provision in the criminal law.[5]

Probably the first recorded use of imprisonment following the judgment of a court was in thirteenth-century England, where a two-year sentence to "prison" was authorized as punishment for rape. The facilities were the same: dungeons, towers, and similar methods of isolation.

The eighteenth century, known as the Age of Enlightenment, was a period of redefinition of the view of man and the rise of philosophy. It was characterized by the growth of natural science, the philosophy of rationalism and humanitarianism, religious tolerance, and movements toward government by consent. Arising concurrently was general opposition to the gallows, the pillory, and capital punishment.

In England two factors contributed to the problem of prisoner disposition. The first of these was the reduction of capital punishment and the substitution of corporal punishment and other detention practices that resulted in an increase in the number of prisoners. The second was the American Revolution, which stopped transportation to the New World. At that time, three-fifths of the state prisoners in England were in custody because of debts. As a

---

[5] Biblical texts referring to "prisons" are usually interpreted as referring to places of detention for the prisoner awaiting execution, exile, or payment of debt.

result, much thought was given to the care and custody of prisoners. This deliberation brought about a study by Eden and Blackstone resulting in the Penitentiary Act of 1779. The report recommended that the institutions should provide for solitary confinement, be inspected weekly, provide a labor force, and use degrading clothing to distinguish prisoners. This report was never implemented because of the discovery of Australia and renewal of deportation in 1787.

In colonial America, there was a general revulsion against the harshness of the English common law, and revisions were made even prior to the American Revolution. In Delaware, the Duke of York's laws, effected after 1676, primarily emphasized corporal punishment and reserved capital punishment only for sinful acts (offenses against God or the church).

Aside from the humanitarian philosophy of some of the early founders of America, lessening the harshness of the law was also a matter of practicality. If the colonists had continued to execute offenders for the same offenses and at the same rate that had been common in England at that time, the Royal Navy would have been hard pressed to transport sufficient numbers of individuals to the new colonies to sustain a viable community on North American shores.

William Penn, arriving at the Delaware River in 1682 with a charter to found the province of Pennsylvania, became a key figure in the implementation of more humanitarian punishments in the colonies. With permission from Charles II to institute a much milder penal code than the English one, Penn decreed imprisonment at hard labor rather than the previously used death penalty for all offenses except homicide. From 1682 to 1718, the jails were, in reality, workhouses for felons and lesser offenders. Pennsylvania was perhaps the most progressive example of the revolution in penology on the American soil at that time.

After Penn's death in 1718, however, Governor Keith was appointed to administer the commonwealth, and he promptly reintroduced the English criminal law sanctions. Capital punishment was reinstated for second felony offenses except for larceny, and corporal punishment replaced imprisonment. Penology continued to regress until the renewal of Quaker influence in 1776, which roughly coincided with John Howard's *Report on Prisons in England* and the abolition of whipping and the pillory. In 1786 the Quakers, or Society of Friends, were able to influence the legislature to pass a law substituting imprisonment for capital punishment for all crimes except murder, treason, rape, and arson. But something had to replace the gallows for other offenses.

The Prison

The result of the Quakers' influence was the creation of the Walnut Street Jail in 1790, where the emphasis was on penitence[6] and solitary confinement. This institution was the forerunner of what became known as the Pennsylvania System: Prisoners were isolated in single cells and never saw or spoke to another human being. (The Pennsylvania System was comprised of the Western Penitentiary of Pittsburgh, built in 1818, and the Eastern Penitentiary at Cherry Hill, built in 1829. The Pennsylvania influence was felt in New Jersey, where this pattern of confinement was incorporated in the state prison in 1833.) Under a Quaker philosophy equating sin and crime, prisoners were allowed to read from the Bible and to walk daily in a yard surrounded by a high wall to "meditate upon their evil deeds." Unfortunately, the concept of solitary confinement ignored the fact that man is a social being who needs to relate to other humans. Many went mad because of sensory deprivation, and the system eventually was abandoned.

Separate confinement represented a major modification in the nineteenth century. It was a practice in the traditional jails in Europe and in America prior to this time to combine male and female, adult and juvenile, the sick and the well, the mentally ill and the sane, all in one dormitory-type confinement facility.

The philosophy of separate confinement was also witnessed in New York in the early nineteenth century. Auburn, opened in 1823, and Sing Sing, opened two years later, became prototypes of the inside cells[7] with a single occupant. In this system, the prisoners worked together in common workshops and ate in congregate mess

Reprinted from Trailblazer's Jaycee Calendar, Leavenworth, Kansas

---

[6] Hence the origin of the word *penitentiary*.

[7] That is, the cells formed a block in the interior of the structure and were not located on the outside wall as in Pennsylvania.

The Evolution of Penology in the United States

halls, but were not allowed to speak to one another. This practice became known as the "silent system," and was enforced by flogging. At the end of work, the prisoners were returned to their cells where they had no communication with each other. All in all, however, cellular confinement was not seen as a punitive measure, but rather as a progressive movement away from a chaotic incarceration situation that spread contamination, vermin, sickness, and criminality. Not incidentally, separation also made control easier.

It is important to emphasize that in the early days of the United States, the prison system that evolved did not come about according to any great master plan. As mentioned above, states imitated each other, and the Auburn System was imitated the most. This trend has continued to the present. State systems vary in that some are more modern than others; and some have only one prison facility, whereas others have a series of minimum-to-maximum security installations. But despite these differences, all prison systems evolved pretty much alike after the Pennsylvania System was abandoned.

National Prison Association

In October 1870, at a meeting called in Cincinnati, Ohio, by Dr. Enoch Wines, secretary of the Prison Association of New York, prison personnel gathered to form the first national prison association. Later called the American Prison Association, and now the American Correctional Association, the first prison congress formulated a Declaration of Principles listing 37 goals. One of the principles advocated the use of the indeterminate sentence, whereby the amount of time to be served by an offender was unspecified but within certain minimum-maximum limits. The first law to that effect

had been passed in New York State in 1869. Prison authorities rather than judges or courts were to determine the exact length of the sentence on the rationale that they could better judge when a prisoner was "reformed." The indeterminate sentence also allowed

The Evolution of Penology in the United States

the concept of parole to develop so that an offender could be released before the maximum sentence had been served, be placed under supervision in the community, and be required to follow certain rules of conduct. Although we are now aware of the inequities resulting from the indeterminate sentence,[8] the overall mood of that first congress was one of reform, not vindictive punishment. Classification, diagnosis, probation,[9] parole,[10] and above all reformation were henceforth to be the goals of penal treatment.

Some members of the professional association view the Declaration of Principles as one of the great documents in corrections. It was updated in 1930 and 1960, then again in 1970 at the Centennial Congress of Correction. It is ironic, however, that only six of the ideal-sounding goals articulated at the first association meeting have ever been realized.

The Reformatory

As opposed to the incarcerated prison population, the offenders sent to reformatories are usually young or first offenders.[11] The first state reformatory in the United States opened in Elmira, New York, in 1876. The youthful adults between the ages of 16 and 30 sent to

---

[8] The American Correctional Association, Ramsey Clark, and others still consider the indeterminate sentence a "reform." In theory, the sentencing of an offender to an indefinite term (as opposed to a fixed term of years) gives correctional officials the flexibility to parole him whenever he is "rehabilitated." However, the same flexibility can be exercised to keep a prisoner in an institution *longer* than he would have served on a definite term. It was such a law that enabled California parole authorities to keep George Jackson several years for a robbery.

What actually happens is that the amount of time a prisoner eventually is required to serve is determined *not* by his offense or criminal record, but by his behavior in prison. Thus an inmate may have his time extended administratively for violation of prison rules far beyond that intended by the court for the offense for which he was committed to prison in the first place.

[9] The idea of probation in the United States is generally credited to John Augustus of Boston. In 1841 he convinced the court to release a man being sentenced on a drunk charge to his care. When he later referred to that experience, he used the word *probation* and hence became known as Father of Probation. By 1858 he had bailed almost 2,000 men and women. Generally, probation is the process whereby the court suspends most or all of a criminal's sentence and allows him or her to live in the community under supervision of a probation officer.

[10] Parole is an administrative procedure by which the balance of a prisoner's sentence to confinement is suspended and he is supervised in the community on release.

Elmira were selected primarily because of their lack of sophistication in criminal matters and because they were fairly easy to handle. The indeterminate sentence that had been so widely heralded at the 1870 meeting was used, there was no intentional degradation, and there was an emphasis on education and prison industries.

Time and again, prison administrators discovered that ideal-sounding programs do not work if there is overcrowding. Too much time has to be spent simply on security. The same was true for Elmira, and the reformatory degenerated eventually into an institution for routine work and mass treatment so characteristic of other institutions both then and now. Of course, the programs for education and meaningful prison work were also curtailed by the legislature's lack of sympathy with such programs. But probation, in growing use as an alternative to incarceration, inadvertently contributed another hindrance—with the more tractable and more intelligent offenders being put on probation, those who composed the prison population were not as easy to work with in programs of "reform." The use of parole had much the same effect.

There are still reformatories across the United States, and their populations are still generally younger and may be composed of first offenders, but the structure and activities therein differ very little from those of prisons.

Prison Labor Systems in America

Historically, the primary utilization of prisoner labor has been for the benefit of the state. This approach was strictly utilitarian, punitive, and, in theory, had some deterrent effect. Viewing man as a sinful creature who should repent, the philosophy changed in Pennsylvania from punishment to penitence in monastic solitude. The introduction of labor in New York was seen as a striking change.

What to do with the prison population has been a perennial problem of incarceration. Prisoner idleness is viewed as problematic, especially by the warden who must concern himself with controlling the energies of inmates. Originally, labor was looked on as punishment in itself—a kind of penal servitude. But it also served to decrease the costs of operating a prison. Today, some therapists view work primarily as a means of rehabilitation.

---

[11] The term *first offender* is a misleading one, because it really refers to the first time an offender is incarcerated in an adult institution. But the offender could have committed innumerable offenses without having been caught; he could have been placed on probation many times; or he could have had an extensive record as a juvenile.

Over the years prisoners have been put to work at various tasks. Between 1786 and 1790, when the Walnut Street Jail opened, prisoners formed road gangs that repaired Philadelphia streets. Because the citizens of that city were fearful of the bedraggled criminals, the convicts ended up being weighted down with iron collars and chains to prevent their "escape." The Newgate Prison in New York, which opened in 1797, introduced industries, and prisoners manufactured goods for the general market. The idea of prison industries spread as other states imitated those that seemed to be working out successful programs.

The six major systems of prison labor that have existed in the United States include, first of all, the *lease system*. Beginning after the Civil War, it was particularly common in the South during Reconstruction and continued until about 1923. Under this system, state prisoners were "rented" to an individual to be worked as that person saw fit.

The *contract system*, now generally abandoned, allowed a manufacturer to set up shop inside the prison and to supervise prison labor in production of goods to be sold in the freeworld.

The third system, or *accord*, is a variation on the above. Under this practice, orders are taken from outside firms and prison officials supervise the production. Such goods are also marketed in the freeworld.

The *public work system* involves prisoners in public road-building and reclamation projects. This practice, which was in operation in Philadelphia as early as 1786, has been common throughout the United States, although road gangs have probably been most extensively used in the South. Road gangs have now largely disappeared and this practice has been discontinued.

One Little Raincloud

by Harold Lee, Texas State Prison,
Ramsey Unit. Reprinted from The Echo,
Huntsville, Texas.

One little rain cloud
Floating way up high,
I wish that over me
It would cry.

Pouring its tears
Upon my back,
To cool me off
Cuz' the boss won't slack.

He works me hard
Throughout the day,
So little rain cloud
For you I pray.

Let the Lord above
Fill you with rain,
Soak my skin
To ease the pain.

You see I toil everyday
In this bountiful field.
The hat on my head
Is my only shield.

There's nothing to protect me
From old Mr. Sun,
He wants to bake me
Till I'm well done.

If God's willing
Let my efforts be paid,
By a cool rain
and a bit of shade.

A fifth method is the *state use system*, where prisoners manufacture goods sold for state use, such as license plates, furniture, and other commodities. Under provision of this system, prison-made goods can be transported and sold in interstate commerce to another prison system if the receiving state has no prohibitions against such acquisition.[12]

The last general system is *public control* (state account). Prisoner labor is utilized freely and the products are sold on the open market. The industry is sustained by competitive sales to the public at large. Minnesota's sale of prison-made farm machinery is an example of this system.

Rehabilitation programs that involve study or other forms of work, rather than labor per se, are increasing, but most states rely on industrial or agricultural work to keep their inmate populations occupied. As we shall see in later chapters, inmate labor has often been exploited to a debasing extent, with inmates today being paid as little as two cents an hour for their work—and some not at all.

---

[12] At the time of World War I, prison labor was used to produce goods for the military. But when the labor movement gained momentum, it was contended that such free labor depressed the job market. And then in 1934, during the Depression, the Hawes-Cooper Act went into effect, prohibiting the interstate transportation of prison-made goods for sale on the open market, with the exception of agricultural products.

Penal Reform

The evolutionary view of progress maintains that it is a result of gradual, incremental changes which result in the steady, but often imperceptible, movement toward some ideal. The forces that bring about this change can be by design or accident.

Although modification of criminal sanctions has sometimes been the result of a changing philosophy, more often than not it has been a function of pragmatism. The "prison" of biblical times and the medieval dungeon both served the same purpose: detention of the offender until he could be dealt with by the legal authorities. The common sanction imposed on the convicted was death by a variety of means.

The impact of the humanists during the sixteenth century resulted in the erection of Houses of Correction. But the abandonment of the galley ships in the seventeenth century was perhaps more significant in changing penal policies. There were no more pyramids to erect, no more cities to build, no more aqueducts or "Appian Ways" to construct, no more ships to row. For the first time, modern nations were faced with the problem of how to use—effectively use—prisoners of the state.

Early Reform Efforts

Although our knowledge is cumulative and may have an effect on historical trends, there are nonetheless points in time when radical departure seems to occur, possibly by a new insight that translates into action what the philosophers have been saying. Hence, the following discussion focuses on the reformers and, with apologies, ignores the philosophers who may have influenced them.

John Howard (1726–1790) was a major contributor to penal reform in eighteenth-century England. He had been a French prisoner of war in 1756 and wrote a report on prison conditions subsequent to his release. As sheriff of Bedfordshire in 1773, Howard conducted the first prison (gaol) inspection in England. As a result of this inspection, statutes were enacted that authorized the release of prisoners at the end of their sentences, even though they might be unable to pay the jail fees.

In 1775 Howard extended his inspections to Scotland and Ireland, and two years later he published his report on the state of prisons. Recommendations of this extensive survey included: housing of prisoners should be in spacious and sanitary, but secure, accommodations; officials of the institutions should be salaried; prisoners should be segregated in cells, although an individual should be allowed to work in groups; torture should be abolished; and work and religious instruction should become the major theme of prisons. By exposing penal conditions for the first time and by suggesting worthy solutions, Howard's report had great impact on subsequent legislation that eventually resulted in the organization of the then-progressive British prison system. Howard continued his interest in institutions by pursuing his inquiry on the Continent, where he contracted the plague and died in 1790.

About the same time as the development of the New York prison, there were efforts at penal reform[13] by legislation in other countries. In England, Sir Robert Peel's Prison Act of 1823, which suggested the creation of nonpunitive prison workshops, is considered by most scholars to be the beginning of English reform in penology. Because most of the reform effort was a reaction to the extensive use of capital punishment, nonproductive activities such as the use of the treadmill were largely unaffected.

The Gladstone Report of 1895, which resulted in the Prison Act of 1898, is the foundation of the present English prison system. Proposing rehabilitation through education and long-term detention of the habitual criminal, this report was viewed as a supplement to the criminal law in the prevention of crime.

It was in Australia that one of the early pioneers of criminology implemented major reforms. Alexander Maconochie (1787–1860) was assigned as superintendent of the penal colony at Norfolk Island in 1840, where he established a "Mark System." From the British prison vessels, a prisoner could be transported to the colony, where he engaged in public employment. As he moved to the next stage, he was granted a "ticket of leave" that became a rudimentary parole system. If he served a period of time satisfactorily in this category, the prisoner then moved into a conditional pardon. The next phase was penal settlement in some type of a civilian communal setting and then retransportation to England and restoration of the prisoner's status as a freeman. This system is an example of the cyclical ritual of expulsion, mortification, penitence, reconstitution, and reacceptance into the society from which the person was originally expelled. Maconochie's experiences as a French prisoner of war had a

---

[13] Penal reform and psychiatry developed simultaneously in the United States. A lesson could be learned from some of the early development of mental institutions. In past times, mental patients were chained to the floor or punished for overt acts considered deviant in the institution. But as progressive elements were introduced into mental health, physical restraints and punishment were removed. Contrary to the dire predictions of the staff of these institutions, there was a reduction in violence, not an increase, as a result of these liberal practices.

profound impact on his rejection of the traditional penal practices. His contributions were implementing humane treatment of prisoners; providing a progression of freedom and responsibility for the inmates; using positive peer pressure; originating the concept of parole; stimulating inmate-operated industries; and providing a mechanism for the prisoner to earn his freedom.

In the 1850s, Sir Joshua Jebb introduced the English "Progressive Stage System" in Ireland, combining the indeterminate sentence and parole concepts. Later, between 1854 and 1862, Sir Walter Crofton implemented his "Intermediate Stage" system there. In that system, a prisoner spent nine months in solitary confinement and was then transferred to a public works project on Spike Island. From there, he moved into the next stage of unsupervised work while residing in a halfway house. After he had satisfactorily completed these stages, the prisoner was transferred into an aftercare program (parole), where he was in the community in which he was released.

Crofton contributed by taking the work of Maconochie and Jebb and creating a transitional system from the "prison to the public." He believed that the prisoner could be reformed through productive work and the development of industrious habits. His greatest insight was that these experiences must take place in the community rather than in the artificiality of the prison.

While innovations were being introduced in Australia, in England, and on the Continent, change was also taking place in the United States. The industrial prison in New York had replaced the theocratic model in Pennsylvania and was destined both in design and philosophy to influence all American prisons as well as those in Europe. However, the Auburn System was no more successful than the Pennsylvania System in "curing criminality." As news of Crofton's work spread to New England, there was a rising dissatisfaction with the existing prison systems.

The reformatory movement arrived in America, but as in most reforms, only portions of the old system were discarded. Thus religion and hard work were retained in the introduction of the educational model at the first reformatory at Elmira in 1876 under the charge of Brockway. But, alas, the reformatory movement was doomed to follow the pattern of other reform movements in that it became neutralized by the larger system and thus failed to attain its objective of becoming the ideal system to reform convicts.

Modern Reform Efforts

The twentieth century has not produced major innovations in facilities designed to treat the criminal offender. The post–World War

II correctional camps are used in only a few states and accommodate a very few inmates. Similarly, halfway houses and, more recently, community corrections centers are not "institutions" in the traditional sense and do not influence a large segment of the prison population.

Significant reform efforts in this century have addressed themselves not to institutions but to differential methods of managing prisoners within existing institutions.

Thomas Mott Osborne (1859–1926) served as president of the Board of Trustees of the George Junior Republic for 15 years and later applied the notions of self-government and self-support to adult institutions. Both the inmates and Osborne were convinced of the value of involving inmates in prison management. Less convinced were the guards and politicians, who eventually brought about Osborne's departure and the collapse of his "Mutual Welfare League" in 1929. Osborne's contribution was in reviving some of Maconochie's notions about participatory management and in believing that the dignity of man was essential to any reformation of an individual.

Howard B. Gill (born 1889) was familiar with Osborne's work in New York when the former was appointed superintendent and given wide latitude in building a new institution in Massachusetts between 1927 and 1933. Gill rejected the idea of inmate government but incorporated a system of committees and a highly structured constitution that provided a great deal of inmate participation in management. Gill's contribution was in demonstrating that work efficiency could be increased, violence reduced, and a more hospitable climate created by the formation of a new prison community including guards and inmates.

There are several common threads in the work of Maconochie, Osborne, and Gill.[14] Each rejected the dictatorial model for prison management, none had training in the field of penology, and each entered a system that was so decadent that "radical" ideas could be tolerated. Also, they focused their attention on the everyday relationships between staff and inmates rather than on architectural renovations or esoteric theories relating to the cure of criminality. Perhaps it is because they were outside the mainstream of penological thought in their own time that the significant work of each had little impact on the direction of penology in the United States.

---

[14] A more detailed discussion of the work of Maconochie, Osborne, and Gill appears in Chapter 9.

General Description of the Penal System Today

Crime Trends

According to the *Uniform Crime Reports*, 172,639,000 offenses were known to the police in 1973. This figure represents increases, compared to 1972 figures, in all categories of crimes, ranging from the lowest (3.8 percent) in auto theft to the highest (12.5 percent) for negligent manslaughter. There was also a marked increase in larceny of amounts over $50 (11.6 percent) and forcible rape (9.2 percent). Overall, violent crimes went up 4.3 percent.[15]

Between 1960 and 1973, there was a 27.8 percent increase in total male arrests. The increase in the arrest rate for those males under the age of 18 years rose 123.5 percent. For female offenders the change was even more dramatic. The percentage increase in the arrest rate for all women rose 95.3 percent, and for women under 18 years of age the increase was 264.1 percent during the same 13-year base period.

Funds expended by federal, state, and local governments on criminal justice in fiscal year 1969–1970 amounted to $8,571,252,000.[16] Of that amount, $1,706,475,000 was spent on corrections. The Law Enforcement Assistance Administration (LEAA) allocated $342,458,000 to state governments in fiscal year 1971; "corrections and rehabilitation" were awarded $46,192,867 of that sum.

Jails

It is estimated that there are about 142,000 inmates in city and county jails in the United States on any given day. For the most part, this constituency consists of misdemeanants serving time of less than one year or awaiting court action. Management of these institutions for minimal care and custody of prisoners is usually at a level below that of the prison.

The United States Bureau of the Census conducted a survey of local jails at the request of LEAA in the summer of 1972 to "assess the socioeconomic characteristics of the country's jail population. . . ."

---

[15] United States Department of Justice, Federal Bureau of Investigation, *Uniform Crime Reports, 1973*, Washington, D.C., September 1974.

[16] United States Department of Justice, Law Enforcement Assistance Administration, *Sourcebook for Criminal Justice Statistics 1973*, Washington, D.C., August 1973.

The Survey revealed that there were 3,921 jails in the United States at midyear 1972, holding approximately 141,600 inmates. Both figures were slightly smaller than those recorded in the 1970 National Jail Census. Approximately 95 percent of all inmates were male, and about 6 in 10 were less than 30 years of age. During the year preceding their admission, almost half earned an income below that defined by the U.S. Government as poverty level for persons without dependents.

About two out of every five were unemployed at the time of admission, and roughly 20 percent of the employed had worked on a part-time basis only. Approximately half the inmates had never been married and slightly more than half reported having no dependents.

Black inmates comprised a proportion of the jail population much higher than the proportion of blacks in the total U.S. population. By geographical region, the South had a larger share of the total inmate population than the North Central region, the Northeast and the West, although the West had a slightly higher ratio of inmates to inhabitants.[17]

Felony Institutions

Another large group of inmates (some 23,500) are incarcerated in institutions under the jurisdiction of the United States Bureau of Prisons. These offenders are located in 39 institutions throughout the United States, and because they are a product of the federal system of criminal justice they are commonly characterized as being a "higher class" of inmates than usually found in state prison systems. A partial explanation for this belief is that the United States Code deals with more sophisticated crimes. The typical federal prisoner probably represents the opposite extreme from the common drunk found in most city and county jails.

The bulk of felony prisoners, however, are housed in state prisons, reformatories, camps, and other facilities. The average state prison population is about 175,000. Thus the total incarcerated adult population may run as high as 340,500 on any given day. Of course, this figure does not represent the total number of offenders who experience incarceration over a year's time.

---

[17] United States Department of Justice, Law Enforcement Assistance Administration, *Survey of Inmates in Local Jails: Advance Report*, Washington, D.C., 1974, p. 1.

FEDERAL CORRECTIONAL SYSTEM

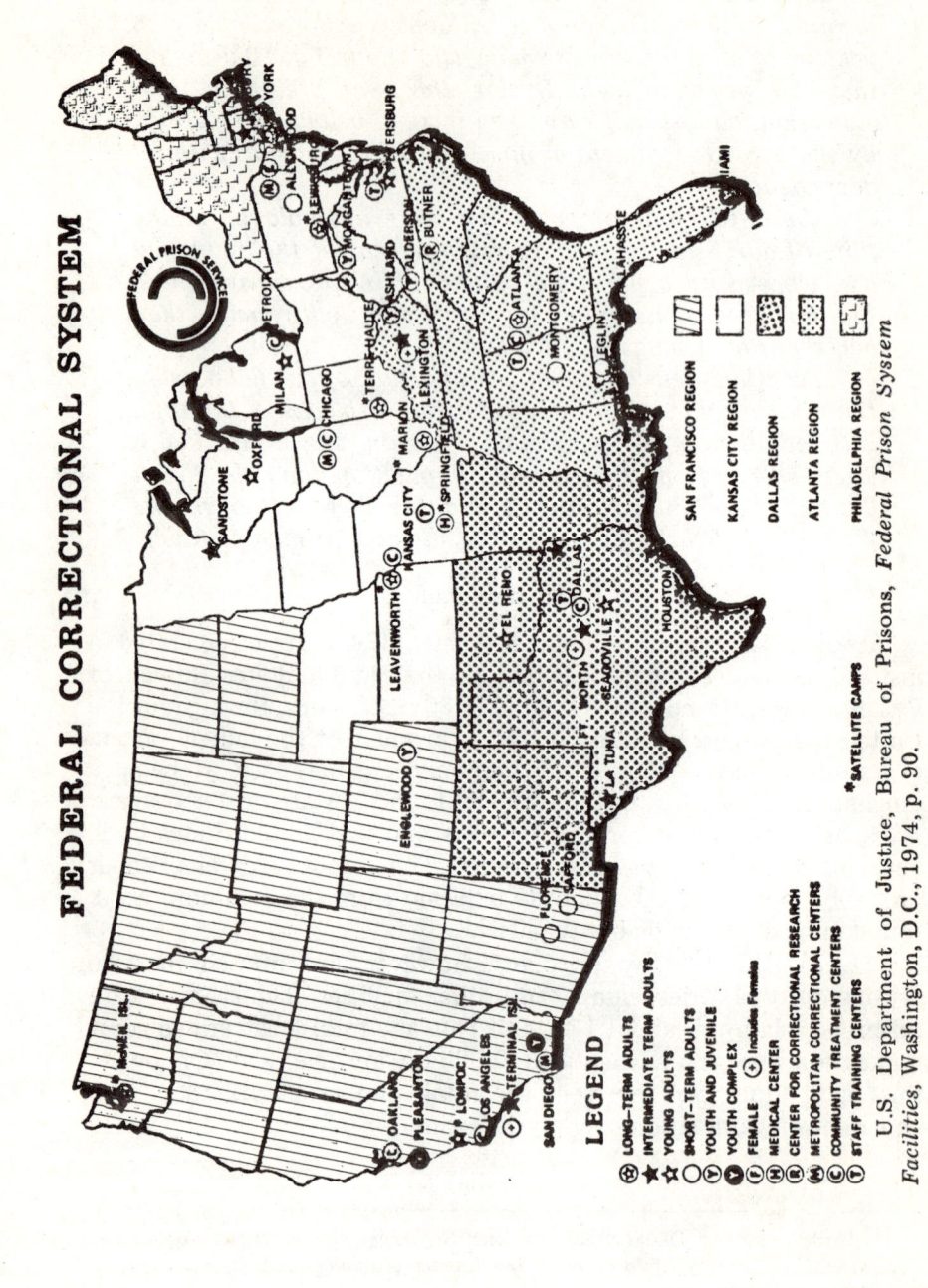

U.S. Department of Justice, Bureau of Prisons, *Federal Prison System Facilities*, Washington, D.C., 1974, p. 90.

Ratio of Prisoners to General Population

The Georgia Department of Corrections reported in the fall of 1974 the results of a survey of the ratio of state prisoners for each 100,000 residents in the general population of all 50 states. During the 3½-year base period (January 1971 through June 1974), 24 states reported a decrease in the ratio. The largest decrease (26.1 percent) was in Indiana. Decreases were attributed by the researchers to use of "shock" probation[18] in Ohio (20.88 percent); pretrial diversion in Minnesota (11.0 percent); more liberal use of probation and parole in Kansas (18.4 percent); and a change in the law excluding juvenile commitment to adult institutions in Pennsylvania (17.9 percent).[19] (See Table 1-2.)

Increases in ratios were ascribed to longer prison sentences in Maryland (20.3 percent); an increase in drug-related crime in New Hampshire (4.4 percent); a combination of "better" police, conservative judges, and more drug-related crime in New Mexico (10.4 percent); and "catching and convicting men more efficiently" in Texas (7.1 percent). Noting that Georgia ranks first in the nation with 214 prisoners per 100,000 population, Corrections Commissioner Allen L. Ault stated that Georgia may be required to spend $2 billion on new prison construction by 1980.

North Dakota reported the lowest ratio of prisoners to population with 22.5 per 100,000. Northeastern states average 73.3 prisoners per 100,000 residents; Southern states 124.7; North Central states 60.2; Western states (including Alaska and Hawaii) 81.0. The number of prisoners per 100,000 population in the South is greater than in any other region of the United States and is more than twice that of Northeastern states. (See the map.)

Prisoner Characteristics[20]

Age. According to the 1970 United States Census, there were 198,831 inmates in federal and state prisons and reformatories. Of that number, 104,019 (52.8 percent) were between the ages of 18 and 29. The number of female inmates in those institutions was 3,278 or 1.6 percent of the total prison population.

---

[18] Under this program, Ohio authorities place the probationer in prison for a short period of time to "give him a taste of prison life."

[19] *Atlanta Journal and Constitution*, Atlanta, Georgia, October 24, 1974.

[20] Taken generally from United States Department of Commerce, Bureau of the Census, *1970 Census Population*, "Persons in Institutions and Other Group Quarters," GPO, Washington, D.C., July 1973.

TABLE 1-2. Prison Population Listed by States

STATE	1974 Population	Prisoners Per 100,000	Percent Increase/Decrease Jan.–June 1971–1974
Alabama	3,523,000	113.5	Not Available
Alaska	337,000	145.0	+ 3.4
Arizona	2,064,000	64.4	−11.8
Arkansas	1,994,000	68.4	Not Available
California	20,853,000	100.0	+ 7.7
Colorado	2,486,000	82.8	+13.5
Connecticut	3,102,000	94.9	−11.3
Delaware	573,000	119.9	+11.7
Florida	7,881,000	137.3	+ 2.9
Georgia	4,800,000	214.2*	+15.1
Hawaii	842,000	26.4	+ 4.0
Idaho	742,200	65.5	+12.6
Illinois	11,273,000	54.0	− 7.4
Indiana	5,344,000	92.8	−26.1
Iowa	2,891,000	51.2	− 5.3
Kansas	2,555,000	63.4	−18.4
Kentucky	3,322,000	92.4	− 2.1
Louisiana	3,799,000	94.6	− 3.4
Maine	1,045,000	75.0	− 1.5
Maryland	4,113,000	147.4	+20.3
Massachusetts	5,822,000	33.2	− 4.9
Michigan	9,101,000	90.8	−12.7
Minnesota	3,947,000	45.8	−11.0
Mississippi	2,288,000	85.0	− .5
Missouri	4,764,000	74.0	Not Available
Montana	726,000	43.0	Not Available
Nebraska	1,543,000	61.1	− 3.9
Nevada	583,000	156.0	Not Available
New Hampshire	788,000	36.9	+ 4.4
New Jersey	7,361,000	84.2	− 5.6
New Mexico	1,090,000	75.4	+10.4
New York	18,292,000	70.7	+ 2.5
North Carolina	5,274,000	202.4*	+12.8
North Dakota	632,000	22.5	+ 3.3
Ohio	10,883,000	64.9	−20.8
Oklahoma	2,692,000	132.0	−19.5
Oregon	2,227,000	73.9	−16.6
Pennsylvania	11,874,000	63.9	−17.9
Rhode Island	968,000	61.1	Not Available
South Carolina	2,700,000	124.5	+10.4
South Dakota	680,000	40.6	−14.2
Tennessee	4,126,000	118.7	Not Available
Texas (1970)	11,196,730	138.9	+ 7.1
Utah	1,160,000	49.1	− 3.5
Vermont	469,000	92.8	Not Available
Virginia	4,849,000	116.9	Not Available
Washington	3,423,000	80.8	− 1.1
West Virginia	1,780,000	84.1	− 2.5
Wisconsin	4,547,000	61.7	−21.6
Wyoming	343,000	91.8	+ 6.7

*As of October 15, 1974.

The Evolution of Penology in the United States

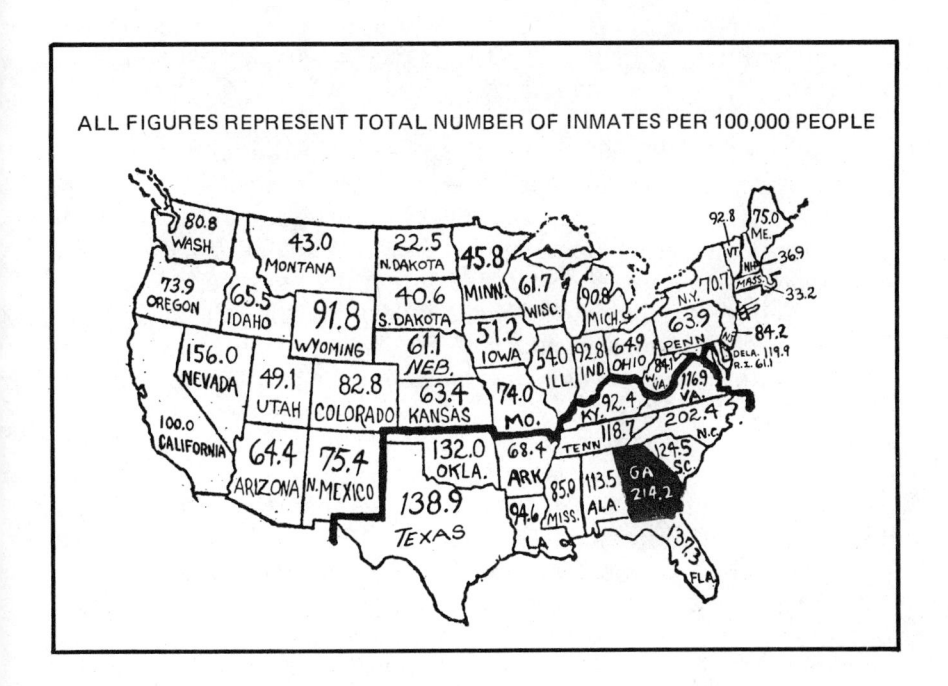

ALL FIGURES REPRESENT TOTAL NUMBER OF INMATES PER 100,000 PEOPLE

WASH.	80.8
OREGON	73.9
IDAHO	65.5
MONTANA	43.0
N.DAKOTA	22.5
S.DAKOTA	45.8
WYOMING	91.8
MINN.	40.6
WISC.	61.7
MICH.	90.8
N.Y.	70.7
MASS.	33.2
ME.	75.0
N.H.	36.9
VT.	92.8
NEVADA	156.0
UTAH	49.1
COLORADO	82.8
NEB.	61.1
IOWA	51.2
ILL.	54.0
IND.	92.8
OHIO	64.9
PENN.	84.1
DELA.	119.9
R.I.	61.1
CALIFORNIA	100.0
ARIZONA	64.4
N.MEXICO	75.4
KANSAS	63.4
MO.	74.0
KY.	92.4
W.VA.	116.9
VA.	202.4
N.C.	118.7
OKLA.	132.0
ARK.	68.4
TENN.	124.5
S.C.	214.2
GA.	
TEXAS	138.9
MISS.	94.6
ALA.	113.5
LA.	85.0
FLA.	137.3

Race. Of the total 198,831 inmates of all ages, 114,608 (57.6 percent) were white; 80,742 (40.6 percent) were black; and 13,596 (1.8 percent) were Spanish-speaking.

Marital Status. Of 198,508 prisoners, 105,878 (53.3 percent) had been married but at the time of the survey were separated, widowed, or divorced.

Residence. Of 198,831 prison and reformatory inmates, 91,193 (45.8 percent) resided in metropolitan areas and the remaining 107,638 (54.2 percent) lived in nonmetropolitan areas.

Of the 21,094 federal prisoners, 98,384 (51.4 percent) were housed in institutions with a capacity of over 1,000 inmates. Of 177,737 state prisoners, 98,384 (55.4 percent) were similarly housed in 578 state institutions. Of 119,359 inmates who were not in the same institutions five years previously (1965), 110,666 (92.7 percent) had been in a different county or state.

Education. Of 400,287 inmates between the ages of 18 and 34, only 10.7 percent had been in school when arrested. Of 1,679,048 inmates over the age of 25, some 7.3 percent had no schooling, 55.9 percent had completed elementary school, and 26.3 percent had not finished high school. The median achievement level was 8.7 years of schooling. Of 202,556 inmates 14 years old or older, 137,199 (67.7 percent) had no previous vocational training.

Employment. Of 1,060,926 male inmates 14 years old and older, 170,884 (16.1 percent) had never worked previously. Of the 962,678 female inmates, 306,436 (31.8 percent) had no previous work experience. Also, 99,081 inmates had served in the military service.

Of the 14-years-old and older group of inmates numbering 198,508, there were 108,484 (54.6 percent) who reported no income in the previous year. In addition, 64,831 inmates (32.6 percent) reported receiving less than $2,000 during the same period of time.

Tendency to Commit Suicide. Two sociologists of Florida Technological University surveyed 100 major male prisons in the United States concerning prisoner suicides. The base period was from 1952 to 1972, the last year for which complete figures were available. Many states and the United States Bureau of Prisons declined to provide information for the study.

In the summer of 1974, the researchers reported there had been 160 prison suicides, which represented "17.5 suicides per 100,000 prison inmates as compared to 11 suicides per 100,000 in the nation's population.[21] The suicidal inmate is young, white, single, poorly educated, and lived in a city before going to prison. He is nonviolent (to others), is serving a relatively short sentence, has few visitors, and kills himself by hanging shortly after entering prison.

In sum, these figures suggest that the "average" inmate in adult state and federal institutions in the United States is between 18 and 29 years of age, is white, is from a nonmetropolitan area, and is incarcerated in an institution housing more than 1,000 inmates. He has an eighth-grade education, received no previous vocational training, served in the military service, and earned no income the year prior to the survey. He has had an unsuccessful marriage, changes residence frequently, and is more prone to suicide than the general population.

The female inmates represent a very small proportion of the total incarcerated population, but once the increased arrest rates are processed through the criminal justice system there will no doubt be an increase in women sent to prison.

Summary

The differing institutional designs and penal practices described previously have been the manifestation of a variety of philosophies relating to the cure of criminality. Strong religious beliefs of the

---

[21] *Atlanta Journal and Constitution*, Atlanta, Georgia, June 22, 1974.

early American colonists had an effect on the structure of the New England communities, and as a result separation between church and state was often vague. The liberalization of the law under William Penn and the strong influence of the Quakers in Pennsylvania pointed toward new methods of dealing with criminal offenders. As noted, these factors gave birth to the penitentiary and what was to be known as the Pennsylvania System of penology.

The underlying assumptions concerning criminality were that there was an equation between sin and crime (a concept still permeating penal concepts in much of the South). The obvious cure for the criminal, then, was his conversion to Christianity. There is some logic to this approach since the criminal code can be traced to the old Mosaic Law. However, this form of treatment ignores such issues as mental impairment, etiology of crime, the negative effects of sensory deprivation, and the fact that some crimes are beyond the scope of religious prohibitions.

Living a monastic existence, reading only the Bible, never hearing the voice of another human being, and "communing" with nature in an isolated yard had the effect of alienation rather than resocialization of the prisoner.

When the New York prisons were erected in the 1820s, the failure of the Pennsylvania System was well known. New York authorities made the assumption that criminality was a function of slothfulness and the absence of acceptable work habits. Consequently, under the Auburn (Silent) System, inmates were disciplined through silence and hard work. Although they ate and worked in congregate systems, they lived separately and were forbidden to speak. Initially, the work consisted of making little rocks out of big ones under the notion that any work, per se, had therapeutic value in teaching the worth of the work ethic. During the Civil War, prisoners were engaged in making products needed by the Northern forces and thus the American industrial prison was born. Although prisoners were once again used for the benefit of the state, there was no evidence to indicate that the work ethic had any appreciable impact in reduction of crime.

The realization that the theological and work-ethic models had failed to achieve the objectives of their proponents, and the knowledge of effective penal innovations in England and Ireland, gave impetus to the convening of penologists at the Cincinnati meeting of the American Prison Association in 1870. The guidelines for prison management that emerged from this meeting focused on humane practices, reform of the prisoner, instilling hope, placing the prisoner's destiny in his own hands, and eliminating political influence in prison management. The indeterminate sentence was suggested, as were strong discipline, protection of society, enhancing the prisoner's self-respect, and elimination of the exploitive contract system.

Emphasis was placed on classification of prisoners, parole, executive clemency, new architectural designs, and creation of strong, professional prison management systems. But the central issues for changing the offender resided in education and vocational training. It was assumed that criminality resulted from a lack of education and training and that prisoners could be reformed by correcting such deficiencies. It was further assumed that reform could be imposed on the criminal; as a consequence, The Reformatory was created in 1876 as an educational model for reforming criminals. Unfortunately, this model ignores the fact that some educated and trained people do commit crimes. Hence it cannot be considered a model having general applicability—or, for that matter, specific applicability.

Although there has been some delay in implementing these concepts, the general trend in stated penal policies has been from retribution toward rehabilitation since "The Reformation" in 1870. Yet the reformatory became what it was supposed to replace: another monolithic bastille wherein the same kinds of degradation persist as in the prison. This situation resulted from overcrowding, emphasis on prison industries instead of vocational and educational training, and the fact that the increasing use of probation placed the best risks on the street and kept them out of the prison. Further, by the 1930s parole functions had become so widespread that all states had some form of parole legislation even though its implementation varied among jurisdictions.

Probation kept the more amenable offenders out of prison; parole removed the better offender from prison through early release; and the residue of less tractable inmates that accumulated in the reformatory caused the original objective to be abandoned.

As new philosophies of penology emerged, the previous ones were not totally abandoned, but rather de-emphasized and retained. Thus, although the educator held predominance under the reformatory regime, the prison chaplain and the industrial foreman retained some influence on prison practices.

Following World War I, there were efforts to coordinate the activities of the theological, work-ethic, and educational models in some penal systems. But it was not until World War II that the fourth major change in prison treatment evolved. Mass testing of soldiers provided measurement tools not previously available, and the importance of social work and clinical notions of treatment of human behavior were becoming commonly accepted in academic circles. Out of these factors grew what is today known as the rehabilitation model.

This model assumes that prisoners are "sick" in the psychological sense and that their cure can be brought about through the application of appropriate diagnostic and counseling techniques. The treatment includes psychiatry, psychology, social work, and whatever may pass for the "healing" sciences. The prison staffs themselves are separated into (1) the "professional," clinical personnel devoted to rehabilitation of the inmates and (2) the custodial staff whose responsibilities are solely the confinement of prisoners and protection of society.

According to the medical model, any treatment method can be justified as a cure for criminality once the presumed psychological sickness of the prisoner is accepted. Under the aegis of this model, a myriad of programs have emerged. Individually and collectively, they constitute the treatment philosophy that exists today. Yet, despite the increased staff, the acquisition of a host of treatment personnel, the creation of innumerable treatment programs, and the well-intentioned interest of society in curing the criminal, we have observed an increase in institutional violence, disorders, rebellion, and riots.

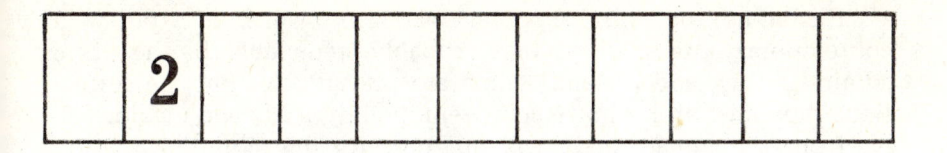

Prisons in America: Conditions after 100 Years of "Reform"

I'm afraid that the men who run the prisons as I have seen them do not share this view with respect to converting prisoners. They do not want to progress and to reform the system. They want to keep the inmates back in an archaic, brutal and inhuman situation because they do not know any better or are afraid of progress.

—Dr. Sam Sheppard[1]

The prison does not readily lend itself to scrutiny by the free world because prison officials successfully thwart all inquiry. Nonetheless, the skilled observer can translate, explain, and interpret the true dynamics of the prison culture in terms that should have meaning, significance, and relevance to the freeman.

Clues to unrest are communicated to the administration by a variety of techniques far in advance of any overt action by the inmates to force change. Disturbances, disorders, and riots in prison, as elsewhere, are symptoms of intolerable conditions within the institution that apparently are not amenable to change by any other method. Currently such disruptions of the prison regime indicate efforts to call attention to the inmates' plight. They are a plea for assistance from the public by appealing through the media. Too few choose to hear that cry; fewer yet respond with help. Often the response is gunfire.

---

[1] *Testimony of Dr. Sam Sheppard* before the United States Senate Subcommittee to Investigate Juvenile Deliquency, Washington, D.C., July 8, 1969, p. 7. Sheppard was one of several inmates or former inmates subpoenaed to testify about prison conditions by Senator Thomas Dodd.

Excluding the truly "spontaneous" riot, which is a rarity in contemporary times, all riots are probably predictable (by the astute administrator), and certainly most are preventable. But the correctional administrator who remains remote, physically and ideologically, from the inmate body will not perceive the mounting tension until the custodial captain begins to issue riot gear. Current prison disorders indicate that the inmates are usually petitioning for humane treatment, better food, adequate medical services, and—incredibly—for "prison reform." Generally, the inmate requests seem to be reasonable, should have been granted *before* the riot, and most invariably are subsequently provided *after* the riot.

Thus the administration clearly informs the inmates that it must be forced to perform its duty. It also indicates that it can be manipulated by intimidation and coercion. From these revelations, the inmates learn the necessity of developing a power base in order to bring about change within the prison.

By anticipating the needs of the inmates, however, the administrator with courage can forestall such disruptive activities, save embarrassment to his regime, and demonstrate to the inmates his true interest in their welfare. By going a step further and sharing decision making with the inmates, he can also redirect hostility back on the inmate group. The skillful administrator can thus *lead* a reform movement rather than be inundated by it. Such insightful approaches to prison management appear to be rare or nonexistent.

Oregon

On March 9, 1968, 700 inmates of the 102-year-old Oregon State Penitentiary took 40 hostages during a riot that lasted less than one day. Twelve hostages were held and later released individually as various demands were met. During the course of the riot, some $2 million in damage was done to the facility.

George W. Randall, Administrator of the Oregon Corrections Division, readily agreed that "mistakes have been made in the past."[2] The riot was brought to an end when Randall agreed to work for increased medical and psychiatric treatment, revision of the visitor system, an elected inmate council, a new canteen, changes in handling prisoner finances, improved recreation programs, and "fair treatment of Negro inmates."

One demand—removal of 73-year-old Warden Clarence T. Gladden—was realized when the warden "resigned" during the course of

---

[2] *New York Times*, March 11, 1968.

negotiations. This news was received by the inmate population with unrestrained cheers. In the aftermath of the riot, Randall also resigned, and state officials pledged to meet the inmates' demands for selection of a "top flight" warden for the prison. The search for someone to reform the Oregon prison system ended with the appointment of John Galvin of the federal prison system. Galvin was described as "the most creative and skillful innovator the Federal Bureau of Prisons ever had."[3]

> **REFORMER AWARD**
>
> *[To point out the benefits to prisoners of continued "reform efforts" in Oregon, this award was given in January 1973.]*
>
> TO: G. E. Sullivan, warden, Oregon Correctional Institution, for his unique use of colored cells and control towers to liven up the institution. Each of the tower's eight sides is painted a different shade of pastel and cell bars come in soft greens, blues and buff. For contrast, cell doors are done in vivid shades of yellow, orange, green and blue. Said Sullivan, "We keep constantly changing to keep this an exciting place to work and live in." [*The Freeworld Times*, Jan., 1973]

On February 6, 1971, 140 inmates began what was to have been a peaceful sit-down demonstration in protest of prison regulations. By the end of the demonstration, some $5,000 damage had been done to isolation cells.

California

The California prison system is impressive in many ways. It contains some 24,000 inmates under the supervision of about 121,000 employees in twelve institutions with an annual budget in excess of $100 million, thus making it the largest prison system in the United States—even larger than the Federal Bureau of Prisons.

California's innovations in corrections have been frequently described in penological literature. Innovations include the creation of the first forestry camp in 1931, establishment of a minimum-

---

[3] *The Oregonian*, Portland, Oregon, circa summer 1968.

custody prison facility by Kenyon Scudder at Chino, and development of a system of minimum-custody camps under the guidance of Richard A. McGee. In corrections, at least, these men have become folk heroes. One certainly cannot dispute that camp programs have spread throughout the West and elsewhere as it has become apparent that not all men require maximum custody.

The large number of correctional institutions in California has provided the opportunity for diversification and experimentation. It would be difficult to dispute the contention that California has produced a wide range of treatment programs that have sought to analyze, evaluate, and categorize the inmate in an effort to construct a personally tailored program that will lead to his rehabilitation.[4] Therefore, in the field of penology, California is generally acknowledged as leading the nation in prison reform and pioneering in correctional treatment programs under a progressive philosophy implemented by creative correctional administrators. Let's examine the fruits of the labors of the innovators in the "most progressive prison system" in the United States.

Several "correctional facilities" have been created that are staffed with "correctional officers"[5] trained to treat the offender with dignity and concern. On January 13, 1970, inmates were allowed into a new recreation yard at a California institution at Soledad. A fight broke out between eight white and seven black prisoners. Without any warning, the tower guard shot into the group, killing three blacks and wounding one white.

Although it is an acceptable rule of penology to use reasonable force to put down violence, there is usually presumed to be some correlation between the offense and the action taken. In the Soledad case, there is no evidence to indicate that there was a warning shot, whistle, or alarm of any type.

Alternatives usually available to authorities in quelling such disorders are the use of reserve forces (commonly known as the "goon squad"), the use of gas or a fire hose to disperse the group, firing of warning shots, or the use of the riot stick, .22 calibre rifle, or shotgun. At Soledad the most lethal weapon in the arsenal—a .30 calibre rifle—was used, with the predictable deaths resulting.

Equally predictable was the killing of a white guard three days later in retaliation. Prison officials laid the blame for these incidents on "outside agitators," "black militants," and the "new breed of

---

[4] See Chapter 3 for discussion of the effectiveness of these programs.

[5] The terms *correctional facilities* and *correctional officers* are euphemisms employed to change the image of institutional treatment.

Prisons in America

inmate" being sent to prison. A grand jury was immediately impaneled; it ruled the shooting "justifiable homicide." Before the end of 1970, a total of five inmates and two officers had been killed.

Three inmates, including George Jackson, were charged with the death of the white guard at Soledad and transferred to San Quentin. On August 7, 1970, Jackson's younger brother Jonathan and two other black inmates attempted to abduct the Marin County judge who was hearing the case about the Soledad killing, in which the San Quentin inmates were defendants. The idea was to hold the judge hostage until the release of George. Instead of securing his brother's release, Jonathan, his two colleagues, and the judge were killed in the shootout that erupted outside the Marin Civic Center.

Two weeks later at San Quentin, three guards and two inmates, one of them George Jackson, were killed in another uprising. Prison officials explained that Jackson had obtained a pistol and was making a break for the wall in an effort to escape. The credibility of officials was diminished somewhat when it was later conceded that Jackson had been shot *in the back*, while inside the yard, by a tower guard.

The reports of assaults, attempted escapes, knifings, and killings in Folsom and San Quentin state prisons are legion. The total number of prison deaths appears to be an elusive figure not readily available from the Department of Corrections.[6] Reportedly there is at least one stabbing a week at San Quentin. However, these facilities are acknowledged by California authorities as archaic, oppressive, and overcrowded institutions that are not conducive to the rehabilitation of inmates.

In the total context of reform movements, California's euphemisms for penal systems are probably of little comfort to the inmate. How much does it help for him to learn that he may well be shot by a "correctional counselor" in a "treatment milieu" at a "correctional facility" as opposed to being killed by an "illiterate guard" in the "sweat shop" of a "penitentiary"? Renaming a skunk a pussycat is not likely to enhance its odor.

Kansas

On June 18, 1969, a riot in the Kansas State Penitentiary resulted in 100 state highway patrolmen gathering to quell the riot under the command of Superintendent Colonel Robert Woodson of

---

[6] Between January 1970 and January 1972 there were 26 inmates and 12 officers killed in California.

that department. A description of the management of the prison prior to the riot is provided in United States testimony in September 1970.

> At the time of the study, the inmates were clearly and obviously the strongest force within the prison. Prison management subtly negotiated the controls with the leadership of the inmate structure. Rackets run by the inmate leadership such as gambling, homosexual prostitution of younger and weaker inmates, drugs, liquor, medical treatment, leather (craft), and other such things were generally overlooked by prison officials in return for the maintaining of superficial control over the inmate population. Radios, cell assignments, work assignments, food privileges and other privileges were used as favors in return for cooperation.
>
> Inmates did the counts on other inmates. Inmates worked the locking systems. Inmates did the clerical work. Inmates ran the hospital and controlled the supply of drugs flowing through the prison hospital.
>
> In June of 1969, over 1,500 capsules of Darvon were being passed out through the dispensary from inmates to other inmates every single day. At that time, there was neither a pharmacist nor a physician in the prison.
>
> The practices of the inmate leadership, however, included at that time murder, maiming, blackmail, extortion, gang rape, physical beatings and bum rap informing to mention only a few things.[7]

In February 1968, a raid on the prison temporarily broke up the inmates' control. In June 1969 another raid was held, and trucks were required to haul away the contraband. This action was followed by six weeks of rioting that resulted in $140,000 damage to the physical plant.

After the riot of June 18, Director of Penal Services Charles McAttee was removed and State Police Director Woodson was appointed as his replacement. What followed was a general "get tough" policy of suppression of the inmate population. Warden Sherman Crouse was transferred to the state reformatory at Hutchinson.

For complex reasons resulting from the difficult transition to the new administration, the internal power struggle, and the efforts to

---

[7] Don Hardesty, *Report to the Senate Subcommittee on Juvenile Deliquency*, Topeka, Kansas, September 3, 1970, pp. 3, 4.

call attention to the need for reform, over 400 inmates mutilated themselves during the subsequent months.

An aftermath of the riots in 1969 resulted in a lawsuit, filed in federal court in Kansas City by 16 prisoners, charging prison officials with cruel and unusual punishment. The alleged events grew out of the June 18 riot and involved placing inmates in "strip cells" for long periods of time and spraying them with a fire hose.

In May 1970, Lieutenant Colonel R. J. Gaffney retired from army service and was appointed warden of the prison to bring about needed reforms.[8] His military heritage is evident in management practices: "If it doesn't move, we paint it." His stated view of the prison provides an indication of his perception of the prison problems:

> *The prison experience can be valuable. Some of these men are a hell of a lot better for having been here. Any prisoner can make this a valuable period in his life and the time he spends here can be constructive and useful.*[9]

During January 1971, some 40 members of the Kansas Legislature toured the prison at Lansing to learn about prison problems. Their orientation consisted of a briefing by prison officials, listening to the prison choir, and lunching in the officers' dining room.

Arkansas

The barbaric conditions in the Arkansas State Penitentiary came to national attention in January 1968 when I (as superintendent appointed by then-Governor Winthrop Rockefeller to reform the prison) exhumed the bodies of three inmates allegedly murdered by prison officials or inmates. Shortly thereafter, I was fired.[10]

In mid-October of that year, national attention was once again focused on the prison when 120 inmates protesting prison conditions were shot at by prison officials. The inmates sat in the main compound to demonstrate their grievances concerning brutality, exploitation, and poor medical care. Instead of attempting to reconcile the complaints, prison officials issued 12-gauge shotguns and riot gear to an increased guard force.

---

[8] *Kansas City Star*, January 22, 1971, p. 7A.

[9] See further text and footnote in Chapter 11 relating to Gaffney's philosophy and termination.

[10] See: Tom Murton and Joe Hyams, *Accomplices to the Crime: The Arkansas Prison Scandal* (New York: Grove Press, 1969).

During negotiations that followed the demonstration, some of the men returned to work in the fields. The remainder were ordered to move to another portion of the compound, but refused and sat on the ground in peaceful protest. They were not attempting to escape; they posed no threat to life or property. Nonetheless, associate superintendent Gary Haydis ordered the shotgunning of these inmates, and 24 of them were wounded. Miraculously, there were no deaths. For his part in the shooting, Haydis was indicted by a federal grand jury in the summer of 1969 on a charge of depriving inmates of their civil rights by his actions. (Haydis had been a lieutenant at Soledad just prior to his appointment in Arkansas; he was the training officer there.)

During the trial in mid-December of that year, George Johnson, Assistant Superintendent of the California Correctional Institution at Tehachapi, testified that Haydis enjoyed a good reputation in the California prison system and that "we always considered him to be very good at handling inmates." Johnson further stated that firing into the air "to quell unruly convicts" is a common practice in California. (However, Johnson's comment was not directly related to the facts in this case because Haydis had ordered the shooting at the men, *not* into the air.) Before the trial was concluded, Federal Judge J. Smith Henley directed an acquittal of Haydis because "the evidence failed to show Haydis acted with bad purpose or evil intent" as required in the elements of proof for this offense by the United States Code.[11]

During the subsequent three and one-half years, there were at least 22 stabbings and 9 killings at the prison. And during this same period, the federal courts in Arkansas ruled three times that specific practices at the prison were unconstitutional because they constituted "cruel and unusual punishment." The first ruling dealt with inhumane practices in the isolation units; the second with cruel conditions relating to the chaining of inmates to a fence for several days; and the third with the shooting of unarmed, nonviolent inmates protesting prison conditions as recited earlier.

On February 18, 1970, Federal Judge J. Smith Henley ruled that commitment to the Arkansas prison system, per se, constituted cruel and unusual punishment and therefore violated the United States Constitution. As Judge Henley observed, "If Arkansas is going to operate a penitentiary system it is going to have to be a system that is countenanced by the Constitution of the United States."[12]

Then-Commissioner of Correction Robert Sarver assessed the

---

[11] *Arkansas Democrat*, Little Rock, Arkansas, December 18, 1969, p. 10A.

current state of corrections in a prepared statement to a United States Senate subcommittee investigating prison conditions: "When I read of an exposé of homosexualities, bribings, escapes, [and] political corruption in prisons, I think most knowledgeable correction administrators think: 'So, what else is new?' "[13]

On November 2, 1970, armed inmates tried to shoot their way out of the isolation unit at Cummins Prison Farm and, before the event was over, Superintendent Bill Steed, Commissioner Sarver, and two inmate guards were held hostage. Between 17 and 20 inmates involved in the incident threatened to kill the inmate guard hostages if their demands for an escape vehicle and safe conduct from the prison were not met.

Sarver and Steed then became voluntary hostages in an effort to resolve the problem. The inmates stated that the uprising was in protest of lack of clothing, eating utensils, and proper sanitation. And they complained about the indiscriminate shooting by inmate guards among the work crews in the field.

Governor Winthrop Rockefeller refused to submit to the intimidation but promised correction of the inequities if the inmates surrendered. Subsequently the hostages were released, the guns were confiscated, and order was restored—for the time being.[14]

Less than three weeks later, Cummins was rocked with the first riot ever to take place in the Arkansas prison system. Some 75 state troopers took over guard towers and provided security inside the prison. Fifty more patrolled the perimeter of the prison and three companies of National Guard troops were activated. Over 500 inmates (40 percent of the prison population) were in open rebellion against the prison system. The riot was suppressed by the troops who remained at the prison for several weeks to maintain control.

Explanations by prison officials of the continuing difficulties at the prison centered around "racial conflicts" and efforts at integration. Meanwhile Judge Henley waited, with enforced patience, in

---

[12] Judge J. Smith Henley, *Opinion: Lawrence J. Holt et al. v. Robert Sarver et al.*, United States District Court, Eastern District of Arkansas, Pine Bluff Division, February 18, 1970, p. 44.

[13] Robert Sarver, "Conditions of Juvenile and Young Offenders Institutions," *Report of Proceedings*, Subcommittee on Juvenile Delinquency of the Committee on the Judiciary, vol. 6, United States Senate, March 11, 1969, p. 447.

[14] The uprising occurred the day before the general election in which Rockefeller was defeated by Dale Bumpers. It was later contended (but never proved) that the incident was planned for the purpose of embarrassing Rockefeller and supporting Bumpers' claim that the incumbent had never lived up to his promise to reform the prison.

hopes that prison authorities would comply with his order to provide a plan for rehabilitating the Arkansas prison system. If one was not forthcoming, he threatened to close the entire prison system. The State of Arkansas had achieved the distinction of being the only prison system in the United States to have been declared by a court to be in conflict with the United States Constitution.[15] The same court accepted a plea of "no contest" by former Superintendent Jim Bruton, who was given a one-year suspended jail sentence and a $1,000 fine for fear that inmates would kill him because of his acts of brutality if he were sent to prison. The court declined to accept a plea of "guilty" because such a plea would have rendered Bruton ineligible to draw his $333.33 a month pension check from the prison system.[16]

Indiana

The largest reformatory in the United States is located at Pendleton, Indiana, about 30 miles northeast of Indianapolis. Until 1970, Pendleton boasted of having the only uncensored inmate newspaper in American prisons. However, like most reformatories, Pendleton had fallen into the same oppressive routine found in prisons with all the attendant hostility, fights, and polarization of staff and inmates.

In the mid-sixties, in an effort to reform the reformatory, a sociologist was appointed as superintendent. His aversion to rules, disciplinary measures, and use of authority in general led to a very permissive atmosphere that demoralized the staff and astonished the inmates.

The guards, stripped of their usual authority, stood by while the inmates conducted themselves pretty much as they chose. There was no adequate preparation of the population for accepting or demonstrating the responsibility that the new privileges entailed. Predictably, many inmates took advantage of the opportunity to escape. Reportedly, 89 inmates absconded from Pendleton in the first weeks of the superintendent's tenure.

As Dr. A. LaMont Smith[17] used to say: "You have to keep'em

---

[15] Subsequently, a circuit court judge ruled on May 7, 1971, that imprisonment in the West Virginia State Penitentiary violates constitutional prohibitions against cruel and unusual punishment. The ruling applied only to a single institution and not to the entire system.

[16] *New York Times*, January 20, 1970; *Arkansas Gazette*, January 17, 1970.

[17] Former faculty member of the School of Criminology, University of California at Berkeley.

to treat'em." The new superintendent demonstrated that he could not keep them so the correctional authorities did not keep him.

At the main prison in Michigan City, 25 inmates rebelled in August 1968 and took two guards as hostages. Their complaints included poor food, excessive prices at the commissary, overcrowding, and lack of treatment personnel. A 50-man force of the Indiana State Police riot squad quelled the disturbance without incident.

On September 26, 1969, several hundred inmates gathered in a fenced recreation area to protest general conditions and what they considered to be placing four inmates in isolation arbitrarily. The inmate body had been led to believe that these inmates were to have been released on the previous day. Instead, two were transferred to the main prison. In defiance, some inmates started fires in the furniture factory while some 230 others sat in protest. The yard was cleared, by armed riot squads, of all but a group of black inmates who refused to talk to the guards.

Eleven white guards (half of whom, it was later revealed, were members of the Ku Klux Klan) and one vocational teacher appeared at the fence in full riot gear bearing 12-gauge shotguns. No effort was made to disperse the inmates with a fire hose, tear gas, smoke bombs, or riot sticks. The guns were stuck through the fence. Captain of the Guard Jason Huckeby ordered a volley fired into the air and instructed the inmates to return to their cells. Instead of moving, the inmates lay on the ground assuming that the guards would not shoot them in the back. One inmate remained standing with his back to the guard force and raised his hand in the black power salute. One of the guards was heard to say "That one is mine!" and the 20-year-old youth fell to the ground, dead, with five bullets in his body. This was the beginning of what was later called the "Pendleton Massacre."

Before the cease-fire order was given, between 15 and 90 shots were fired into the demonstrators lying on the ground. (The discrepancy in the number of shots fired is the result of conflicting reports from witnesses.) In addition to the death, the results were described by one investigator as follows:

> *Forty-six men were wounded, many critically, from shots in the head, in the back, through the chest, in the legs, feet, thigh, through the groin, in the side—in fact some who tried to throw up their hands in traditional gesture of surrender had their hands shattered and are minus fingers. Many of the injured had multiple wounds.*[18]

---

[18] Luther C. Hicks, *Testimony before the Senate Subcommittee to Investigate Juvenile Delinquency*, Washington, D.C., September 29, 1970, p. 5.

There was no disciplinary action taken against either the guards who did the shooting or those who later gassed the demonstrators while forcing them to disperse and return to their cells. The grand jury was quickly impaneled and ruled that:

> From all the evidence submitted, the Grand Jury has concluded that the guards were in the performance of their duties at the time of the incident; therefore, there is insufficient evidence to place criminal responsibility on any of the reformatory personnel involved.[19]

The superintendent stated that he backed the action 100 percent. Governor Edgar D. Whitcomb stated that no reformatory personnel would be suspended or released. Subsequently, a federal grand jury intervened and indicted eight guards and a plumber from the prison maintenance crew on charges of violating the civil rights of the inmates who had been shot.[20]

Once again, inmates peacefully protesting conditions were shot down for their "crime" by prison officials who were neither being threatened nor endangered in any physical way.

Ohio

During an attempted escape from the Ohio State Penitentiary in 1930, a fire swept through the cell block and claimed the lives of 322 inmates. These men burned or suffocated in their cells because the guards were afraid to unlock the cell doors.[21] The death toll constitutes the greatest single disaster in Ohio—and in the annals of American penology.

Relations between staff and inmates have not materially improved over the years. Accounts of prison conditions since that time have been a recitation of archaic, if not barbaric, treatment of prisoners, resulting finally in a major riot in June 1968 that injured fifty persons and caused an estimated $1 million worth of damage. It took 150 National Guardsmen, backed up by 800 additional troopers at a nearby fort, to establish order.

The warden was fired and a new one appointed. But the new warden was accused of showing "too much concern for the inmates"

---

[19] *Ibid.*, p. 6.

[20] On November 18, 1971, all eight defendants were acquitted by a federal court jury. See *The Indianapolis News*, Indianapolis, Indiana, November 18, 1971, p. 1.

[21] Harry Barnes and Negley Teeters, *New Horizons in Criminology* (Englewood Cliffs, N.J.: Prentice-Hall, 1947), pp. 592, 593.

and met considerable resistance from the guard force in his efforts to reform the prison. On August 21, 1968, some 300 inmates seized a cell block and took nine guards hostage. The principal demands were for a federal investigation of prison conditions and removal of sadistic guards. After a 30-hour impasse, Commissioner of Corrections Maurey C. Koblentz ordered an assault to retake the cell block. Ninety pounds of plastic explosives were detonated, blasting holes in the side and roof of the cell block. Concussions shook windows within a one-mile radius of the prison. Lawmen swarmed through the holes with shouts of "Kill the bastards!" and launched a two-hour shooting spree, although the hostages were taken to safety within a few minutes. By the time the episode was over, 70 shotgun blasts and five bursts of machine-gun fire had raked the prison. The toll: five inmates dead; ten seriously injured.

Eyewitness reports by civilian observers in adjacent buildings indicated that uniformed officers herded the inmates from the cell block into the yard, stripped them naked, and forced them to lie down on the ground. "I've never seen anything like it. The prisoners were naked on the ground, face down, and were being hit in the head by rifle butts. I saw one man shot as he laid on the ground naked."[22]

Columbus Police Major Dwight Joseph emerged from the hole in the wall and commented: "A lot of them were shot. They were shot for *refusing to obey orders.* We had to shoot them. Nobody was shooting warning shots. We were shooting people. That was the order and that is what we did." [Emphasis added.][23]

Major Harold Cardwell, in charge of the State Police detachment that shot up the prison, denied that more than five inmates had been killed. "We don't have any bodies buried in the courtyard. This is not Arkansas."[24]

REFORM RHETORIC

"I don't believe in tear gas. It's too indiscriminate. I prefer to use a gun."
—*Harold Cardwell, formerly warden, Ohio State Penitentiary, shortly after he assumed command of the Arizona State Prison.*

---

[22] Dale Huffman, *Statement before the Senate Subcommittee to Investigate Juvenile Deliquency* (quoting Charles R. McNeil, observer), Washington, D.C., July 8, 1969, p. 9.

[23] *Ibid.*

[24] *Ibid.*

Inmate Thomas Bradshaw, Jr., was shot to death in the back as he lay naked for "raising up to assert authority."[25]

Inmate Walter Baisden was shot to death in the back while lying naked because he "raised up when he was supposed to be lying down."

Inmates Burton Anderson and Jesse Wade were shot to death in their cells for "refusing to obey orders."

Inmate Wesley Neville, Jr., was shot and killed for "attempting to resist arrest," according to lawmen. Neville had been a polio victim from birth, could not walk without braces, and had difficulty raising his arms.

The Ohio State Patrol was assigned the task of investigating charges of brutality and the deaths of the inmates.

Dr. Sam Sheppard gave his analysis of the difficulty with the Ohio prison system:

Mr. Maurey Koblentz, the head of the system, is like a cruel emperor who has life and death power over his subjects. He has inherited and continues to perpetuate a system that is entrenched in the dogma of punishment as a positive force. He is blind to the fact that punishment can only deform rather than reform. And in some ways he and his underlings are victims of this dogma; they are men who have become insensitive to human needs and human emotion because they have become conditioned by the system which they operate. Of course the real victim is the inmate who is handled on a subhuman level. Under this system he can be degraded, punished and even killed with impunity.[26]

An Ohio newsman worked as a guard at the Ohio prison for several months during the winter of 1969-1970. His formal training consisted of the following admonitions:

Don't wait for an inmate to hit you before you hit him. If he looks as if he is going to hit you, hit him.

By law, all we have to give inmates are housing, food, clothing and medical attention. Anything else — mail, visits, movies and rehabilitation — is a privilege.[27]

---

[25] For this reference and those following, see Huffman, pp. 9, 10.

[26] Dr. Sam Sheppard, *Testimony before the Senate Subcommittee to Investigate Juvenile Delinquency*, Washington, D.C., July 8, 1969, p. 5.

[27] *NCCD News*, New York, March-April, 1970, p. 15.

Sheppard recited an account of a demand by Koblentz that Sheppard get rid of that "S.O.B. Bailey" (his attorney) or he would be in "a world of trouble."

> *I naturally refused, whereupon I was chained with leg chains, chains around the neck and I don't know where all else. I was then given the treatment known as being placed between the doors for six days. These were two metal doors and were less than 12 inches apart.*
>
> *There was no food. There was no light and little air, and I felt I would suffocate. I couldn't sleep, I would just pass out. I was allowed to wear my shorts, shoes and socks. I had no toilet privileges and just stood in my own excrement.*
>
> *After six days they removed me from the doors and Koblentz asked me if I had changed my mind. I made a rather unfortunate comment about Mr. Koblentz' heritage whereupon I was placed between the doors for three more days.*
>
> *When I came out my ankles had swollen so large the shoe strings had split on my shoes. I should add that during this time I was beaten with rubber hoses.* [28]

Major Cardwell, who led the prison attack resulting in five deaths, was appointed warden three days after the August riot. He later stated his philosophy of prison management before the United States Senate:

> *I believe in being firm but fair—in equal rules equally enforced—that every person should be treated with courtesy and dignity—that he should be encouraged to develop pride and self-respect—and I am unalterably opposed to brutality or discrimination by anyone, anywhere, at any time.* [29]

An Ohio prison reform group made up of citizens conducted an independent investigation and made the following report on Cardwell's "treatment" program:

> *The Governor appointed a new warden, Maj. Harold J. Cardwell of the State Highway Patrol. He at once built two machine gun towers in the middle of the courtyard, and cut down all the trees and bushes, to assure a clear line of fire. He armed his guards, not only with their usual clubs, blackjacks,*

---

[28] Sheppard, *op. cit.*, p. 3.
[29] Harold Cardwell, *Statement to the Senate Subcommittee to Investigate Juvenile Delinquency*, Washington, D.C., September 28, 1970, p. 6.

and canisters of chemical Mace, but with pistols and shotguns as well. And he built special shotgun emplacements inside C and D block, where the bad guys were. For many months the Warden himself wore a pistol everywhere. He might not understand penology, but as an ex-Marine, he certainly understood war.[30]

Florida

The Florida prison system has inherited a somewhat deserved reputation of not having progressed much beyond the days of the notorious chain gangs.[31] Despite professions of prison reform in the 1960s, continued reports of prison mismanagement reached the freeworld. In 1970, an investigative reporter was allowed to visit the main prison at Raiford to talk privately to inmates and probe prison records. His findings seemed somewhat inconsistent with the officially stated "correctional" policy of the division of corrections. For example:

The prison records show [medical technician] Murphy diagnosed the swollen, gangrenous [inmate's] hand as a fracture and sent [inmate Milt Frank] to the university hospital for treatment. There, the records show it was 40 hours after a fall caused his hand to swell before he reached the university hospital only 35 miles away.

...Frank, a convict with half his hand gone...swore that a medical technician, J. J. Murphy, had refused him adequate treatment. Murphy, in a long interview, denied it.[32]

The investigator uncovered many instances of inadequate medical treatment and reported that "despite fear of retribution, [inmate Tony Antone] said roaches had crawled down his face twice after his head bandages were unwound. On one occasion, he swore, hospital personnel had to pick the insects out of the wound."[33]

On May 7 of that year, inmate J. C. Reid of Raiford prison had

---

[30] Ysabel Rennie, *Statement to the Senate Subcommittee to Investigate Juvenile Delinquency*, Washington, D.C., September 28, 1970, p. 7.

[31] One account of the savagery and brutality of the road camps (which still exist as part of the prison system) was documented in a book entitled *Cool Hand Luke* by Donn Pearce, a former inmate of the road camp. His account was later made into the movie of the same name.

[32] *Atlanta Journal and Constitution*, Atlanta, Georgia, October 3, 1970.

[33] *Ibid.*

Prisons in America

an asthma attack, was treated as an outpatient at the prison hospital at 5:05 P.M. and returned to his cell. The next entry in the medical record is a notation the following day at 6:20 A.M. that he had died. The same investigator reported that:

> *In a shocking attempt to whitewash a prison death, Florida prison functionaries have falsified medical records and tried to hospitalize a corpse....*
>
> *Sometime after his mysterious hospital trip, Reid returned to his cell where he had an asthma seizure on the night of May 7th. He repeatedly rattled his cell door for more than an hour, appealing for help. Then he fell, in a fit of wheezing, to his cell floor....*
>
> *Since Reid had friends and relatives on the outside who might ask questions, prison officials sought to cover up the awkward fact that he had died in his cell, calling for help, after being turned away from the hospital.*[34]

Two inmates and a prison official issued sworn affidavits substantiating the information reported. They also confirmed that correctional officers had attempted to have the corpse admitted to the hospital so that it could later be identified as deceased in the hospital. The hospital administrator who provided the information was ordered to resign or be suspended for "smearing the institution." The inmates who testified were harassed. That has been the net result of efforts and promises by prison officials to provide a "total and thorough investigation."

Tensions over prison conditions increased during the subsequent few months, resulting in a so-called riot on February 13, 1971. The "riot" was preceded by a 72-hour hunger strike and work stoppage by inmates of the maximum-security section of Raiford. The inmates were simply asking for improved prison conditions. This protest was on the way to being peacefully resolved when an estimated 600 inmates, who were gathered in the recreation field, began destroying property in the yard and proceeded toward the fence.

Major Curt McKenzie, Raiford's chief custodial officer, explained, "[W]hen the men got within 30 yards of the fence [I] ordered eight officers to fire a warning volley from a submachine gun. Two more blasts of grapeshot followed from .12 gauge shotguns."[35]

---

[34] *Atlanta Journal and Constitution*, Atlanta, Georgia, October 5, 1970.

[35] *Daytona Beach Sunday News-Journal*, Daytona, Florida, February 14, 1971, p. 2A.

It was reported that about 100 inmates were beaten or shot. "This riot was building up over the past few months," Director of Corrections Louis Wainwright said. "How can we expect the prisoners not to feel this way if they don't think they're getting a fair shake?"[36]

The FBI conducted an investigation into the prison violence. If the report has been completed, it has never been released.

A month later the NAACP claimed that some inmates were still not accounted for. Governor Reuben Askew suspended three officials and seven guards three months after that for "using excessive force" against the inmates. The governor's action was protested by State Representative Gene Shaw, who feared that it might "hurt morale among the law enforcement men." One hundred fifty prison guards voted to assist the defense of the suspended officials.

Mrs. Carl Scott, a lawyer working for the ACLU, filed suit in federal court on behalf of 36 Raiford inmates asking for federal takeover of the prison a week after the uprising. A few days later an unidentified man entered her home and shot her in the chest with a .38 calibre revolver.

Later, in commenting on prison racial difficulties, Director Wainwright stated that black inmates got a fair share of the good jobs and training positions at the Apalachee Correctional Institution. But his own total at the time showed that only two blacks had administrative jobs as compared to 21 whites.

A state senator who toured the Raiford facility commented, "The egg-pickers were mostly black, the vocational programs mostly white." Wainwright's response was that "people should be assigned to jobs based on their qualifications."[37]

New York

On October 2, 1970, rebellious inmates in the Manhattan House of Detention known as The Tombs rioted and took eight hostages. The uprising quickly spread to institutions in all five New York City boroughs. A group of inmates in the Queens prison sued the City of New York to enjoin prison officials from perpetuating the "cruel, unusual, uncivilized and unlawful conditions"[38] in the institution.

---

[36] *Ibid.*

[37] *St. Petersburg Times*, St. Petersburg, Florida, March 22, 1971. Wainwright served as president of the American Correctional Association during 1970–1971.

[38] *Atlanta Journal and Constitution*, Atlanta, Georgia, December 27, 1970, p. 16C.

The federal judge hearing the case granted an interim restraining order prohibiting guards from mistreating the inmates. Riots in the five institutions lasted about 110 hours and involved approximately 6,000 prisoners who took a total of 32 hostages. The prisoners surrendered on October 5 after officials promised there would be no reprisals. The inmates were then herded into a courtyard and what followed was reported by reporter Michael McCardell:

> *It was a gruesome scene. About 250 prisoners were sitting on the grass. Behind them, 30 Correction Department guards were lined up, all of them holding weapons—ax handles, baseball bats and nightsticks.*
>
> *One inmate was dragged out a doorway onto a loading platform and five guards attacked him with their clubs. They battered his head and face, and blood flowed over his face and body. He was kicked off the platform, and several other guards pounded him again with their clubs.*[39]

The cause of the riot on October 2 was demands for speedier trials, lower bail, and improved prison conditions. Three State Supreme Court Justices promptly held bail hearings and released some inmates on their own recognizance.

Another reporter gave an eyewitness account of the beatings from the ninth floor of a nearby warehouse:

> *The beating started as a prisoner was pushed through a doorway onto a loading dock where there were a couple of guards armed with axe handles, bats, and nightsticks. A few smashes to the head and a doubling-over blow to the stomach, then on to a hungry mob of about 25 or 30 guards armed in the same manner as their aides on the platform. The inmate fell into the mob and they beat him to a bloody pulp and stomped him a few times before throwing him into a van.*
>
> *The next inmate was beaten on the platform with the same intensity, blow after blow that I could almost feel myself a few hundred feet away. A ramming axe handle to the groin and down he went to the concrete, only to be pulled up and knocked down again for the kicks which would send him through the air to the now re-grouped mob for their licks, and then on to the van—not an ambulance but a Correctional Department prison on wheels.*[40]

---

[39] *Ibid.*
[40] *Village Voice*, New York, February 4, 1971, p. 46.

One month later, on November 5, 1970, inmates of the Auburn Correctional Facility rioted and held 50 hostages for eight hours. Damage was estimated at $500,000. Although the inmates' grievances were not published, prison officials attributed the riot to lack of training and racial tensions between inmates and guards. A grand jury laid the blame on inadequate training for guards and judicial "interference" in prison management.

State Correction Commissioner Paul D. McGinnis later listed the demands as better clothing, protection from reprisals by guards, revision of rules on letter writing, more programs (unspecified), and more liberalized prison rules.

City Commissioner George F. McGrath observed that "you get basic reform and appropriate attention only after riots and other disturbances. This has always been so in the prison field."[41] Prison officials promised to relieve overcrowding and to improve conditions.

After one year's effort by correctional administrators to fulfill this promise, the population of The Tombs numbered higher than the day of the riot. Commissioner McGrath reported to the City Board of Correction that 25 inmates had died in the institution during the one year since the riot.

The Attica Atrocity

"If we cannot live as people, we will at least try to die like men."[42]

Events leading up to, during, and after the Attica Correctional Institution riot of September 9–13, 1971, will probably remain unclear for some time. This recent outbreak of prison unrest was born in obscure circumstances, confused by conflicting reports during the revolt, and lost in a fog of "explanations" after its suppression. The drama retained aspects of a Laurel and Hardy travesty with a touch of incredibility more characteristic of fiction than of fact.

One thing is clear: the riot didn't "just happen." In July, two months before the riot and six months after Russell Oswald became Commissioner of Corrections for New York, Attica prisoners had sent a petition to his office asking for improved prison conditions. Oswald pleaded that he "needed more time" and apparently took no action.

Some news telecasts reported that 12 hours before the Septem-

---

[41] *New York Times*, October 23, 1970.

[42] Attica inmate Charles Horatio.

ber riot, prison guards had been informed of the pending event and had so informed the warden's office. No action was taken to head off the uprising. Much of the rest remains unclear.

Commissioner Oswald taped himself talking about projected prison reforms, and his remarks were played for the inmate population on September 3. Oswald spoke in general terms of installing law libraries, training personnel, establishing four community correctional centers as soon as practical, encouraging volunteers to visit the prison, and implementing vocational and academic training programs for the inmates. Most of the balance of his remarks fell into the category of "reform rhetoric" so often heard by the inmates. One of Oswald's main difficulties was that he lacked credibility with the inmates. Julio Carlos, among the first inmates to be interviewed after the riot, told newsmen that the prisoners did not trust Commissioner Oswald because he had made "too many promises" without fulfilling them:

> *The first time he came in [to negotiate with the rebels], he told us a lie. We knew he wasn't gonna come through, that he was going to promise and promise and in a year's time he might come up with a little better food and books.*[43]

Because inmates lacked faith in the prison administration, a negotiating committee of 17 members was created to deal with prisoner demands. Unfortunately, this group was more distinguished for its concern for the lives of the inmates and hostages than for its knowledge of penology. Further, according to Parkinson's Law, any committee consisting of more than 13 members is foredoomed to failure because it will never agree on anything. The Attica committee was destined to follow this mandate.

REFORMER AWARD

TO: The entire membership of the E. R. Cass Award Committee, American Correctional Association. Members Stanley Brodsky, E. R. Cass, Edna Goodrich, Bruce Johnson, Oliver Keller, Jr., Thomas Mangogna, Sanger Powers and Richie Turner showed remarkable judgment in selecting Russell Oswald, of Attica fame, as recipient of the ACA's highest award. [*The Freeworld Times*, Aug.–Sept., 1973]

---

[43] *New York Times,* September 23, 1971, p. 67.

Oswald agreed to grant or support 28 of the 31 inmate demands, denying only amnesty, removal of the superintendent, and prisoner transportation to a foreign country. He noted that these demands should have been met before the riot. (Oswald later observed on national television—in what appeared to be an argument against himself—that it did not seem unreasonable for the inmates to protest their allotment of only one roll of toilet paper every five weeks and only 52 showers a year.)

As a result of complex determinations not readily apparent at this time, Oswald ordered several hundred armed troopers into the prison to retake the facility and rescue the hostages. Ten guards were killed by the assaulting troops (nine died at the time and one died of wounds nearly a month later). And in the process of "rescuing" the hostages, 28 inmates were also killed. The death of one guard during the uprising and the killing of three inmates by their fellow prisoners brought the toll eventually to 43 deaths in what has become known as the "Attica Massacre."

If possible, the aftermath of the riot proved to be more confusing than the riot itself. The predictable investigations were begun ostensibly to discover the truth but more probably to affix blame for the Attica bloodbath. One of the investigators even rendered a conclusion before he began the investigation. Representative Claude Pepper of Florida was appointed chairman of a congressional panel to make the inquiry into the riot. Five days after the riot (and prior to his inquiry), he stated that "had there been enough money, much of this tragedy could have been prevented."[44]

The McKay Commission, appointed by Governor Nelson Rockefeller, rendered its report on the Attica riot one year later with somewhat different conclusions as to the causes: "Despite vows of reform, appointment of commissions, and visits by legislators and special committees, there was no improvement in conditions at Attica for months."[45]

In March 1972, the inmates were allowed to elect a liaison committee to establish "a formal channel of communication with the institution concerning grievances and common problems. But the inmate grievance committee, while providing a forum for discussion of complaints, gave inmates no sense of participation in the important decisions affecting their lives.[46]

---

[44] *Arkansas Democrat*, Little Rock, Arkansas, September 19, 1971, p. 2A.

[45] Robert B. McKay, Chairman, *Official Report of the New York State Special Commission on Attica* (New York: Bantam Books, 1972), p. 467.

[46] *Ibid.*, p. 470.

Superintendent Vincent Mancusi resigned rather than implement this plan. By August 1972, half the inmates on the committee had been transferred to other institutions, had quit, or had been released from prison. "Less patient inmates began asking what had become of the 28 points to which Oswald had agreed in D yard and began talking about their readiness to risk their lives once again if change did not come."[47] Forty-three victims of Attica have been buried, but the rumbles of dissent are heard once more.

> *Thus, the cycle of misunderstanding, protest, and reaction continues, and confrontation remains the only language in which the inmates feel they can call attention to the system. The possibility that Attica townspeople will again hear the dread sound of the powerhouse whistle is very real.*[48]

To which the inmate adds: "How much money does it require to stop the killing of inmates; to stop brutalizing them; to treat them as human beings?"

This reform odyssey through American prisons in the 1970s indicates that we have not come very far from the barbarity of the 1870s when concerted reform efforts first began. It is also obvious that it really makes no difference whether one examines prisons in the western, southern, midwestern, or eastern sections of the United States; regardless of the relative sophistication of the system, there seems to be no significant difference in the way prisoners are treated.

In Chapter 3, we shall examine the traditional prison in an effort to determine why this uniformly negative impact is pervasive throughout our American "correctional" system.

---

[47] *Ibid.*, p. 467.
[48] *Ibid.*

3

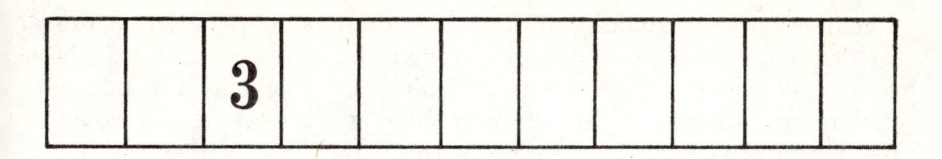

The Traditional Prison Model

> We trained hard... but it seemed that every time we were beginning to form up into teams we would be reorganized.... I was to learn later in life that we tend to meet any new situation by reorganizing; and a wonderful method it can be for creating the illusion of progress while producing confusion, inefficiency, and demoralization.
> —Petronius Arbiter, 210 b.c.

Criminality is probably one of the few social phenomena that is studied by analyzing those who are the failures of their "profession" —the ones who get caught. By definition, the skillful perpetrator of a criminal act is the one who, at the very least, prevents his own discovery. Thus the one who is not skillful in accomplishing this feat is set apart; he is not representative of the definition. Yet the only opportunity we have had to study criminals has been to look at these failures in the controlled environment of the prison.

Sampling the failures in a prison setting, of course, has many shortcomings. Not only does it fail to take into account those criminals who are neither apprehended nor convicted, but it also does not include those criminals who, for a variety of reasons, are excluded from the prison system. Those convicted of white collar crime, for example, tend to receive fines or very minimal jail sentences. Prostitutes tend to be fined instead of imprisoned. Many crimes are not reflected in the prison population because the laws governing them are generally ignored by the society. Adultery, fornication, and so-called aberrant sexual behavior rarely result in prosecution, conviction, or incarceration.

It is fairly obvious that although studies of prison populations may be informative in specific areas of interest, they fail to demarcate the boundaries of the true criminal population in the larger society simply because the sample is not representative. Efforts to define the attributes of the criminal by analyzing the prison inmate are as confusing and unproductive as a trip to the zoo would be in providing an understanding of the characteristics of animal life in the natural habitat. A study of a lion reared in captivity and conditioned to respond to an imposed structure is not very useful in understanding why he was captured in the first place. Nor is such a study of much assistance in attempting to explain or modify behavior of the free lion in the jungle. Since the true criminal population has thus far escaped identification, research must remain incomplete and inconclusive because most theories of criminality have relied upon suppositions based on observations of the captive criminal population.

The Dogma of Penology

A major penological assumption is that prison research reveals the etiology of crime. As mentioned above, such a view does not materially contribute to an accurate understanding of crime because the individuals studied do not represent criminals in general. Since it has been estimated that only about 2 percent of those arrested eventually go to prison, it is unwarranted to generalize findings in prison studies to the other 98 percent; certainly these findings do not apply to unidentified criminals. Unfortunately, this erroneous assumption has led to some dubious notions about penology that generally have been accepted as dogma. Some people even refer to them as the *tenets* of penology.

Generally, these notions can be summarized as follows: (1) the criminal is a deviant, and (2) he needs to be incarcerated, but (3) because he will be returned to society some day, he needs rehabilitation, and (4) the people to do this rehabilitating are those on the prison staff. To cope with these four notions, criminologists have reacted with (1) models to explain the deviancy, (2) facilities to incarcerate the deviants, (3) methods of rehabilitating them based on the deviancy models, and (4) employment of treatment staffs to carry out the rehabilitation programs.

The first of these notions is that convicts represent a deviant segment of the larger society and as such are depraved individuals. Because they constitute a threat to the "good" citizens and to the value system of the majority, these deviants must be confined for the protection of society. Throughout history, punishment—whether banishment, exile, branding, transportation to penal colonies, prison

The Traditional Prison Model

—has been aimed at ostracism. Label the deviant as such, then keep him away from others he might contaminate. Some observers argue that society must have a system of labeling and processing deviants for its own psychological stability. It is easier, of course, to create a schism between "good" and "evil" by demeaning the evil ones than it is by elevating the good ones. The deviants have been generally considered by the larger society as moral paupers having "no redeeming social qualities" and as degenerates incapable of functioning adequately or properly. Evidence of this outlook is explicit in efforts to "reform" the criminal.

A second notion is that the potential threat of the convict to the free society is a physical one and he must therefore be confined in a maximum-custody facility. The sheer force of prison walls and the presence of armed guards are credited with preventing the inmates from breaking loose from their cages and perpetrating their vile acts upon the righteous.

The layman's concept of a prisoner invokes images of a rapist, a murderer, or, at the very least, a violent, vicious, aggressive person. But men can also go to prison for nonpayment of fines, contempt of court, tax evasion, civil disobedience, nonsupport, abandonment, and writing worthless checks. Although none of these acts constitutes violence per se, there is a tendency nonetheless to generalize the violence potential of a few to all who are incarcerated.

For those who acknowledge the responsibility of the prison to reform the individual, a third notion is that the criminal offender needs "rehabilitation." As other authors have noted, the use of the term itself is confusing because rehabilitation suggests a "restoration to the former self" (in this case, criminal), and this is not really a desirable objective for a correctional system. If the correctional administrator accepted this definition, he would be admitting what many critics already contend: that the prison is a crime school.

What both the layman and professional usually intend rehabilitation to mean is for the prisoner to be redirected by some unspecified method so that when he is released from prison, he will not return to his criminal activities but will become a useful member of society. Some people advocate these efforts out of humanitarian concern or from a desire to "help" the unfortunates, although a few endorse rehabilitation as a means of self-preservation. Others have realized that since about 95 percent of the prison inmates will one day return to the community, it is to the advantage of the freeman that the cycle of criminality be broken.

And, finally, the fourth notion is that prison staffs are the most appropriate tool for bringing about change in the inmate. In other words, there is presumed to be something inherent in staffing patterns, qualifications, training, and concepts that uniquely equip correctional personnel with the right, wisdom, expertise, and motivation to "rehabilitate" their subjects. The implicit assumption is that there are essential differences in behavior patterns, personality traits, and value systems between the guards and the inmates.

Dealing with the Dogma

These four notions should be examined in light of how penologists have attempted to deal with them in practice. First of all, almost every theory of criminality has assumed that there is some deficiency in the criminal; that he is a deviant. These theories have given rise to models designed to cure deviancy. The equation between crime and sin under the puritanical ethic of the eighteenth century gave rise to the model of correction through penitence, prayer, and conversion to religion. The idea that slothfulness was an explanation for crime resulted in the model that would cure criminality through hard work. It has also been assumed that criminals are such because they lack education and training, and hence we have the educational-training (reformatory) model. And, finally, the medical (rehabilitation) model postulates that the criminal is sick but could be cured through the proper psychological treatment. Many varieties of the pleasure-pain principle and reward-punishment theories have been tried in an attempt to reform the convict so that he would be able to return to society and "sin no more."[1] These models and their attendant philosophies of how to correct the deficiencies of the criminal have been distinguished by their uniform failure.

Second, what about the notion that the convict poses a physical threat to free society? Prison officials suggest that probably only 10 percent of the prison population requires the level of custody imposed on all inmates because of the overall custodial requirements of the institution. The remainder, by far the majority of the inmates, present little risk for escape or potential for violence to the free-world community if they do escape. It is a sad fact that the

---

[1] What type of rehabilitation can be provided for the professional criminal, the white collar criminal, or those convicted of so-called political crimes such as draft evasion? Since the "error" of "deviance" of the draft evader was a result of a specific way of thinking about human life and did not fit the classic theory of etiology of crime, the only "solution" for this "problem," or problems caused by others who challenge the system, would be the one applied to Murphy in Ken Kesey's novel, *One Flew Over the Cuckoo's Nest*—a lobotomy!

The Traditional Prison Model

"overkill" of custodial considerations inhibits the majority of the inmates in both a negative and an unnecessary way.

In fulfilling the custodial responsibilities of the prison, a philosophy of security and protection has been embedded in the concrete and steel structures that closely resemble medieval fortresses. Even "reformatories" are formidable in design and present an austere, repressive image to those inside and out. These bastions of security came into being to fit the level of custody presumed to be required by the freeworld designers. Consideration of other functions of the institution and consultation with prison officials prior to architectural design have been fairly recent developments. In other words, the design of prisons traditionally has been a function of the prejudicial and fearful concepts of the layman as interpreted by the architect.

Most of the "innovations" in the treatment of criminal offenders in the United States have been well intentioned but nonetheless negative in result. The penitentiary, America's "contribution" to criminal justice, was meant to be a place for penitence and salvation, but as was mentioned earlier the structure and management practices resulted in a high ratio of mentally deranged inmates.

Third, even assuming that the criminal needs education or training, such programs for inmates generally are unrealistic in terms of the "rehabilitating" they accomplish. When prisoner idleness was replaced with work projects that served some useful function for the state, it soon became apparent that work could not only provide needed goods and reduce the costs of imprisonment but would also lessen the amount of time available for the inmates to cause problems for the administration. The reformatory movement was really the first effort to retrain inmates. Academic education was a primary program of the reformatory until the extensive use of probation and demands for industrial production forced educational programs into a secondary priority. But it has been only recently that sincere, concerted efforts have focused on "treatment" of the criminal offender. Past efforts at treatment really have had as their goal protection of society, punishment of the deviant, or retribution.

Unfortunately, vocational training programs today too often involve either industrial or housekeeping functions of the prison and are not geared to occupational realities. In theory, prison industries are designed to provide income for the prison; at the same time it is hoped that prisoners will develop skills that will be useful on the outside. The classic flaw in this notion is demonstrated by the manufacture of license plates that, with rare exception, can only be made in prison. Many other activities are equally lacking in realistic employment opportunities for the inmate. Even when a training program does equip a man with a real trade, he often cannot practice this skill outside the prison because of prejudice against those convicted of felonies or because of lack of employment opportunities in his specialty.

[Cartoon: A prisoner works on a machine under a sign reading "NOTICE YOU ARE HAVING A MEANINGFUL WORK EXPERIENCE —OR ELSE!" while two officials look on. Caption: "WHAT'S ALL THIS TALK ABOUT SLAVE LABOR? THESE MEN ARE EARNING .08¢ AN HOUR!"]

Educating the inmates would appear to be worthwhile if the criterion is the general notion of education held by the free society. Yet, in prisons today, programs—vocational training, industries, education—are not addressed to two central problems of the offender: he needs to change his attitude and to learn how to survive in the free society.

If education in its various forms is a cure for criminality, then one would have to believe that educated and trained people do not commit crimes. Realizing that this conclusion is patently false, one must then challenge the hypothesis. Another difficulty is that because of security, institutional maintenance, and lack of facilities, only a small fraction of the inmate population can participate in the programs. And, of course, there is the unproductive fallacy of providing a cure without a prior diagnosis.

Educational and training programs may be "good," may keep the inmates busy, may employ additional staff, and may create the impression that inmates are being reformed. But they are tools that can be useful only *after* the offender has changed his view of himself, his peers, his society, and his relation to that society. If he is unwilling (or unable) to accept and demonstrate self-responsibility, the acquisition of knowledge or skills will only enhance his competence as a criminal offender.

Evidence that treatment programs leave something to be desired came out of the Annual Congress of the American Correctional Association in 1970. Warden Wayne Patterson of the Colorado State Penitentiary addressed the Wardens' Association on the efficacy of reform efforts and reminisced nostalgically about the "good old days" and cited one case to demonstrate the "value" of such programs.

Patterson related the criminal history of an inmate who had been sent to prison several times for blowing open safes with a variety of explosives and stealing the contents. After the rehabilitation philosophy was imposed on the prison, the treatment staff diagnosed this inmate's problem by saying that he lacked trade skills. Consequently, he was programmed to complete his high school education and was placed in vocational training programs. He eventually received his high school certificate and completed a course in welding. It was then determined that he had been rehabilitated, and he was promptly paroled.

Subsequently, however, he was returned to prison "for cracking safes with a blow torch."

Finally, consider the reaction to the fourth notion that prison staff people are the ones who should undertake the rehabilitation of the criminal. Traditionally, it has been the guards who provided the prisoners' main contact with the freeworld, but whether or not they ever did any "treating" is another question. Although Beaumont and de Tocqueville reported in 1833 that the "most distinguished persons offered themselves to administer a *penitentiary*"[2] this has not been the case with all employees: prisons have seen more than their share of sadistic personnel. One can debate whether sadistic people tend to seek out prison employment or whether prison employment tends to make people sadistic. Those who are cruel to others become brutalized through their own acts. A strong argument can be made that the prison has a negative effect on the guard as well as the inmate. As the inmate frequently says to the guard, "I have to walk

---

[2] *Ibid.*, p. 133.

these tiers for five years before I get out, but you have to walk them for twenty-five years." That is, the inmate will be paroled eventually, but the guard must serve his time until retirement, which is much longer than the average prison sentence.

In this century, we have seen the rise of "treatment" staffs that encompass not only the academic and vocational training programs but have been expanded to encompass religion, counseling, and diagnosis. At the present time in more "progressive" systems, it is not uncommon to have a prison staff consisting of a psychiatrist, psychologist, caseworkers, chaplain, educators, vocational experts, and "rehabilitation counselors." The general approach to treatment is the team concept. This method ostensibly assures that the expertise of people in many disciplines is brought to bear in order to evaluate the needs of a particular individual and to recommend a total program of rehabilitation encompassing parts of many, if not all, of these available services.

It should not be surprising that even progressive systems have fallen short of achieving their goal of rehabilitation. The efforts of treatment staffs are based on notions of dubious worth, since they, in turn, have been based on the fallacy that the prison population is representative of criminality in general.

The Reality of Rehabilitation

The notion of prisoner rehabilitation implies that the inmate *needs* to be changed. From this notion, it follows that the prison is an ideal place for this change to take place. It is assumed that intensive techniques that will reconstitute the offender so he will live "responsibly" in the freeworld can be imposed on the inmate in a highly structured situation. Such notions are not illogical if one believes there are specific factors that can be administered to bring about "rehabilitation." And it is helpful if one ignores basic inconsistencies in the environment in which these programs are to be instituted—an environment of fear, aggression, totalitarianism, and exploitation.

Data on the number of ex-convicts returned to prison are usually cited as the measures of success (or failure) of prison systems. Defining success in this way assumes a simplistic view of crime and correction. The responsibilities of other aspects of the society and variables beyond the control of the warden are ignored. Evaluating a prison on the number of returnees also does not take into consideration the fact that former inmates may commit crimes but not be caught. Also, others may be caught but be reinstated on parole, fined, or placed on probation and thus not be returned to prison.

Even if one could accept the return-to-prison definition, there are other difficulties. There is no uniform agreement among correctional administrators as to what the time period for following up on ex-inmates should be. For example, if a parolee is not convicted within three months in some jurisdictions, he is considered a "success." Other states may use a one-year period of study. Still others consider it a success if the parolee does not return to prison before the end of his parole. If he commits a crime after release, he is still considered to be a success. If he goes to prison in another state or in the federal system, he is still considered a success in the original jurisdiction. Frequently, success is assumed if there is no positive information that he has been returned to prison.[3]

Several prison studies have demonstrated that treatment programs have uniformly failed.

Dr. Robert Martinson headed a four-year research project that analyzed all studies published between 1945 and 1967 of the various institutional programs designed to "rehabilitate" convicted offenders. A total of 231 such programs were discovered and critically examined. Martinson observed that:

> *Although the overall conclusions of a work of this magnitude and complexity are difficult to convey in a few words, I think it is fair to say that there is very little evidence in these studies that any prevailing mode of correctional treatment has a decisive effect in reducing the recidivism of convicted offenders.*[4]
>
> *...I am bound to say that these data, involving over two hundred studies and hundreds of thousands of individuals as they do, are the best available and give us very little reason to hope that we have in fact found a sure way of reducing recidivism through rehabilitation.*[5]

---

[3] Professor David A. Ward has told me that in the course of his investigation of parole effectiveness in California, the researchers found that six parolees were listed as successes although they had been deceased for some time. It is true that they did not return to prison and thus statistically qualified for the honor, but their demise eliminated that option for them.

[4] Gene Kassebaum et al., *Prison Treatment and Parole Survival: An Empirical Assessment* (New York: Wiley, 1971), p. 309.

[5] Robert Martinson, "What Works? Questions and Answers about Prison Reform," *The Public Interest*, no. 35 (1974):49

An independent study of the California Department of Corrections prepared at the request of the California Assembly dealt, in part, with treatment program effectiveness:

> *These [California Department of Corrections] rehabilitation efforts are either not being directed at the problems which are associated with eventual parole adjustment, or are ineffectual in producing results which last after the man is released.*[6]

Another four-year study of an experimental educational program in a Pennsylvania institution was reported by Dr. Morgan V. Lewis in 1973 under the auspices of the National Endowment for Humanities. The purpose of the grant was to evaluate the exposure of youthful male inmates to programs in music, writing, and theater. The assumption was that such involvement "would help them achieve a sense of personal identity and develop more socially approved values."

Dr. Lewis found that although three-fourths of the inmates stated that they had positive feelings about the programs, follow-up interviews over a three-year period revealed that "almost one-third of those released were returned to prison." Another one-third remained unemployed, and of those who had employment, many expressed dissatisfaction with their jobs.

Psychological testing revealed no significant differences between the experimental group and the two control groups that did not receive the treatment. The inmates exposed to the enriched environment "were no more likely to read books, write essays or poems, or attend concerts and plays" than those not in the program.

Contrary to the contention of "prominent figures in the American correctional system, they [the educational programs] can accomplish almost nothing within the traditional prison environment," according to Dr. Lewis.

> *The inability of the prison to produce positive changes in the inmates lies not in the characteristics of the staff but in the nature of the institution itself.... Since the inmates typically outnumber the staff, methods of social control based on coercion are adopted. Inmates are reduced to the status of nonpersons (Sykes, 1958) and made dependent upon their keepers for the basic necessities of life. These conditions*

---

[6] "Order Out of Chaos," *Parole Board Reform in California* (Sacramento: Assembly of the State of California, 1970), p. 13.

obviously produce many changes in inmates but hardly the type of positive personal growth assumed under the term "rehabilitation." As long as prison is a prison, that is, as long as it confines inmates, it seems very doubtful that honest rehabilitation is possible.[7]

Recent research[8] in Florida focused on attitudinal changes attributable to work release[9] programs in that state. Pretests and posttests were administered to 193 randomly selected medium-security inmates in an effort to assess expected changes in perceptions.

Work release is the practice of allowing selected inmates to leave the institution during the day in order to be an employee and then to return at night. The concept was inaugurated, in modern times, with the passage of the Huber Law in 1913 in Wisconsin that allowed misdemeanants to be temporarily released from jails for this purpose. It was subsequently extended to include felons and over the past ten years has become a major "reform" advocated by most penologists.

It is generally believed that during the transitional period, the trauma of moving from the autocratic prison to the democratic society will be lessened by the inmates' change in attitude through the work release experience. In Florida, however, it was found that:

> *Contrary to expectations, there is* no *discernible improvement over the duration of the work release experience in the levels of perceived opportunity, achievement motivation, legal self-concept, and self-esteem expressed by work release participants.*
>
> *Further, at the end of final discharge from prison there is* no *significant difference between work release participants and non-release controls with regard to perceptions of legitimate opportunity, achievement motivation, legal self-concept, and focal concerns.*
>
> *Finally, the only attitude change apparently attributable to the work release experience is* unfavorable. *That is, the*

---

[7] Morgan V. Lewis, *Prison Education and Rehabilitation: Illusion or Reality?*, Institute for Research on Human Resources, Pennsylvania State University, University Park, June 1973, p. 126.

[8] Gordon P. Waldo, Theodore G. Chiricos, and Leonard E. Dobrin, "Community Contact and Inmate Attitudes: An Experimental Assessment of Work Release," *Criminology*, vol. 11, no. 3 (1973):345–381.

[9] According to Waldo (p. 375), "most [correctional observers] express a *belief* that work release will prove to be a significant step forward in modern corrections."

level of self-esteem expressed by work release participants at the conclusion of the work release experience is significantly lower than that expressed [before the experience] and is significantly lower than that expressed by the control group at [the end of the experimental period].

In sum, at the conclusion of work release, the responses of participants to fifty attitude items were more or less identical to those of nonparticipants, and, where significant differences were found, they uniformly reflected "less favorable" responses from those who had the "benefit" of the work release experience.[10]

There is yet another example that so-called rehabilitation programs are not the "men-savers" they are claimed to be. As a result of the Gideon v. Wainwright decision by the United States Supreme Court in 1963 concerning the right of indigent felons to counsel, 1,252 Florida inmates were discharged from prison outright before completing their treatment programs and without any supervision by parole officers. The Florida Division of Corrections conducted a follow-up study after 30 months. It compared the findings with a comparable group consisting of the same number of prisoners who had been released from prison after completing prison programs and who had been placed under parole supervision.

Of those discharged by order of the court, 13.6 percent again returned to prison. Of those who were discharged under the treatment programs and continued under parole supervision and casework counseling, 25.4 percent returned to prison. In other words, those who received treatment were twice as likely to return to prison than those who received no treatment.[11]

In sum, there may be some confusion over the semantic meaning of the term *rehabilitation*, but it is generally assumed that it exists, that it is a commodity which can be isolated, encapsuled, and injected into a human being as an antidote for crime. It is unfortunate for penologists and prisoners that reality has not borne out this assumption.

---

[10] Waldo, pp. 368, 369.

[11] On August 13, 1971, Georgia Governor Lester Maddox released 750 inmates whose discharge dates would have been before February 28, 1972. Governor Maddox also released randomly a large number of prisoners each Christmas. Georgia authorities report that of over 3,000 inmates thus released only 2 percent have returned to prison. The period of follow-up, characteristics of the prisoners, and the methodology used were not reported.

The Traditional Prison Model in Practice

The notions of penology discussed earlier, and the models and treatment programs they have generated, all add up to a very traditional approach in the administration of this country's "correctional" system. The "deviancy" of the criminal is not a new concept; the medical model for treating it is just the latest variation on other models. In terms of physical facilities, "custodial security," and penal philosophy in general, prisons are more similar than dissimilar to prisons 100 years ago. Historical antecedents are allowed, often unconsciously, to limit thinking, innovation, and departure from tradition. The "system cannot change" because "it has always been done this way." This justification was given for turning off the television at 10:15 each evening (15 minutes before the end of the program) at the Women's Reformatory in Shakopee, Minnesota; for having five inmates supervise the work of three others at the granary in the Arkansas prison; and for feeding the evening meal at 3:30 P.M. in the Alaska jail system. What are the results of this continued adherence to tradition?

The Fiction of Prison Control

A system evolves in which both the inmates and guards assume roles that allow guards to act "as if" they are actually in control of the prison. In the final analysis, the amount of authority exercised by guards is no more than the amount granted by the inmates. The inmates allow the guards to remain ostensibly in control as long as the inmate power structure is allowed to function sub rosa. It is advantageous to both groups that the fiction be maintained.

The inmates, of course, realize that the free community will not tolerate their running the institution openly, so they settle for the next best thing—the appearance of good order. In varying degrees, inmates affect management of all correctional institutions by this method. The prison officials serve a very real purpose for the inmates in that they create the facade of good order, thereby appeasing any societal anxieties and making it possible for society to rest comfortably in the fiction that the prison is under control. At the same time, some inmates are able to achieve a fair number of rewards by exploiting their fellow inmates. The inmates know; the prison staff members know. Only the occasional pilgrim is deceived.

Without an effort to restructure the organization of the prison community, the only alternative left to the staff is accommodating to the situation. The rookie guard soon learns that both his physical and his professional survival depend on the vagaries of the inmates' attitudes as well as the philosophy of the prison administration. Realizing that the prison system will not tolerate any reordering of the prison society, he is faced with the first of many dilemmas in prison reform: Should he do what is "right" now and risk negative sanctions from the prison officials and inmates? Or should he do what is expedient for the moment until the time when he has gained sufficient power to do what is "right"?

The officer quickly learns that if he attempts to enforce all the rules of the institution, the inmates will devise a series of rather simple actions that will reflect negatively on his competence. If this happens, he will be reassigned to another area of the prison to determine whether he "can adapt to prison life." This phrase is a euphemism that actually means: Can he strike the delicate balance between enforcing the rules just enough to maintain the fiction of staff supremacy (which is essential for the institution to function) and at the same time not antagonize the inmates to the extent that they refuse to cooperate in the charade? As former Arkansas Commissioner of Correction Robert Sarver stated on national television, "If I'm not in it [the system], I can't change it."[12] The officer thus succumbs to the system by rationalizing about his inevitable collaboration with inmates.

If the rookie tries to maintain his role as an ideal officer, he will be transferred to new assignments until he is finally removed from the roster. Realizing that his personal integrity poses a threat to the system, he quickly agrees to adjust to the inmate power structure enough to survive—or else he leaves. He apparently must compromise his principles so that some semblance of order can be maintained.

The Case of Harold A. Porter

Harold A. Porter faced the dilemma of compromise soon after his appointment as a guard in the Georgia prison system in the spring of 1968.[13] Porter was first assigned to a cell block where, one evening in the fall of that year, he prevented a white officer from beating an unresisting black inmate. He was promptly called to the office of the lieutenant in charge of the shift and advised that his conduct constituted "interfering with an officer in the line of duty." Porter was admonished not to do it again; then he was transferred to the kitchen stockroom.

---

[12] Transcript of comments by Robert Sarver, Arkansas Commissioner of Correction, on the Dick Cavett Show, October 21, 1970, New York, p. 9.

[13] Porter had just been fired from the Arkansas prison system. He had been in charge of the detail of inmates that had excavated the graves of three inmates who allegedly had been murdered by prison officials and trusties.

In the kitchen, he "caused trouble" by preventing food rackets on his shift and by treating inmates with some fairness and humanity. Although such efforts had popular support among the general population, they did not favorably impress either his fellow officers or the privileged inmates. With another reprimand, he was transferred to the telephone switchboard.

> *[One day] I reported all to the superintendent [Jack Caldwell] who said he would investigate, only to be informed by him [two weeks later] that they were moving me to Waycross Prison.... I let it be known that if I was forced to transfer I would talk to the news media.*[14]

In January 1969, Porter discussed the proposed transfer with Caldwell at the latter's home. "My main worry," Porter stated, "was the fact [that] if I was moved from [the Georgia Industrial Institute at] Alto, there wouldn't [be] anyone whatsoever to guard the inmates from the guards."[15]

Prison officials hoped that the boredom of his new assignment would prompt Porter's resignation. If not, at least it would remove him from any direct contact with other officers and inmates. But this punitive assignment was not totally successful in isolating Porter from the prison community:

> *The mistreatment of inmates kept up ... and one night an officer came to me and was very upset; telling me that he had just seen seven inmates being beaten [to the extent] he was scared they might be killed.*
>
> *Of five officers ... the Lieutenant was hitting the inmates in the back of the neck with a tape-wrapped chain; one was hitting in the same area with a stick; another in the back of the inmate's neck with the side of the hand as in Judo; and the fourth officer was hitting the inmates in the back of the neck with the edge of his elbow.*
>
> *He said they tried to get him to go away while all this was going on, but he refused.*[16]

As a result of his experience in Arkansas, Porter was well aware of the personal and professional dangers of exposing prison brutality. The choices open to him were these: to take no immediate action; to remain in the system and attempt to gradually prevent the brutality

---

[14] Written statement of Harold Porter to Tom Murton, October 1, 1969.
[15] *Ibid.*
[16] *Ibid.*

by being an example to other officers; or to take overt action to stop it and risk being removed from the system—thus losing the power to prevent *any* of the brutality. Porter debated the issue with his conscience for a year. Then he made his decision.

Porter decided that "all this mistreatment had to be stopped no matter what it cost me. I also knew I could no longer trust my superintendent 'cause the last time I reported mistreatment, he tried to transfer me far away and under the leadership of a very tough warden."[17]

Porter submitted a "confidential" report to State Representative Jack Gunter, who had been critical of the institution and had publicly urged reforms. But "Gunter turned the statement over to the chairman of the prison board [who in turn gave it to Porter's boss, superintendent Caldwell in mid-July 1969] without my permission."

> *The next day, Mr. Caldwell called me into his office where he had one GBI [Georgia Bureau of Investigation] agent and one FBI agent waiting. Later the chairman of the prison board came in [and] right off promised me that I would not lose my job; that I would not be fired.*
>
> *During the talks, Mr. Caldwell told me that I was "not worth a shit." [He] called in a few of the officers and one even admitted hitting inmates.*
>
> *And, while I was waiting outside as requested, he said he was going to beat me up and even later said I wouldn't get home alive.*[18]

Porter was immediately suspended. Two days later he was terminated. He released his statement to the press and was promptly subjected to Georgia "justice."

On July 22, 1969, Porter was arrested at his home, handcuffed, and taken to the county jail. He was not arraigned, not permitted to post bail, and not allowed to exercise any other constitutional guarantees. Four days later he was released on bail and subsequently learned that he was charged with four counts of "defaming public officials"—a felony under the Georgia Penal Code—as a result of exposing the four officers who allegedly beat the seven inmates. Porter said he was well treated in the jail, enjoyed the rest and safety, and "made quite a few friends among inmates in the population."

---

[17] *Ibid.*
[18] *Ibid.*

Commenting on Porter's arrest and his allegations concerning brutality at the institution, Governor Lester Maddox stated that he thought Porter was trying to "use" the prison to write sensationalized material for profit:

> It seems to me there was a story to be sold to discredit the prison, which is one of the finest in the world. Of course when you have a prison you've always got problems. In fact, we have some in my church.[19]

Maddox's admission probably is true; but the church "problems" probably do not center around the deacons beating the parishioners half to death.

Director of Corrections Robert J. Carter filed charges against Porter on August 15—nearly a month after his dismissal. Charge 29 (of 51 charges brought against him) is one commonly cited to explain the "deviance" of those who challenge the system:

> Inefficiency in performing the duties of the position held in that your working relationship with your fellow employees and with inmates has been abrasive and disruptive, necessitating your constant reassignment from one department to another.[20]

One irony in the aftermath of Porter's dismissal and jailing was the appointment of Jack Gunter (the one who had betrayed Porter's confidence and precipitated the subsequent events) as Porter's defense counsel.

The Case of Edward F. Roberts[21]

Edward F. Roberts was 23 years old, had graduated from high school, had completed his military service, and was looking around for a job. He had relatives working in the Florida prison system.

"Momma called on [State Representative Gene] Shaw and that sure enough got me the job," he said.

His three-year tenure at the Raiford State Prison ended abruptly after his testimony before the federal grand jury on February 16, 1971. Roberts had violated the unwritten code of corrections—he had betrayed the residents of the surrounding community to

---

[19] *Atlanta Journal and Constitution*, Atlanta, Georgia, July 21, 1969.
[20] Robert J. Carter, "Specification of Charges Against Harold A. Porter," Atlanta, Georgia, August 15, 1969, p. 7.
[21] *Freeworld Times*, Minneapolis, Minnesota, April–May 1972.

The Traditional Prison Model

outsiders; he had betrayed his fellow officers by exposing brutality; and, to a lesser extent, he had betrayed the inmates by inadvertently placing them in jeopardy by his actions.

What caused the transformation within a local political hack who embarked on a course of action not only antithetical to his heritage but destined to place him in ultimate conflict with the system?

His first assignment was in the prison wing that housed the homosexuals, cop killers, and wife murderers. "It wasn't hard to hate them," Roberts admitted. He contended that it was part of the socialization process for new officers that teaches them to think of inmates "as the lowest thing on earth."

"You get your mind set right in the beginning," Roberts said, "and I was as rough as any man out there. I wasn't at all permissive."

Then Roberts enrolled at Lake City [Florida] Junior College and the metamorphosis began. "I woke up to what was happening to me (at the prison)—I was being dehumanized," Roberts said. "I had been brought up to believe there were good people and bad people and criminals were hardcore bad. I came to think there were a lot inbetween."

The changes in Roberts' attitude were reflected in his work and were not looked upon favorably at the prison despite the system's stated goal of encouraging officers to continue their education. "What was going on in my head started causing problems with other officers," Roberts said. "It was easy to do the job and not think and be confident that convicts are scum. It was harder with my new attitude. . . . There's a chain gang mentality there [at Raiford]. They don't believe in rehabilitation. Their idea is to make the prison so bad no one will ever want to come back."

This attitude resulted in increased tensions at the prison and, in turn, some form of protest was frequently the outcome. The prison protest of February 1971, as recounted earlier in Chapter 2, resulted in some property damage and the wounding of 74 inmates by gunfire from guards. Roberts found the shootings very disturbing but the injuries suffered by 26 inmates, who were allegedly beaten after the uprising was put down, caused him even greater distress.

Roberts was called before the grand jury to relate what had happened. He explained that unresisting inmates had been beaten unconscious by prison officials; that they had been forced to "run the gauntlet" between armed guards; that he had seen blood on the walls where inmates had bled and run—prior to the yard disturbance that resulted in the shooting.

He explained to the grand jury that this was the way "correctional officers" had reestablished control over inmates who were engaged in a peaceful work stoppage to protest prison conditions. When the grand jury acknowledged that excessive force had been used but ruled there were no indictable offenses, Roberts took his case to the public and repeated his charges.

He was given an unsatisfactory career service rating and was confronted by his superiors, who charged him with violating prison rules. The list of derelictions included eating in the inmates' canteen, spending too much time talking to inmates, not being "authoritarian," and "telling an inmate he was an important person," according to Roberts.

"It got to the point where they didn't trust me more than the worst inmates. They never left me alone," he said. "If I was seen talking to an inmate, the inmate was called up before the prison brass. The inmates didn't want to talk to me because they didn't want any trouble, and I can't blame them."

The surrounding community came down on him. He was denied gasoline from local service stations; other guards' wives stopped talking to his wife; even Roberts' family said, "You ought to be ashamed of yourself." After coping with such harassment for eight months, Roberts quit in September 1971 and became a full-time student at the University of Florida. His hope was to return to prison work after graduation.

"In a funny way, I loved every day I was out there. It was probably the most productive three years of my life," Roberts said.

Why does Roberts no longer work at the prison? There is no evidence that he ever beat an inmate. No one contends that he oppressed inmates. He did not abuse his authority. To the contrary, it appears that he cared for the inmates and placed that concern above loyalty to his fellow officers or his own job security. Yet he is gone.

Roberts no longer works at the prison. Not because he was a threat to the inmates but because he constituted a threat to the correctional power structure. And that is the unforgivable sin of corrections.

In conclusion, too few guards demonstrate the integrity of men like Porter and Roberts, and so the prison environment is shaped more by those who compromise their values than by those who "fight the system." And, unfortunately, the compromises guards make result in an illegal form of government, an exploitative dictatorial system based on brute power and without the consent of most of the governed. Such systems are perpetuated through the moral corruption of the guard force, deceit of the administration, timidity of correctional officials, and the relative powerlessness of the larger inmate body. It is based on fear, coercion, intimidation, and brutality.[22]

From this experience, the inmate learns quite well that democracy is a fiction; that the treaters speak of treatment but treat not; that they profess to believe in the rights of man while tolerating and promoting the indignity of totalitarianism. Deceit, the art of exploitation, and the advantages of power are well-learned lessons—and the functional aspects of this experience are not totally lost on the inmate. He is conditioned to a value system precisely the opposite of that desired. He is influenced through rewards and punishments to reject any vestige of decency he might have had on entering the prison. He perfects the ability to lie, steal, cheat, and manipulate others—and, if he does it skillfully enough, he will be paroled.

The Medical Model: The "Treatment" Game

The medical (sickness) model, in combination with the theological (confessional) model, has become an essential ingredient in the ceremony of rehabilitation. Since it is most difficult to force a remedy on one who views himself as healthy, it is essential in most treatment programs that the inmate must first recognize his deficiencies and then accept the remedy as corrective of his deviant behavior.

The medical model is best implemented in a total institution that limits freedom of choice, reduces variables to a minimum, and leaves the subject with few options. The prison has been particularly well suited for application of this method, and a host of cures have been instituted to bring about the healing process. These cures have included group therapy, individual counseling, behavior modification, electroshock treatment, drug therapy, and training. In this process, the inmate will be subjected to a ritual of degradation and alienation and will be forced to defer to the professional treaters. After the confessional, the professions of being sick, the self-acceptance of depravity and worthlessness, and the acknowledgment of the wisdom of the healers, the inmate is ready to begin the arduous trek through the intricate maze of complicated maneuvers

---

[22] In *The Penitentiary System in the United States and Its Application to France*, Gustave de Beaumont and Alexis de Tocqueville observed: "While society in the United States gives the example of the most extended liberty, the prisons of the same country offer the spectacle of the most complete despotism." Things haven't changed much since 1833. H. R. Lantz, ed. (Carbondale, Illinois: Southern Illinois University Press, 1964), p. 79.

that will assure the healers that his behavior has been changed and that his "illness" of criminality has been cured.[23]

What most supporters of the medical model fail to recognize is that inmates quickly learn to play whatever game the treatment staffs devise. Under the medical model, the patient (inmate) is expected to accept the diagnosis (sentence) and to submit to treatment (manipulation) by the treaters (staff) until he is cured (paroled). The inmate soon becomes painfully aware that his personal success in obtaining release from prison is directly related to the personal successes of the professional staff assigned to correct him. Refusing to acknowledge that one is "sick," or questioning the ability of the "physicians" to administer the appropriate "medicine," will ensure a longer residency while the "final cure" is being sought. The inmate thus chooses the game most likely to gain his ultimate release. He "wins" the game when the "rehabilitator" declares that the "rehabilitatee" has indeed been "rehabilitated."

Thus each individual can fulfill the immediate needs of the other. The treater gains success by healing; the treatee gains freedom by being healed. Each has perfected or improved his techniques in playing the game, and it is suspected that each knows that the other is playing a game: but the fraud cannot be exposed because to do so would deny mutual success to the players. It is a game where every player can be a winner.

Of course, the treatment is not directed toward attitudinal change, but the facade of behavioral change. Although it can be argued that presenting a good image is functional in real-life

---

[23] A former officer of the California Institution for Women at Frontera reported an incident that points out the necessity for all participants to play their assigned roles in the ritual of the reform game. A certain prisoner had been in and out of the institution many times and never appeared able to succeed after release. In the mid 1960s, she escaped from the prison and was at large for a number of years.

When arrested on the escape charge, she was working, had a husband and children, and was demonstrating responsible, crime-free behavior. Nonetheless, she was returned to prison to serve the balance of her original sentence as well as additional time for the escape offense. There is no question that the law had been violated and that she "owed" the state more time.

If one really believes the rehabilitation rhetoric of prison officials, then prisoners should be released when they become responsible citizens. When a formal rehabilitation ceremony is instituted, however, complete with professional treaters, it is very discomforting to have a patient demonstrate that she can rehabilitate herself where the officials fail.

Thus the woman was returned to prison, her rehabilitation voided, and she was forced to submit to the prison games so that the official rehabilitators could demonstrate their prowess.

situations, it is doubtful that a life style based primarily on deceit, deception, and fraud will assure sustained success in a nonprison society.

Those who become the most proficient in the art of lying are able to function most effectively within the prison and to respond most efficiently to the authoritarian (dictatorial) system. Those who succeed in the dictatorship are conferred the "degree" of "rehabilitation" and are graduated to the freeworld, where their preparation, training, and *modus vivendi* are in fact dysfunctional to democracy. Being unable to function in the foreign environment of the free society, the inmate falls back on his previous skills, turns to the deviant acts that were reinforced by the prison environment, and eventually returns to the prison—where he will be subjected to more intensive "treatment" since the first dose was obviously not strong enough.

Confrontation Is the Norm

Another result of the present model of institutionalization is that two warring factions are created—the staff and the inmates. This situation is perplexing in view of the fact that the goals and objectives of each group in relation to the inmate body are apparently the same. The inmates' objectives are to obtain release as quickly as possible with the least number of negative experiences and with no permanent damage. The staff goals for the inmates are identical. Yet these two groups (with the same avowed goals) are at constant war with each other. Thus the energies of both groups are dissipated on the surrogate enemy of real prison reform—namely each other.

The criminal gets into trouble by committing acts prohibited, or required, by the penal code. But the actual conflict is not between the offender and some abstraction known as The Law, or the legislative body that enacted the code, or the victim who is the recipient of the action. The confrontation is between the criminal and the police officer. But the officer only represents The Law; he did not create it. Street violence in opposition to "unfair" laws is nonetheless directed at the policeman as a symbol of the official power structure.

Similarly, the correctional officer did not create the rules governing the prison. As will be discussed in more detail later, the oppression of the inmate originates at the administrative level both inside and outside the prison. Since inmates do not usually have physical access to the warden or those outside the prison, their

The Concept of Implementation of Rehabilitation by Means of the Medical Model as Perceived Both by Staff and Inmates in the Traditional Prison Setting

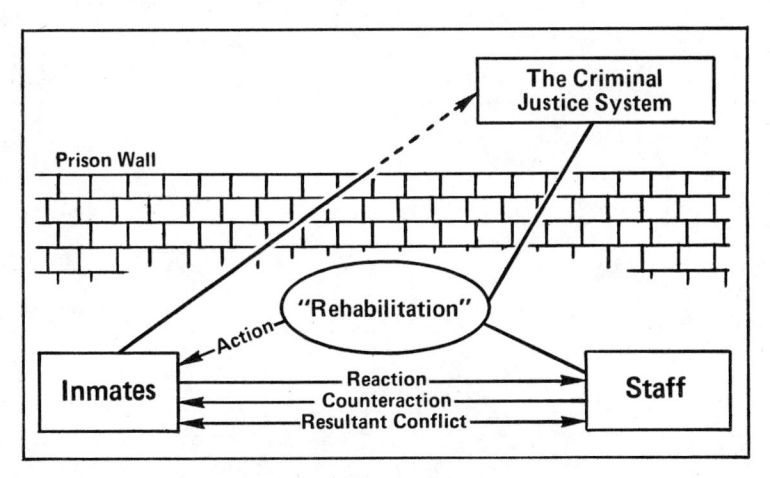

```
                    ┌─────────────────┐
                    │  The Criminal   │
                    │ Justice System  │
                    └─────────────────┘
  Prison Wall  ══════════════════════════════════════
               ══════════════════════════════════════
                      "Rehabilitation"
   ┌─────────┐   ◄──Action──                ┌───────┐
   │ Inmates │   ────Reaction────►          │ Staff │
   │         │   ◄──Counteraction──         │       │
   └─────────┘   ───Resultant Conflict──►   └───────┘
```

The power of the criminal justice system and the prison staff (without inmate participation) coalesces into "rehabilitation programs" that are imposed on the inmates.

According to a "Law of Correctional Physics," there will be an unequal and opposite reaction.

Because the avenue of reaction against The System is blocked by the prison wall, inmates therefore react against the only vulnerable component of the system: the prison staff. The guards retaliate by meeting force with force. Under the "best" conditions, this confrontation is only ideological resistance of "treatment"; at the worst, a riot will occur.

The attack and counterattack between inmates and guards, unfortunately, never engages the real opposition to reform because the fundamental issues are obscured by the heat of battle between the two surrogate enemies.

hostility is vented on the correctional officer—the policeman of the prison society. This conflict eventually results in intolerable conditions, resentment, dispute, disorder, disturbance, and riots, all of which lead to scandals of varying proportions—depending on the skill of the prison system in suppressing the truth.

The cycle of oppression, revolt, reform, and oppression is a common phenomenon of the traditional prison model and most, if not all, prisons fit into this mold. An examination of prison reform strategy is necessary to determine why intervention in the cycle has, in nearly 200 years of prison "improvements," never provided real prison reform.

4

The Facade of Reform

> It's the facade of reform, but it's better than the facade of reform other people have. It's a long ways from ideal. At least, we provide a reasonably high-quality warehousing service for bodies.[1]
> — Thomas R. Branton

It should not be surprising to discover that the citizens of the prison community do not always live in peace and harmony with one another. The overcrowding, the enforced idleness, the regimentation, the monotony, and the exploitive government that exist within the prison all foster a climate of hatred and hostility which, from time to time, erupts into conflicts. To a large extent, these confrontations between inmates, or between inmates and staff, are handled routinely as an anticipated aspect of imprisonment.

A glance at any training curriculum for correctional officers reveals that methods for controlling "disturbances" (a prison administrator's euphemism for a riot) are an essential part of the correctional officer's education. Most disorders are "minor" and do not reflect a concerted effort by the inmates to achieve a specified objective. Such problems are fairly easily suppressed by a variety of techniques using any of several options available to prison officials such as a show of force and isolation of the dissidents, or, in more extreme cases, the use of night sticks, gas, fire hoses and other devices commonly used in police tactics. Such "minor incidents" as work strikes, fights, stabbings, boycotts, and even deaths are "dealt

---

[1] Acting Director of Corrections; statement made to Tom Murton, Wasilla, Alaska, July 15, 1969.

with" internally. Prison deaths in the federal system are only infrequently revealed to the outside world, and then, more often than not, only through informal channels such as visitors or released prisoners and not through any pronouncement by the warden.

When such information becomes known outside the prison, by whatever method, it is the warden who is called on to explain what occurred. Of course, the warden has a vested interest in maintaining the status quo and is not generally inclined to expose real prison problems by the indiscretion of actually revealing the truth. To do so might call into question the myths that support the basic tenets of penology, such as the assumption that the majority of inmates are vicious, dangerous, and unreasonable. And therein lies one of the subtle roadblocks to reform: *society* generally accepts the warden's explanation without further inquiry; that is, without seeking information from other officials or from the inmates themselves. Thus, as citizens, we have little opportunity to gain access to the information that is necessary for a complete and accurate understanding of the dynamics of the incident.

Frequently, however, problems at the prison reach such magnitude that attempts to keep the matter secret are futile. The resulting manifestation may take the form of a riot, sitdown, brutality, reprisal, or possibly corruption in the prison. When such an event reveals a problem that no longer can be contained by the prison administration, a scandal ensues that must be dealt with by officials outside the prison structure.

Every prison riot carries with it political overtones. As far as the governor is concerned, there is no good time for a riot, but some times are less uncomfortable than others.

After the "Disturbance": Initial Reforms

State governors normally express shock (perhaps sincerely) over prison conditions that precipitate an incident, disavow any prior knowledge of the situation, and call for a complete investigation with the promise to "let the chips fall where they may." At this point, the political rhetoric has the desired initial effect on the electorate without unduly alarming the prison officials. The latter are aware that it is not usually expedient for an elected official to participate in his own ruin by conducting a thorough investigation of his own administration in such a manner as to bring about a negative reflection on his office. Then, too, most prison officials rest comfortably in the knowledge that they can "explain" their conduct and assign any dereliction as the outgrowth of actions emerging from the "degenerate nature of convicts."

The investigation usually is conducted by police agencies that may or may not be competent and objective in rendering a report. Assuming that most state police agencies have adequate investigative techniques, there is no assurance that the information they gather will ever be acted on. The governor may suppress certain portions of the report, release an edited version, issue a statement based on portions of the report, or ignore it altogether. One thing is fairly certain: whatever action the chief executive takes, it will be one that attempts to exonerate the current state administration from any act of impropriety.[2]

Methods of Reform

Although the governor officially and publicly reacts in a manner designed to calm fears and bolster the public's confidence, he will privately urge prison officials to take the necessary action to ensure that the incident is not repeated. The governor, in good faith, may well believe that the warden's explanations are adequate and accept his reasons for the uprising. But the message is quite clear: "Hold the fort at all costs."

But the effort to hold the fort only serves to cover up the sore that continues to fester until it erupts later with greater violence. If a subsequent incident is great enough to indicate a general sickness of the system, there may be a demand to "throw the rascals out." A candidate can usually be found who is willing to adopt a reform platform.

The scandal—reform—scandal cycle is not an isolated phenomenon. The state of Illinois, for example, has a history of "reform" candidates being swept into office by voters indignant with existing conditions—only to be defeated at the next election by yet another "reformer."

Arkansans, disgusted with what they perceived as pervasive government corruption and inefficiency, rejected a century-old tradition and elected a Republican governor (Winthrop Rockefeller) in 1966. With a mandate from the electorate, he promptly set about reforming the prison system when he took office in January 1967. Yet four years later he was defeated by an obscure country lawyer, Dale Bumpers, who campaigned on a reform platform. Bumpers argued (with obvious success) that Rockefeller had never fulfilled his campaign promise to reform the prison. In fact, he correctly

---

[2] To cite but a few examples, grand juries were impaneled immediately after the shooting of inmates in Soledad, Cummins, Pendleton, and Attica (previously described in Chapter 2).

The Prison Reform Scoreboard

In the fall of 1971, penal institutions throughout the U.S. experienced unrest. The protests took differing forms but could all be grouped under a desire expressed for prison reform. Following is a tabulation of these incidents:

PRISON LOCATION	DATE	INJURIES DAMAGES	THOSE INVOLVED	DEMANDS COMPLAINTS	RESULTS, COMMENTS
Indiana Reformatory Pendleton, Indiana	9/16 6 hrs.	6 inmates gathered in one cell, teargassing, minor injuries	16 inmates in segregation	Brutality, poor food	Donald Phillips, Assistant Corrections Commissioner, believed reaction to Attica partial cause; inmate council to investigate
Glades Institution Belle Glade, Florida	9/19 1 day	Nonviolent work stoppage; no injuries reported	100 inmates	Poor food	28 inmates transferred, others "disciplined." "Disciplinary action can run from a simple oral reprimand...to segregation or restricted diet." (Diet--food canned by Corrections Division especially for disciplinary purposes containing all the nutrition an adult needs to survive.)
Civic Center Jail San Jose, California	9/20 2 hrs.	Mattresses and blankets burned, broken windows. No serious injuries reported	"100-500" inmates 44 guards	602 prisoners confined in facilities for 480	"The reason we started burning and screwing up is it's the only way we can get anybody to listen." —San Jose inmate Officials looking for additional facilities
State Penitentiary Lansing, Kansas	9/27-9/28 2 days	Food strike No injuries reported	900 inmates	Low inmate pay and pork served every day	"We will tolerate absolutely no inmate control or nonsense in this prison." —Warden Gaffney No settlement publicized
State Prison Norfolk, Massachusetts	9/27-9/28 2 days	None reported	764 inmates	Trained guards, no mail censorship, amnesty	"The trouble with these men is that when they are on the streets, they act like animals and not men, and they must be treated like animals." —Middlesex County Dist. Atty. J. Droney No results publicized
State Prison Walpole, Massachusetts	9/27-9/28 2 days	Peaceful work stoppage No injuries known	280 inmates	Abolition of "2/3" law, work release, better wages, food and counseling, death row allowed into population	"This is one of the most disgraceful prisons ever built...you could have an Attica in any maximum security prison in the country." —Superintendent Robert Moore Asked how long lockup would be on, Moore replied, "Maybe until Christmas...They're (work stoppages) caused by a small hard-core group of agitators."
	10/5 4 days	Peaceful work stoppage No injuries reported	All inmates (570) locked in	140 demands--authority to transfer guards who harass inmates, visiting privileges, continued to ask for improvements	Death row "abolished October 5 by federal magistrate.
	10/29	$30,000 Injuries not reported	Unreported	Same	Weak version of "1/3" law passed. Mass shakedown of prison, bombs and drugs found.
	11/5-11/6 2 days	Work stoppage Injuries unknown	All inmates locked in	Inmates complained that the demands were repeatedly denied	Moore refused to reveal what actions were being taken regarding the demands
State Prison Windsor, Vermont	9/29	Work stoppage No injuries reported	About 110 inmates	14 demands--higher pay, less pork, hot water (granted) Parts of 164-year-old prison have been condemned	"It isn't so much that we aren't trying to be progressive..it's just that all the unrest across the country and all the protests have had an effect on them, and that was the cause of what happened." —Warden Smith

The Facade of Reform

Prison	Date	Damage/Injuries	Inmates/Guards	Demands	Outcome
Pontiac State Prison, Pontiac, Illinois	10/2	Damage unassessed 11 inmates shot 10 guards injured	300 inmates	'Street/gang confrontation" No demands publicized	Situation was handled "effectively," according to Governor Ogilvie. No results publicized.
Dallas County Jail, Dallas, Texas	10/4 3½ hrs.	$20,000 1 inmate died	500 inmates 50 guards	Overcrowding, poor medical attention and food	$20,000 worth of riot control equipment purchased. Dallas Legal Services initiated probe
State Reformatory, Green Bay, Wisconsin	10/4 4 hrs.	Damage unassessed 11 inmates hurt	200-400 inmates	Guard brutality	"Extreme polarization" between inmates and guards; governor's task force recommended greater involvement of inmates in developing rules...no settlement reported
Lehigh County Prison, Allentown, Pennsylvania	10/5 2 hrs.	Benches broken 1 officer and 1 inmate suffered scalp wounds	168 inmates 30 police, state troopers, guards	Mistreatment, bad food, little recreation	District attorney called for officials conference Warden Larry Nero attributed causes to "everything in general."
State Prison, Santa Fe, New Mexico	10/6- 10/7 2 days	$65,000 Strike and work stopped; 100 inmates injured, 10 hospitalized	500 inmates refused to leave cells 200 placed in segregation	Legal representation at parole board meetings, resignation of staff and board, pay for work, more clothing, no censorship, a full-time doctor	Warden Rodriguez refused to accept unsigned demands but said later that he had received lists and "there's always room for improvement." 150 inmates in segregation.
Suffolk County Jail, Boston, Massachusetts	10/8 4 hrs.	None reported	90 inmates Guards, 12 riot squad members, 50 policemen	Asked that press be let in to investigate conditions.	"As far as I'm concerned they have no grievances and I have no plans to talk to any of them...We can't run our institution if we provide a platform for them." —Sheriff Eisenstadt
San Joaquin County Jail, Stockton, California	10/12 1 day	Mattresses burned Teargassing, minor injuries	10 inmates refused to leave cells, 250 rioted	Investigation of conditions, improved food and recreation, help from public defenders	Jail was "modern," according to Sheriff Canlis, who did not report any settlement
Cumberland County Jail, Bridgeton, Pennsylvania	10/13	Peaceful sitdown No injuries or violence	10 inmates	Needed exercise, better mail service, public defender allowed in jail	Warden refused to publish demands except major grievances. New facility being built.
Joliet Prison, Joliet, Illinois	10/16 3 days	Reports unknown; damages unassessed	47 inmates 50 guards	Brutality, inadequate food and medical attention 88 of 90 inmates in "special program unit" (lockup) are black	"If they beat me any more just because I'm black, I'm ready to die fighting back..." —letter from inmate in segregation No settlement reported
State Penitentiary, Omaha, Nebraska	10/18 1 day	Work stoppage; no violence	205 inmates	Warden Charles Wolff gave answers to 27 demands; 205 inmates refused to work in protest	When threatened with misconduct reports, inmates returned to work; missed meals
Solano Jail, Fairfield, California	10/18	Burned bedding, broken windows and toilets No serious injuries	19 inmates	Sheriff refused to divulge demands	"I told them we're not going to discuss anything with them in hostility. We're going to wait until things cool down and discuss this thing objectively and constructively." —Sheriff Cardoza
Contra Costa Jail, Martinez, California	10/19 2 hrs.	Fire and other damage reported in thousands	100 inmates 40 riot deputies	210 inmates confined in space for 165, bad conditions	Voters subsequently turned down jail bond
Rahway State Prison, Rahway, New Jersey	11/24 1 day	Damage unassessed 7 guards injured, 6 hostages taken	150-500 inmates	14 demands—better medical care and drug rehabilitation program	"To be treated as human beings is all that we ask of this administration..." —Inmates' petition No results reported

The Facade of Reform

observed (as discussed in greater depth in Chapter 8) that the prison system was so bad under the incumbent administration that it had been condemned by a federal court as violating constitutional guarantees against cruel and unusual punishment.

If reform appears to have popular support, the candidate will not be negligent in assuming the posture of a reformer. He will condemn prison conditions, blame the incumbent for all the deficiencies, and promise to eliminate evil, correct prison problems, and provide "prison reform." If reform indeed becomes a mandate from the electorate, if the candidate is able to convince the voters that he can correct the problems, and if he indeed is successful in his campaign, the "official reformer" will be swept into office with a commission from the electorate to provide reform. Once installed, the official is faced with the problem of defining reform and developing a strategy for attaining it.

Although most executives may have certain expertise in administrative problem solving, they rarely have realistic notions about prison administration. This lack of experience is understandable in view of the fact that the route to political success is not usually through the warden's office. Nor should it be. Politicians, whether governor, legislator, congressman, or President, are usually elected through their ability to convince the majority of the electorate that their programs will provide "the solutions." Since their job is to lead, coordinate, and direct programs, more importance (and rightfully so) will be attached to their general administrative ability and not to their demonstrating expertise in a specific area of government. Being unknowledgeable in the area of penology, officials must rely upon their advisors and may fall victim to the "committee, consultants, and concrete" syndrome that promises a solution to prison problems.

The "Blue Ribbon Committee"

The official reformer may select an individual to investigate the prison situation and report the findings to him so that he can develop a plan of implementation. However, the usual form of inquiry results from the appointment of a group of prestigious citizens, representing a cross section of the community, to investigate the prisons and report their findings and recommendations to him. And thus is born the ever-present accoutrement of reform movements—the "Blue Ribbon Committee."

Unfortunately, more often than not, the principal attribute the members of the Blue Ribbon Committee share in common is their abysmal ignorance of penology. But then they are not appointed for their knowledge of the area under study; they are appointed for their credentials of demonstrated "success" in a cross section of "professions." The inference that competency in one discipline is transferable to another unrelated field defies logic. Although the process of a committee implies democracy at work and the pooling of The Best Minds, it is not particularly suited to accomplish the mission at hand: analyzing prison conditions and offering workable remedies.

This group knows little more about prisons or reform than the official reformer, yet this does not deter the members from trying to provide solutions. They are liable, of course, to be manipulated by both the official reformer and the consultant whom they will retain to give them a clue as to the direction in which they should be heading. The number of members usually is so large that the commission cannot function; certainly a large commission does not lend itself to a consensus on any phase of the effort other than that there should be reform—and even that is sometimes not totally agreed on.[3]

The committee, floundering in bureaucratic procedures, succeeds (not entirely by accident) in clouding the issues. Polarization of thought between the "coddlers" and the "beaters" results in each group striving to reinforce its point of view by selective data. Thus efforts to pursue the actual facts with some aura of objectivity are really impossible.

The committee performs an auxiliary, but essential, function in addition to developing information. The appointment of the committee, per se, is an act well calculated to assuage demands for immediate reform. What reasonable executive would proceed without sufficient information on which to base a plan of action?

---

[3] The McKay Commission report on Attica, *Official Report of the New York State Special Commission on Attica*, (New York: Bantam Books, 1972), pp. 209–214, made some findings relative to the observer team that conducted the negotiations during the uprising in September 1971. "[T]he observers were placed in the position of acting as intermediaries between the parties. The observers' committee was not, however, constituted to serve a mediation function. The committee was unwieldy in number—over 30 members—and racked with ideological differences between those who identified completely with the inmates and those who were proponents of the position of the state." (p. 209)

"The Commission believes that direct negotiations between inmates and the state are preferable to the use of outsiders. However, if outsiders are required in the negotiations, their function and authority must be clearly defined and agreed upon by them, the state, and the inmates. A large panel cannot function effectively and should be avoided." (pp. 213, 214.)

Criticism of a governor for inaction tends to fall on deaf ears if he has instigated a "thorough inquiry" through his committee.

The two purposes of the committee are to gain time and to diffuse responsibility. It would be presumptuous for the official reformer to usurp the committee's function by prematurely announcing his reform plans. Thus the official is granted a "stay of execution" in the mandate for reform and can turn his attention to other areas of concern that may be less complex and contain greater promise for more dramatic success. He is thus given "time out" in prison reform efforts while the committee seeks "the truth."

The diffusion of responsibility is no small item for consideration. By appointing respectable and successful citizens to the board, commission, or committee, astute politicians are able to create a buffer between themselves and their constituents. Impatience, frustration, and hostility are then directed toward the committee instead of the governor, who merely shrugs his shoulders in a gesture of benevolent deference and vows that he will act promptly after the committee completes its study.

At the first meeting of the committee, it will be observed that "the torch has been passed" and the question will arise as to the best method to shed light on prison problems. The fact that few present might be able to find the prison without a map provides the first clue that the group does not contain the knowledge essential for an objective inquiry. Realizing that the onus for change rests on their shoulders, and needing both time and knowledge, the committee members borrow a chapter from the executive manual and further diffuse responsibility by engaging a consultant who is an "expert" in the field of penology.

The Consultant

By the strategy of appointing a committee, the official reformer is absolved of taking immediate action and can blame the committee if nothing constructive emerges. The committee can blame the consultant, and the consultant can blame the committee and/or the governor. But after the exercise is over, only the inmates will be aware that the real prison problems were never addressed.

An inquiry to the American Correctional Association will ensure that a consultant will be dispatched with a "do-it-yourself" prison reform kit complete with copies of the *Manual of Correctional Standards*. Objectivity dictates that sources other than prison officials be engaged to ascertain the true situation. It is assumed that the correctional consultant will provide this objectivity because he is "not part of the system"—a contention that merits further examination.[4] The consultant is retained to provide some order to the proceedings and to serve as a professional arbitrator and truth-seeker. He plays a different role than most people involved in the investigation in that he is independent of the system and yet exerts influence disproportionate to those who have been granted official power.

Although he has no authority to implement, neither does he have responsibility when "things go wrong." Nonetheless, he can control the input of data into the committee machinations so that the end result can be not only predicted but predetermined. He molds thinking in a committee that can have a lasting impact on the direction of reform. The consultant draws on his experience both to serve as a consultant and to ensure that the recommendations will be of the dimension that "offendeth not." The purpose of the latter consideration is to ensure his continued occupation as a consultant by receiving a favorable endorsement from his committee.

The consultant will lead, guide, cajole, and endeavor to move the committee toward accepting first his analysis of the prison and then his recommendations. The traditional assessment includes an evaluation of the physical facility, the presence or absence of "programs," the size of the guard force, and other such factors that can be easily reduced to specific terms of evaluation. It is more than likely that the consultant will use as his hypotheses the sacred (but undemonstrated) tenets of penology—that is, one or more of the notions discussed in Chapter 3. It is fairly certain that his inquiry will challenge neither the essence of the prison community nor the rationale of management.

The Recommendations

The consultant will provide the committee with a written report containing certain negotiable recommendations. These will consist generally of suggestions to upgrade facilities, personnel, and programs. The report will also urge that additional funds be acquired to institute these changes. The final report, delivered to the governor for action, will be couched in terms that will not appear offensive—except, perhaps, to the inmates, who neither vote nor hire consultants.

The governor's recommendations will be essentially those of the committee—that is, "more of the same." With enthusiasm the governor will declare that prison reform cannot become a reality

---

[4] See the discussion in Chapter 6 about consultants who act "as if" they are indeed a part of the system.

unless more money is provided so that more people can be employed with more training to do more things to more inmates. He may emphasize higher qualifications for staff, more education, more training, higher pay, shorter hours, better uniforms, increased professional staff, more staff, more concrete, more institutions, higher fences, more Mace—all of which are equated with more "rehabilitation."

The final step of the initial phase of fulfilling the campaign promise to reform the prison is accomplished by appointing a "prison reformer" to a policy-making position. This appointment may reflect a sincere desire on the part of the official reformer to reconstitute the prison, or it may be only a gesture following recommendations that a "professional" be put at the helm of the prison ship. The ramifications of this appointment depend to a large extent on whether the official reformer is committed to real reform or whether he is willing to settle for the *facade* of reform. Assuming he knows the difference (which is not usually the case), his definition of reform will be made explicit when he selects either a mock reformer or a real reformer to chart the new course for the prison.

Pseudo-Reform

If the new prison administrator is not committed to real reform, the traditional myths of penology will be perpetuated. That is, the "danger" of the average inmate will be emphasized, the appropriateness of the correctional (medical) model will be accepted, and the ability of staff to impose "rehabilitation" will be assumed.

The arrival of a conventional reformer poses no real threat to the guard force once it is clearly understood that he does not intend to change the prison staff structure. Staff can quite readily adapt to a new mode of performance once terms are defined and purposes made explicit. Basically, all that is involved is the acquisition of a new jargon and possibly other outward changes such as physical improvement of the facility or creation of highly visible, but ineffective, programs. There may be some grumbling and dissatisfaction over the inconvenience of moving inmates around for a variety of new "programs," but as long as control is maintained the guard force does not see this change as a personal threat to its safety or potency.

The inmates will also move cautiously in accepting the new regime. It will be a time for testing the quality of reform and the implications for their own welfare. Any real effort to change the basic structure of the prison community will be readily recognized, and staff and inmates may even cooperate in helping such programs fail. This is not to say that the bulk of the staff and inmates would not welcome real reform, but they lack the capability either of indicating or effecting their desires because of the autocratic structure of the existing prison society that suppresses freedom of expression.

The staff will, perhaps grudgingly, tolerate "newfangled ideas" in order to secure tenure, promotion, and retirement. Staff objectives are not unlike those of the inmates: they wish to survive the prison experience with the least trauma and to attain eventual release from the institution. These goals may require the officers to develop new roles under the new order, but once these roles are clearly defined there will be general compliance in order to survive.

Likewise, the inmates will adjust to the fact that they must pursue a different route in order to escape legally (be paroled) from the institution once that route is clearly defined. The progressive system (characterized by use of the medical model) invariably is more complex, and the route to success is not apparent. In the unsophisticated system, release is earned by meeting production quotas (such as picking 300 pounds of cotton per day in Arkansas) and "not causing any trouble." In the advanced system, it may not be so simple. The new passage to parole may involve participating in a combination of several treatment programs (such as attending daily group therapy sessions) that will supposedly "cure" the inmate—a prerequisite for discharge. But essentially, both staff and inmates will become adept at role playing through participation in some form of the ritual of "rehabilitation." They will make the transition to the new regime with little difficulty as long as no real effort is made to modify the basic organization, concept, or structure of the prison.

Lest one should think too harshly of the prison staff, it should be observed that they, as well as inmates, are products of their environment.[5] The belief system of the middle-management and lower-echelon personnel in a prison may not reflect malice or cynicism, but they may nonetheless limit the number of options for change available. It is generally assumed that prison staff members are sincere in their beliefs about prisoners and that the methods of control they impose on them result from those basic concepts. The idea that the hypotheses at work in the prison may be in error probably does not occur to the officer because he is not encouraged to challenge the prison structure.

---

[5] Correctional officers also suffer as a result of alienation by those in power. During the uprising at The Tombs in New York in the fall of 1970, it was the officer hostages who urged the inmates not to release them until the inmate demands were met.

Although the staff may unwittingly, or by design, participate in securing the failure of reform movements, a major responsibility for failure lies with the professional reformer, be he warden or consultant, who has the insight, experience, and training to *know* that his efforts will not be productive because they evade the central issues of reform.

The reformer long ago came to realize that chief executives, prison boards, prison staffs, and most inmates are not willing to risk the consequences of seeking real reform. A real reform venture must include plans to engage other agencies in the political-economic-social system that spawns criminality. In light of the limitations imposed on the reformer by conflicting power structures, it is not surprising that his pledge to "renovate" the prison often gets circumvented. The reformer learns that he is required to act "as if" the prison exists in a vacuum, and therefore he is required to stop short of making any changes that would have an effect beyond the prison walls.

The conventional reformer realizes that real reform is probably not attainable solely within the system, and since he is precluded from changing the system, he settles for what appears to be reform. His tenure, professional status, and impact depend on his ability to bring about only that amount of change which will be tolerated by the existing system. The alternative is to forge ahead toward the goal of real reform with the risks involved in changing the structure.

Because of the hazards of real reform, the conventional reformer settles for the fiction of reform instead of the fact. Consequently, he focuses on the symptoms and not the causes of prison problems. Accepting that he cannot achieve real reform, he is then content to accept changing the image of the prison. Real reform, in contrast, must be directed toward those activities that are *for* the ultimate benefit of the free society and, hence, for the ultimate benefit of the inmates. The real reformer believes, "How I treat the inmate is how I treat Everyman." It applies not only to prison reform but to most phenomena: one can either change the *nature* of a phenomenon or its *appearance*—sometimes both. But if one cannot really change the system behind the phenomenon, then he has the choice of maintaining the status quo or creating the impression that it has been changed.

In 1967, then-Governor Walter J. Hickel of Alaska wished to change the citizens' negative perceptions of the State Police. By executive order, he changed the name of the organization to "State Troopers," had the patrol cars painted dove gray, and spent $38,000 to acquire different uniforms. Apparently Governor Hickel was under the impression that "ugliness is in the eye of the beholder" and thus concentrated his reform efforts on changing the public image of the state's principal law enforcement agency. However, he ignored the obvious fact that the quality of police services was more a function of the character and competence of those wearing the new uniforms in the newly painted patrol cars than of the visible accoutrements of reform. Since he was not interested in changing the personnel composition of the police force, and could not change the personal characteristics by fiat, Governor Hickel chose the less traumatic course of action and changed the image and not the essence of that agency. Predictably, the people's perception of the quality of state law enforcement did not significantly improve.

Similarly, the prison may appear to become more humane, more professional, and even more therapeutic through traditional approaches to reform. But, in fact, no real change may have occurred. One travesty of such movements is that the charade is perpetrated with such finesse that most staff members and many inmates actually believe that change constitutes reform. Thus those who could become major agents of change for prison and prisoner alike are duped into supporting a fraudulent system inherently incapable of providing the real reform that is not only a reasonable demand but the right of both the captives and the captors.

> *Pseudo-reform is the thalidomide affecting the gestation period of real reform.*

The Reality Is a Facade

The pseudo-reformer strives for the appearance of reform without reform; the ecstacy of reform without the agony of revolution; the baby without the birth pains. The result is the facade of reform. The Texas Department of Corrections, for example, takes pride in the high attendance at "voluntary" church services in its youthful offender unit. Only the persistent investigator will learn that most of the points required for parole eligibility can be earned by weekly attendance at church services.

The Arkansas Department of Correction built a prison chapel at Tucker Prison Farm, ostensibly for providing counseling, educational, religious, and other services for the inmates. Yet it was located *outside* the security perimeter of the prison, where it could not be used by most of the inmates. Is it only by accident that it is situated immediately adjacent to the visitors' parking lot?

The Alaska Division of Corrections opened a multi-million dollar "Reception and Diagnostic Center" for juveniles in 1968 to remove them from the negative conditioning of jail confinement. Because I had known him both personally and professionally for some years, I confronted the acting director of the division, Tom Branton, with the contention that political expediency within the state government had resulted in the abortion of reform, and that all which remained was the facade of reform. The following exchange ensued:

BRANTON: *It's the facade of reform, but it's better than the facade of reform other people have. It's a long ways from ideal. At least, we provide a reasonably high-quality warehousing service for bodies.*

MURTON: *You mean like chaining inmates to the radiator of M.Y.C. [McLaughlin Youth Center]?*

BRANTON: *Well...*

MURTON: *How is that different from handcuffing them to the bars of the Fairbanks (Alaska) jail in 1961?*

BRANTON: *There's less of them that have it happen, I'll put it that way. That is...*

MURTON: *...it's just an occasional thing and not a routine one?*

BRANTON: *Yeah!*

MURTON: *Well, I guess you're right; that's an improvement.*[6]

Tokenism

Another aspect of mock reform is the way in which programs appear to be progressive through the practice of tokenism. The California Department of Corrections boasts of a work release program that, in theory, is an effective tool to help the convict make the transition from the walls to the street. Yet of some 24,000[7] inmates in custody on June 30, 1974, only 116 were participating in the program statewide. While there have been at least 60 years of experience with conjugal visiting programs in Mississippi, California has chosen to move cautiously in this area, and, as of the summer of 1974, family (conjugal) visits were allowed so infrequently that on the average an inmate is entitled to one visit every three and one-half years.

Correctional administrators have been inconsistent in admonishing employers not to discriminate against convicted felons in hiring practices while the correctional agencies themselves fail to employ

---

[6] Branton to Murton, July 15, 1969.

[7] *The Nation,* July 21, 1974.

ex-offenders. The U.S. Bureau of Prisons made a gesture to reconcile this conflict by hiring one token inmate in 1966 to work in the central office in Washington, D.C.; of course, he had no contact with the federal prison inmates.[8]

What frequently happens is that those programs which have some prognosis for success are systematically neutralized by timid correctional administrators who provide only token involvement designed to satisfy both the inmate and the liberal reformers. Tokenism is no more valid in prison reform than "taking a nigger to supper" is in improving race relations.

Fraud

As devious as tokenism is in perpetuating the mythology of prison reform, outright fraud is a more deliberate deception. The Ohio Department of Mental Hygiene and Correction announced that a federally sponsored training program for inmates had been instituted in 1968 to qualify them for trade union membership. The commissioner's office stated 18 months later that 60 inmates were in the program, and the associate superintendent of the Chillicothe Correctional Institute advised that "the program is doing pretty well."

It was revealed in October 1969 by an investigative reporter that with a single exception *no* inmate had been given any such courses or received any training. The one exception was an inmate who had qualified as a machinist and had been transferred to the Ohio Penitentiary. Undaunted, departmental brochures nonetheless proclaimed that Ohio "continues to gain national prominence and recognition."[9] Although it could be argued that Ohio has not gained prominence in prison reform, there can be little dispute that it has received recognition of a different sort.

Even where legitimate training programs exist, it is not always practical to place the inmates according to what they need or have an inclination to learn. Although prison authorities have constructed an elaborate classification system, ostensibly to better program the inmate, one finds that the institution has an overriding need for

---

[8] On June 10, 1974, the Bureau of Prisons reported that "accurate data on ex-offenders who are working for the Bureau of Prisons is not easily obtained.... We do not maintain on-going statistics about employees with a criminal background." However, it was stated that both male and female ex-offenders are engaged in a variety of activities "in the Central Office at an institution, or in a Community Treatment Center."

[9] *NCCD News*, National Council on Crime and Delinquency, New York, January–February 1970, p. 17.

prison labor and thus it is high on the priority scale. An inmate at the California Institution for Men at Chino reported in the spring of 1970 that he had taken a two-year introductory course in welding at Deuel Vocational Institute. He was then transferred to Chino to take the advanced course, which would lead to a certificate as an apprentice welder coincidental with his eligibility for release from the institution.

INMATE: *Guess what they've got me doing?*

MURTON: *Chopping cotton.*

INMATE: *No, hoeing corn.*

Other ruses such as hiring "professional staff"; creating an inmate newspaper, inmate council, band, panel; conducting guided tours; and introducing "programs" are all assumed to be indicators of reform. And although they may reflect change, they do not necessarily constitute reform.

Consequences of the Facade

Because the real issues are not addressed, the problems of the prison are not solved and the tyranny of treatment is substituted for the former simplistic system of confinement. The mock reform system lends itself to the moral corruption of both inmates and staff. Both moral and physical exploitation continue, and the brutality includes mental anguish as well as physical acts of violence.

The facade of reform may temporarily deceive the inmates sufficiently to prevent any major disturbance until they become painfully aware that, under the guise of "treatment," psychological brutality has been substituted for physical brutality. The fact that picking 300 pounds of cotton a day will result in parole, and that not picking 300 pounds of cotton a day will result in being beaten, is easily understood. Many an inmate prefers to serve time in the primitive, albeit brutal, system rather than submit to the professionals' "messing with my mind," as the inmates refer to "treatment." Nature tends to heal the wounds of the body, but the repair of the mind does not appear to be as automatic.

While conditions at the prison may improve under the guise of reform, the real horrors of imprisonment inadvertently remain as inmates continue to be manipulated. Although true conditions are often hidden from the layman, the legislator, and the concerned citizen, the inmates are not deceived; and realizing that they have once again been cheated, they will adapt to a mode of life that seems to be most productive for them individually. But as conditions worsen and reform fails to become a reality, factions within the inmate body again become a source of tension that mounts until a "disturbance" again forces public attention on the prison.

"IF ONLY WE HAD MORE MONEY..."

[Excerpted from The Luparar, Vermont State Prison, January 1972.]

We repeat. Perhaps the printed word is stronger than the spoken word. Perhaps we have been misunderstood. If this is the case, we then submit for our readers' consideration some of the problems we face, some of the questions that have gone unanswered.... Some of the questions have been answered since our last issue.... Others have brought comment, but whether or not they have truly been answered, we'll let you decide.

Questions

1. Why must we continue to put up with dirty dishes and cups on the mainline?
2. Why do we receive only one hot dog on Saturday night?
3. Why is the entire amount of allotted good time not used to provide incentive for kitchen help?
6. Why was pork completely deleted from the menu?
8. Why, in a hundred-man institution, are we given dish towels to take a shower with?
10. What ever happened to the fire escape for the hospital and visiting room that we were promised?
12. Where is the librarian and why isn't the library open?
14. Why does industry take priority over education here?
21. Why won't the dentist fill a tooth?
29. Where are the toilet seats promised in 1966?
34. Why can't exhaust fans be put in the visiting room so visitors can smoke?

Answers

1. Mr. Stone informed Phillip Creaser of this paper's staff that the Teflon plates in the institution are cracked and in such bad condition that they will not clean properly. He suggested that any resident who is willing to give of his yard and/or free time to wash dishes may do so and then we can have clean dishes. This accounts for egg, coffee, and other stains on the dishware we eat off.
2. As of December 18, 1971, we began receiving two.
3. Mr. Stone has informed the Editor that items like this should be put through channels, that it should not have been printed because of causing confusion that may be detrimental.
6. Pork has been returned to our diet; pork chops, bacon, etc.
8. Hooray, Hooray. Bath towels are back.
10. No answer.
12. No answer.
14. No answer.
21. No answer.
29. No answer.
34. No answer.

The Facade of Reform

The result of this disturbance will be public awareness of prison problems, an expression of shock from the governor's office, denouncement of conditions, demand for an investigation, and a pledge for reform. A committee will be appointed to investigate and report to the governor. It will conclude that prison officials recognize there are certain deficiencies in the prison. But the excuse for bad conditions will be the familiar apology that "we are doing the best we can with the tools we have." The committee's final analysis suggests that prison officials provide that level of corrections demanded and made possible by the public. Final recommendations can be distilled to the single argument that the prison officials could rehabilitate more prisoners if they were given more money to employ more guards with better training to work in more institutions.

The inmate turns off the television newscast somehow feeling he has heard it all before. And he shuffles toward his cell pondering the many unanswered questions that continue to haunt him. Will members of the guard force be more competent if they are paid more money? If not, is there a plan to fire the guard force and replace them with more competent officers who presumably will be available at the higher pay scale? Does employing more guards to do the same kinds of things to inmates, but more proficiently, really enhance the prospect for a better life in the prison? Would substitution of a 110-volt alternating current for the 6-volt direct current of the Tucker Telephone[10] have been perceived as an improvement by the inmates receiving an electrical charge to their genitals?

It is doubtful whether an increase in salary for the Kentucky correctional officer described below would have produced an improvement in inmate care:

> *One guard recently terminated was rather brutal, slovenly and obese... hence, the reference term for him was "The Pig." This guard set quotas for "white helmets" and instructed his guards to provide them. Subsequently, the guards would move among the population and, with the judicious use of the club, dispatch the prescribed number [of inmates] to the infirmary where their bandaged heads would provide the necessary "white helmets."*
>
> *Reportedly, one day he gathered the inmate population together in the [prison] yard and proclaimed as follows: "Ah*

---

[10] The Tucker Telephone was a torture device used to punish or extract information from inmates at the Tucker State Prison Farm in Arkansas prior to 1967. The instrument was an adaptation of a rural telephone. Wires were connected from the telephone terminals to the inmate's penis after he had been strapped naked to an operating table in the hospital. Another inmate or free-world guard would then sit at the subject's feet and rapidly turn the hand crank thus generating a current of electricity through his genitals.

know you fellows call me The Pig. Now there's just one thing ah want you to remember. Ah may be The Pig, but this is mah pigpen!"[11]

The basic question that must precede any serious reform movement is rarely verbalized: "How much money does it require to treat an inmate as a human being?"

---

[11] Tom Murton, Institutional Visit, Kentucky State Reformatory, Carbondale, Illinois, December 14, 1966, p. 6.

5

Anatomy of Reform Efforts

> Far better it is to dare mighty things,
> To win glorious triumphs, even though
>   checkered by failure,
> Than to rank with those poor spirits who
>   neither enjoy much or suffer much,
> Because they live in the grey twilight
>   that knows not victory or defeat.
> — THEODORE ROOSEVELT[1]

Most reform efforts result in more humane conditions, better control, and increased opportunities for the inmates—at least temporarily. But they do not contain the ingredients of real reform because the real reformer poses a threat to the "reform" administration by resisting the governor's efforts to manipulate the prison for his own political expediency. Governors, in general, probably would like to do what is right for the prisons; they also want to remain governors. If they find it impossible to do both, they will probably do what is required to continue in office.

Reformation movements are a classic example of the confusion that results from semantic difficulties in defining terms, or perhaps objectives. And it is possible that the discrepancy between the ideal-sounding pledges of reform and what actually takes place is not an intended one, but that it emerges gradually as the reform movement escalates. Because "reform" of the prison is more often a remnant of a campaign promise rather than a whole hearted effort to revise the system, the inmate is forced to conform to arbitrary

---

[1] Remarks made in a speech before the Hamilton Club, Chicago, April 10, 1899.

standards of conduct while the administration actually *deforms* him by concentrating on appearances.

> *"Progressive" correctional systems differ essentially from the archaic prison system in that the former are more sophisticated in their degradation.*

The real reformer studies the political system in order to understand its operations and to determine possible points of vulnerability, points at which he can intervene. When the official reformer is subjected to sufficient pressure, a real reformer may be able to infiltrate the prison system at a policy-making level. If so, his objective is to use the power structure in order to overthrow the current system and replace it with one that is reformist and will not perpetuate the cyclical nature of most reform movements.

It is difficult, if not impossible, to establish a correctional system immune from the political-social-economic power structure within which it must exist. Regression is difficult to prevent, and erosion of good correctional techniques for political gain appears to be the rule.

Many factors inhibit reform. As prison apologists are quick to note, programs for inmates are the last to be funded and the first to be curtailed. The basic prison problems have been attributed to insufficient funds, inadequate facilities, untrained personnel, and limited programs. Prison tradition, based largely on mythology and implemented by staff resistant to change, is another obvious factor. In addition, the high job mortality rate in the ranks of reformers contributes to the situation in which real reform is so often stunted before it can be nurtured.

Also inhibiting reform are the correctional structure of the prison system, political considerations, "professional" compartmentalized thinking, lethargic legislatures, timid administrators, overreaction to incidents, and deference to the misconceptions of public relations. Further, administrators frequently fail to provide leadership until forced to do so by outside pressure groups. The approved "reform posture" is one which contends that the prison officials only reflect public attitudes toward the prisons. The implication is that any defects in the prison system can be attributed to the attitude of the public.

> **REFORMER AWARD**
>
> TO: Rhode Island Governor Noel for his enlightened views on inmate rights. Announcing a "get-tough" policy toward inmate disturbances, Noel authorized correctional officers to take "whatever means necessary," including death, to control prison riots. Noel added that officers ignoring court-ordered procedural safeguards for inmates would have his full support and said that he himself would accept a contempt citation if necessary. [*The Freeworld Times*, June–July, 1973]

Abdication of Leadership

One apparent reason why prison officials abdicate leadership is their absolute adherence to carrying out responsibilities as supposedly defined for them by the free society. Former Warden Clinton Duffy of San Quentin used to advise his prison critics to take their complaints to the state legislature because he was only a "caretaker of the prison" working with "the tools provided by society." Most wardens see themselves as being responsive to the wishes of the community.[2] As good civil servants, they believe they are fulfilling their obligations by implementing the philosophy enunciated by the electorate.

The Correctional Administrator

The administrator religiously disclaims personal liability for prison defects and thus fails to provide leadership. What passes for the modesty of a civil servant can be unmasked by careful examination to reveal simply a device for maintaining the status quo. If there is a body of empirical knowledge embodied in the field of penology; if this knowledge can be acquired through study and experience; and if one can become competent in dispensing this expertise in such a fashion that organizational systems and individuals can be positively affected—then penology is a profession. And the professionals should be expected to provide leadership, innova-

---

[2] Donald Cressey made similar observations about the self-perception of workers in probation and parole services. See: Donald R. Cressey, "The 'Square' Theory of Probation and Parole," address before the 30th Annual Training Institute and Conference, California Probation, Parole and Correctional Association, Long Beach, June 9, 1960.

tion, and guidance through better methods and systems of dealing with human behavior.

How would society react to a parallel situation in the field of medicine? A medical student serves his internship, is licensed to practice medicine, and eventually becomes a surgeon. Through medical techniques, the medical staff of a hospital ascertains that a patient requires surgery to remove the appendix. The patient is wheeled into the operating room. The surgeon pauses with scalpel in hand ... and instructs the nurses to conduct a survey at the next meeting of the town council so it can be determined whether the public would perhaps like the gall bladder removed instead. In a self-effacing role, the doctor stands with bowed head awaiting the approval of the laymen in order to proceed with the operation—while the patient suffers.

If such action were to occur, the physician would probably be referred to a clinic for psychiatric evaluation. At the very least, he would be removed from his position. Yet the prison administrator—and the public—fail to see the fallacy of such a posture in the area of penology. If laymen are more capable of making policy determinations than prison officials, then we no longer need prison officials. The prison warden can be replaced by a committee of citizens who will meet periodically to issue decrees.

Once it is understood that prison administrators view themselves in responsive rather than creative roles, it becomes apparent why change is retarded. In general, administrators do not innovate, they do not foster change, they do not act—they only *react* to demands for change from outside pressures.[3] This pressure may be from an investigative committee, concerned citizens, the legislature, the press, or the inmates[4] themselves. Power structures have demonstrated that they only respond to another base of power. As Cressey observed:

In probation and parole, it appears, we have become housekeepers rather than reckless, wild-eyed experimenters. Perhaps this is in part why outsiders are likely to view us as "weak sisters" and "old women."

Research and experimentation have traditionally involved individualistic processes quite different in nature from

---

[3] According to Russell Lash, former warden of the Indiana State Prison, "You get prison reform one of two ways: a disturbance, which puts pressure on political and bureaucratic officials for changes, or by a court action, which gives an edict for change." (*Chronicle-Tribune*, Marion, Indiana, February 3, 1974)

[4] While inmates are a part of the system, physically, they are considered outside the system because they are not a part of the decision-making body of the prison power structure.

bureaucratic administrative process. It is important to observe that some of the most significant discoveries in the last two centuries were made by men who did not have the necessary qualifications for making them! That is, they were individualistic and creative, but not formally trained nor employed in the area of science in which their discoveries were made.[5]

Innovations in corrections have been as diverse in origin as scientific discoveries. The penitentiary came into existence because of pressure from the Quakers. Educators suggested the reformatory. Correctional camps came into existence as a result of legislative efforts in California. Halfway houses were instituted by religious orders. Probation came about through the efforts of a shoemaker. Parole was first used by a British naval officer.

The reason why individuals from fields other than penology have made the major contributions to corrections is simply because the official posture of the penologists has created a void that concerned citizens have filled. Instead of innovating or leading reform movements, most penologists have been content to become busily engaged in focusing attention on "improvements" or maintenance of order.[6]

Bureaucratization

The same conditions that spawn prison chaos, excessive corruption, and brutality also contain the ingredients that could make great strides in prison reform possible. Most antiquated prison systems are primitive societies and, therefore, do not have sophisticated personnel, finance, building, and purchasing agencies. Although these archaic prison systems easily lend themselves to corruption, they also can be revitalized to produce maximum, efficient, good organizational change and optimum reform in a short period of time.

But since the official reformer often believes that organizational structures, per se, hold the key to reform, he may concentrate on structure exclusively and consequently bargain away real prison reform in exchange for a more sophisticated bureaucracy. It is with this "progress" of bureaucratic structuring that reform measures wane, change is hindered, and achievement is thwarted by state agencies that tend to perpetuate themselves rather than to serve the needs of the citizenry.

---

[5] Cressey, p. 14.

[6] Refer to the chart in Chapter 11 noting the American Correctional Association's "achievements."

> *When the creature controls the creator, the creation becomes corrupted.*

Certain conclusions about organizational systems in relation to reform can be derived from the example of corporate machinations. The bureaucratic process is selective, and the incompetents are often promoted, transferred, or retired in order to avoid "airing dirty linen in public."

In the summer of 1962, an officer was transferred from the Youth Conservation Camp and School in Alaska to the Adult Conservation Camp because he had demonstrated to four successive superintendents that he was ineffective in dealing with either inmates or officers. But rather than remove him from the agency, the director ordered his transfer. This officer again demonstrated his ineffectiveness and incompetence in working with inmates at the Adult Conservation Camp, so he was promoted to associate superintendent where he would no longer be in direct contact with them. In that capacity, he interfered with other officers and undermined the authority of the superintendent. Consequently he was promoted in 1964 to deputy director of the corrections agency.

A probation and parole officer at Ketchikan, Alaska, who could not get along with the court or the community was promoted to chief probation officer and transferred to the largest and most influential office in the state. It was subsequently found that he was unable to work with the court or his colleagues, and so he was promoted to interstate compact administrator for the entire state.

A vocational rehabilitation counselor assigned to work with inmates and staff at the Adult Conservation Camp in Alaska demonstrated his incompetence and was given two weeks to find another job under threat of dismissal. He found one. He became the training officer of the Division of Corrections with statewide responsibility for inmate and officer training.

No Room for Dissidents

Unlike the incompetent people in the previous examples, those who challenge the system through their competence and/or integrity are terminated because they constitute a threat to the established order.

Alexander Maconochie instituted some major reforms at the Norfolk Island Penal Colony off Australia in the 1840s. He stopped the torture, brutality, and exploitation of inmates and implemented significant innovations. During his four-year tenure, there were only one killing, four escapes, and no uprisings by the inmates. He was subsequently fired in 1844 for allegedly offending the sensibilities of the freeworld citizenry. The instructions for his dismissal read more like a letter of recommendation than an indictment of wrongdoing:

> *From all the means of information within my reach I am happily able to ascribe to Captain Maconochie a most earnest solicitude for the welfare of a class of society, whose claims to compassion and benevolence have seldom been so keenly felt by persons in his station of life. From the same means of knowledge, I am able to give Captain Maconochie the fullest credit for having declined no fatigue, privation or responsibility, which was requisite for carrying into effect his views for the moral and physical improvement of the convicts at Norfolk Island. In estimating the success of his endeavours, I do not forget that the scene of action assigned to him was not that he would himself have chosen, and was not exempt from some peculiar disadvantages which might have been avoided in a more favourable situation. Neither am I at all disposed to depreciate the results of his experiment for improving the character and the condition of the convicts under his charge. On the contrary, I gladly acknowledge that his efforts appear to have been rewarded by the decline of crimes of violence and outrage, and by the growth of humane and kindly feelings in the minds of the persons under his care.*[7]

I met with the Arkansas Board of Correction on March 2, 1968, to discuss, among other things, my future with that prison system:

HALEY: *If you are scuttled, I assure you it will not be for purposes of political expediency.*

MURTON: *Well, let's include competency then. Will I be scuttled for competency?*

HALEY: *I think that is the only question. . . . In my opinion you have demonstrated near genius in doing what you have been able to do at Tucker. You have made drastic reforms, you have completely turned over an inmate society in a period of a year, probably more effectively than anybody else could. I don't know very many penologists, but I do know that you*

---

[7] Extract of a letter from Secretary of the Colonies Lord Stanley to Sir George Gipps, Governor of New South Wales, April 29, 1843, H.R.A., vol. 22, p. 691, as reported in John Vincent Barry, *Alexander Maconochie of Norfolk Island* (London: Oxford University Press, 1958), p. 147.

> *are extremely capable and have done a fantastic job. As concerns the relationships with the inmates, as concerns dealing with an inmate population, an inmate society, I cannot conceive of how anybody could find any substantial quarrel with what you have done.*
>
> *My personal opinion is that, when it comes to dealing with the inmate population, you are superb.*[8]

Five days later I was terminated.

John Boone was appointed Commissioner of Corrections for Massachusetts in January 1972. The formidable resistance to his efforts to reform that most difficult system came from politically powerful and diverse groups. On June 21, 1973, Governor Francis Sargent appeared on television statewide to report on the status of prison reform efforts of his administration.

> *John Boone gave his every waking hour in the time he has been here to changing a correction system that really didn't work.*
>
> *In fairness... you should hear the record of achievement:... a work release program... [where] ... hundreds of people, many first offenders... now are learning how to become better citizens; dozens of people in educational training in our prisons; new training for guards; the separation of first offenders from hardened criminals; and the new approaches to rehabilitation that don't just return an inmate to society, but restore self-respect to a human being.*
>
> *This is the record of John Boone.... He is a brave man and he has done his very best... and his best has been very good, very good indeed.*[9]

The public thought it was witnessing yet another of Governor Sargent's statements of complete support for Boone. The concluding remarks of that telecast were, therefore, somewhat surprising:

> *John Boone is not the cause of the problem at Walpole [State Prison]; he is the victim of it. He must go because his effectiveness has been crippled by the onslaught of the assault upon him. He must go because he can no longer*

---

[8] Extract from the transcript of an executive session of the Arkansas Board of Correction at Cummins Prison Farm, Grady, Arkansas, March 2, 1968, pp. 73, 74. The dialogue is between Board Chairman John Haley and then-superintendent Tom Murton.

[9] "Sargent Ousts Boone From Massachusetts System," *The Freeworld Times*, Minneapolis, Minnesota, June–July 1973.

maintain a working chain of command. He must go because his ability to do the work he began has been destroyed.[10]

In what has become a refrain frequently used when official reformers remove the reformers, Alex Rodrigues, member of the governor's ad hoc prison investigating committee, succinctly stated the reason for Boone's firing: "In order to salvage the reform movement, the governor had no alternative [but to fire the reformer]."[11]

These examples give some insight into the paradox of correctional practices that contrast the interests and welfare of the inmates (and society) with the self-preservation of the system—a system that frequently appears to have been designed to reward the incompetents and punish the competents.

Those who are a threat to the inmates are promoted; those who are a threat to the power structure are fired.

This axiom of reform differs from that enunciated in the Peter Principle[12] which contends that competent persons are rewarded by promotion until they reach their level of incompetence. In contrast, the preceding axiom contends that some people are promoted *because* they are incompetent—often more satisfactory than the unpleasantness of dismissal proceedings.

Another option available to a supervisor in eliminating an undesirable employee is to issue glowing letters of recommendation to prospective employers. It is reasoned that it is far better that the incompetent leave a prison system voluntarily than involuntarily. The fact that he may then reappear in another system to affect it adversely is of no consequence to the present supervisor. The important thing is to "solve" the problem and stabilize the situation.

Conformity of Thought

There are many ways in which reform efforts, perhaps unwittingly, become neutralized, diverted, or diminished. In addition to those methods cited above, one of the most common is exemplified by the "management by consensus" syndrome common to bureaucracies but foreign to dictatorships.

---

[10] *Ibid.*

[11] *Ibid.*

[12] Laurence J. Peter, *The Peter Principle*, (New York: William Morrow, 1969).

To teach conformity of thought is to advocate maintaining the status quo and to assure stagnation of both the individuals and the agencies in society. It is antithetical to progressive thought and to the evolution of civilizations. Few of our major achievements have been a result of conformity. It has been those who challenged existing ideas who have pointed us toward progress. The heretics of one age are often the heroes of the next.

It is not deviance, per se, that should be eliminated; only deviance that is *destructive* to society needs to be addressed. Societies disregard the fact that there is *positive* as well as *negative* deviance. Controls established to limit excesses of human behavior inhibit creativity in some people while simultaneously suppressing destructive tendencies in others. Unfortunately, we are apparently willing to sacrifice the fruits of genius to the gods of deviance.

We have branded the visionaries as sorcerers and have scoffed at their creative notions, analyses of the present, or perceptions of the future. One example: Billy Mitchell was tried by a military tribunal, convicted, and disgraced for advocating emphasis on air power in our defense system and predicting attack by the Japanese at Pearl Harbor. Twenty-five years later he was reinstated in the military service and promoted; and one of the first attack bombers built during World War II—the B-25—was named in his honor.

Those who have deviated from the mainstream of mediocrity; those who have leapt the chasm of tradition to achieve a higher plateau, those who have risked failure in an effort to achieve success often have been subjected to negative sanctions, ferocity on the part of the leaders, and ostracism by society.

In our fanaticism for conformity of behavior, we have insulated our philosophies from most assaults. We have created institutionalized barricades under the guise of "religion," "education," and "professionalism." In our churches, our schools, and our occupations we have endeavored to stifle every deviant thought. It is indeed a wonder that man is not still obtaining his meat by assaulting a saber-toothed tiger with a tree limb.

The standard procedure in our society for "solving a problem" is to appoint a committee, but the creation of a committee, as was discussed earlier, is often a diversionary or delaying tactic. (But one must also acknowledge that revolutionaries tend to take on the characteristics of what they seek to replace.) The underlying assumption for doing so is based on a belief that creative thought is a result of cumulative efforts of many people.

> *People talk loosely about teams, and sometimes it seems to be that they are implying that when you take any 10 people*

and put them together in a conference room for awhile they are inevitably capable of coming up with a better solution than any one of them could have conceived by himself. Nothing can be farther from the truth.[13]

It is a sad fact that superstition arising from conformist thinking is a powerful force in human behavior, and most persons would rather retreat to the solace of an erroneous belief system than deal with the facts as revealed in a rational inquiry.

An Answer Without a Question

A major difficulty in bringing about change in the archaic prison system are the peculiar thought processes involved in approaching the problem. Joe Lohman[14] used to speak of the foredooming of reform movements because of an erroneous "view of the view," that is, an inability to postulate the right questions to elicit answers that will be materially related to the problem. In addition to this inability to postulate the questions needed in order for reform to be achieved is an apparently uniform characteristic of "reformers": at the time of their appointment, they announce that they are uninterested in the antecedents of the current problem. As C. Robert Sarver stated at the time of his appointment in 1968 as Commissioner of Correction in Arkansas: "I don't care at this point what went on before. I don't intend to waste my time pulling skeletons out of closets."[15] This statement was no doubt reassuring to those in Arkansas who had killed over 200 inmates and buried them in a prison mule pasture. It was perhaps less comforting to those who feared being killed.

"Reformers" proceed to provide the "solution" to prison problems without knowing the cause of them. They reject the real reformer's contention that it is essential to know where one has been in order to understand where one is and to provide the remedy to get to where one wants to go. When correctional rationale is placed in the context of the law it "comes unglued."

---

[13] Roy P. Jackson, "Missiles and the Professional Engineer," a paper read at the meetings of the American Rocket Society, San Diego, June 8–11, 1959, p. 10, as reported in Cressey, p. 16. See also: C. Northcote Parkinson, *Parkinson's Law* (Boston: Houghton Mifflin, 1957). Parkinson contends that any committee consisting of over 13 members is doomed to failure because it is incapable of reaching any conclusion.

[14] Former Dean of the School of Criminology, University of California, Berkeley; now deceased.

[15] *Pine Bluff Commercial*, Pine Bluff, Arkansas, November 22, 1968.

A law student graduates, serves his intership, and is admitted to the bar to practice law. Eventually he may be elevated to the bench and be required to dispense justice based on his knowledge of the law and the facts of the situation. One cannot envision a judge saying, "Well, folks, I am just a moderator. I just make decisions that reflect society's attitude. Instead of ruling on issues myself, I fulfill my role by deferring to the wishes of the people. We will hold a public opinion poll at Joe's Bar and Grill to determine the issues at law in this case."

Envision the improbability of this courtroom drama: An individual accused of a criminal offense is brought before the court for trial. The judge ascends the bench, seats himself underneath the American flag and gazes down upon the defendant standing before the bar of justice.

JUDGE: *It seems to me that five years on probation would be an appropriate sentence in this case for your rehabilitation.*

DEFENDANT: *But, judge, you don't even know yet what the crime was.*

JUDGE: *Let's get on with it; I have a busy calendar. The judgment of this court shall be . . .*

DEFENDANT: *Your honor, I have not even been convicted yet!*

JUDGE: *If you don't quit interrupting this court I will cite you for contempt. As a layman you cannot be expected to understand the intricacies of the law.*

DEFENDANT: *You're right, your honor, I don't understand what is going on, but I thought you had to be convicted before you could be sentenced.*

JUDGE: *You're wasting the time of this court. It is immaterial what you did or whether you have been found guilty. You probably have gotten away with other things. Besides, a law journal article the other day suggested these methods to unclog the backlog of court cases.*

Perhaps, 20 years would be a better . . .

DEFENDANT: *What's this crap about "individualized justice"? How can you sentence me to prison for rehabilitation when you have no evidence that I committed a crime?*

JUDGE: *We are not concerned with what transpired before this hearing. The important thing is to provide the proper remedy. The more I think about it the more I believe your case is hopeless because you keep bringing up these strange notions. It may be that a lobotomy is called for in this situation.*

It is the order of this court that you be committed to the state hospital for . . .

Such conduct on the part of a member of the legal profession would no doubt prompt demands for remedial action from both colleagues and professional organizations. At the least, professional (and probably mental) competence would be questioned.

Not so in penology. The penologists who function within the framework of the criminal justice system and who also have otherwise adopted the medical model of treatment reject the basic requisite for treatment—diagnosis. One could argue that this anomaly only lends credence to the argument that penology is not as precise a "science" as medicine or law. Some would go further and suggest that penology is also less rational than these other disciplines.

6

Functional Roles in Prison Reform

"What I was going to say," said the Dodo in an offended tone, "was that the best thing to get us dry would be a Caucus-race."

"What is a Caucus-race?" said Alice.

"Why," said the Dodo, "the best way to explain it is to do it."

First it marked out a race-course, in a sort of circle ("the exact shape doesn't matter," the Dodo said), and then all the party were placed along the course, here and there. There was no "One, two, three, and away," but they began running when they liked, and left off when they liked, so that it was not easy to know when the race was over.

However, when they had been running half-an-hour or so, and were quite dry again, the Dodo suddenly called out, "The race is over!" and they all crowded round it, panting and asking, "But who has won?"

This question the Dodo could not answer without a great deal of thought, and it sat for a long time with one finger impressed upon its forehead . . . while the rest waited in silence.

At last the Dodo said, "Everybody has won, and all must have prizes."[1]

An abundance of criminological literature describes the variety of roles fulfilled by the "kept" in prisons, such as "merchant," "square-john," "right guy." But the same literature neglects to define a similar variety of roles for the "keepers." Any serious study of the prison will reveal that correctional personnel tend to perform their functions according to rather clearly definable categories. From grouping these responses, one can develop a typology of various roles for the free personnel in the prison system.

---

[1] Lewis Carroll, *Alice's Adventures in Wonderland* (New York: Cupples & Leon Company, 1917), pp. 21, 22.

Internal Roles

The following descriptions encompass certain distinct types that have evolved from the traditional prison model discussed previously. Additional roles might possibly exist within the prisons. Some caution should be exercised in casting all actors into any single one of these roles because many officers are still defining their roles, others are in transition between roles, and a few may perform more than one role simultaneously. Beyond that, these general descriptions are apt.

The Neophyte

Entering the correctional field as a career, in most jurisdictions, depends initially on meeting certain selection criteria. After appointment, the officer must complete his probationary period if he is to attain civil service status. It is during these first six months that he faces his most severe trials as he is tested by both inmates and staff. For reasons that can be challenged, the neophyte officer is frequently assigned to the tiers—one of the toughest assignments in the prison. He there undergoes a baptism of fire from the experienced inmates. One could argue that it is the inmates who really orient the new officer.

The officer faces two options: he can decide to enforce the institutional rules or he can decide not to enforce all of them. If he chooses to fulfill the role as he personally views it, he immediately encounters resistance from his fellow guards as well as the inmates. Other guards resist him because they fear change, or desire to continue a profitable relationship with inmate bosses, or are unable to cope with inmates if the rules are enforced.

The inmate tier boss will approach the new officer and advise him that there are certain activities he wishes to continue on the tier. If the officer refuses to cooperate, the inmates will rattle their cages, flood the cell block by flushing their stopped-up commodes, and otherwise disrupt the harmony of the tier to the extent that the guard's "failure to maintain control" is brought to the attention of his superiors.

The derelictions of the new officer are attributed to lack of experience, and he may be transferred to the laundry. Within the laundry, he is approached by the inmate boss who explains how he will get the work done for the guard-foreman if the latter allows him to continue his rackets. If the officer agrees, he will survive as a laundry foreman. If he does not agree, he will find laundry returned to the inmates without buttons, mismarked, improperly cleaned, and burned with the irons. A discontented population causes other more serious problems.

The officer is gradually learning: he who has no inherent power can gain it by invoking the power of others. If the officer is astute, he soon ascertains that this charade can continue until a third reassignment may well strike him out of the correctional game.

One option available to a man of integrity is to maintain his idealism as long as he can function within the system. Once he realizes that the power structure represents an immovable object, he may make a few abortive attempts to penetrate the defenses, become frustrated, and withdraw from the encounter as a satisfactory resolution appears to be futile. For his own peace of mind, such a move is fortuitous because had he persisted, the organization would have suppressed, inhibited, and eventually ejected him as a foreign organism. But by leaving the organization at an early time, he abandons the system to those he holds in contempt and by default they gain additional power to preserve the defenses of the system. His effectiveness as a gadfly[2] is lost; his impact is nil; and he may have forfeited his chance to bring about change.

The Neophyte, who can be viewed as a Correctional Virgin ("one free of impurity or stain"), might be a student of penology who naively enters the career idealistically committed to righting wrongs, defending the downtrodden, breaking the cycle of criminality, and thereby assuring the triumph of justice. But he soon learns that his survival in the system depends on abandoning such ideas or, at least, on his ability to hide them from the correctional administrator. Somewhere in the training process, the Neophyte gains insight and comes to realize that there appear to be only two viable options available to him if he wishes to remain in the prison system. He must either accept it (become a Careerist) or challenge the system itself[3] (and become a Warrior).

The new officer soon learns that he will not receive support from his superiors and he may go about the prison business unilaterally attempting to do what appears right. If he succeeds, he will embarrass his fellow workers and disrupt the prison routine by interfering with the delicate balance between staff and inmate power

---

[2] "Person who annoys or stirs up from lethargy." Definitions in quotes here and hereafter are taken from A. Merriam-Webster's *International Dictionary*, 1972 edition.

[3] Some optimistic neophytes reject this "either—or" position and posit a compromise solution presumed to lie somewhere between the two extremes. See p. 122 for additional discussion.

structures. Hence his co-workers and superiors take those steps required to suppress any notion of literally following the rules.

The Careerist

The career officer is pragmatic and benefits from his probationary period. He accepts his function as one of many cogs that keep the prison machine operational. He accepts the ambivalance of the formal and informal rules existing simultaneously. He views the formal rules as an ideal tempered by reality. He quickly learns what amount of accommodation to the inmate power structure will be accepted by his superiors.

His goal is to minimize conflict, maintain a semblance of control through alliance with the inmates, and gain acceptance in the profession by demonstrating consistent allegiance to the prison administration; even though this loyalty is not always reciprocated. As a career officer, he sees his role as carrying out orders, not questioning them. He does not concern himself with the issues of philosophy, which he leaves to the warden. He resolves the dilemma of inconsistency between what he should do (in relation to what is "right") and what he actually does (to survive). The Careerist in reality becomes a Correctional Drone ("one who has no sting and does not gather honey") and is another casualty of the prison system.

He, like the inmate, is merely serving time. His abdication of responsibility results in a premature decision not to use whatever power he might have for improving or changing the system. In many ways, his position is one of on-the-job retirement. He is there solely to assist the larger mechanism in functioning in whatever fashion deemed appropriate by his superiors. If he becomes a "good officer" (meaning that he follows orders, does not ask challenging questions, is able to maintain order), the Careerist will receive promotions. But in positions of higher authority, he will be no more effective in modifying the prison environment than before because he perceives his duty as using increased power to maintain the prison corporation.

The Warrior

An alternative for the Neophyte is to pursue the role of gadfly in conflict with a system characterized by significant disparities between what is being done and what (in his opinion) should be done. The Warrior ("one engaged in warfare") differs from the Careerist in that he does not perceive the situation as hopeless and feels a personal obligation to attempt to improve the prison. He carries over the idealism of the Neophyte and tries to use his power for change.

The Warrior is an officer of personal integrity who endeavors to preserve his idealism while continuing to function within the system. The prison world offends his sensibilities and he tries to introduce the concept of justice into a despotic regime—an effort doomed to failure because monarchs do not willingly surrender power and neither are they accustomed to having their authority challenged. Nonetheless he continues to be incensed by daily operational events of the prison and expects a more definitive reason for procedures beyond "it's always been done that way" or "those are the orders from above." He uses what little power he possesses to prevent daily abuses and inequities. His value system will not allow him to become "just a little bit corrupt."

The Warrior will be viewed by staff as abrasive, politically stupid, and masochistic. Inmates may admire his refreshing courage but, at the same time, pity his reckless abandon in rushing to inevitable conflict with those on whom he must rely for professional nurture and sustenance.

Without a change in behavior (if not attitude) the Warrior will not long survive. If he possesses an unusual base of power, he may continue in this role. However, the usual result of such activities is that the officer is either neutralized within the system or expelled from it. He may choose to mask his integrity for a time[4] and "go underground" or become "realistic" and undergo conversion to become a Careerist. He may retain his sense of outrage at certain practices but successfully inhibit it for his own professional tenure. This role is usually a transitional, short-lived one. Under the right set of circumstances, however, the Warrior may manage to endure while being an outspoken critic of certain practices he believes to be improper.

The Therapist

Ostensibly, the rest of the prison hierarchy exists to provide custody, services, and support for the treatment staff in their primary role of treating the offender. Those committed to "rehabilitation" concepts would contend that the treatment staff is the nucleus of all other activities in prison management.

---

[4] See the discussion later in this chapter concerning the Clark Kent syndrome.

> **PSYCHIATRISTS HINDER BLACK INMATES' PAROLE**
> *Baltimore, Maryland*
>
> A former Maryland prison official revealed in February that "a great many of the black inmates are ready to be paroled or transferred out of the penitentiary but are hindered by negative psychological reports issued by white psychiatrists who are obsessed with sexual fantasies regarding black people."
>
> According to the official, the situation is "cruel because the psychological reports have such a far-reaching bearing on [the inmate's] lack of movement in the system, especially parole. The source stated that the parole board "leans heavily" on the reports from psychiatrists in determining releases for prisoners.
>
> 85 percent of the Maryland inmates are black, said the official, yet all the staff psychiatrists are white. [*The Freeworld Times*, March 1974]

The treatment group—counselors, psychiatrists, psychologists, case workers, group leaders, and other assorted therapists—have secured for themselves the private domain of "curing" the inmates. Often included in this group are the chaplains and medical staff. A guard who demonstrates some compassion for the inmates and who has the appropriate academic credentials may be inducted into the priesthood of treatment as a counselor; but a therapist rarely achieves this status by promotion from within the prison. The infrequency of the combination of these requisites makes this source of therapists minimal, because treatment appointments are the result of lateral entry into prison service and do not result from internal promotion.

The corrosive process of attempting to graft a "treatment" program onto a hostile, rejecting prison organism compels the treaters to modify their ideals. The Therapist often becomes a Witchdoctor ("a professional worker of magic in a primitive society") and resolves the pervasive dilemma (of whether to compromise to survive or to resist and end up expelled) by allowing the warden to dictate the parameters of the treatment philosophy and practice.

Therapists operate inside the walls (and therefore are generally accountable to the warden) but constitute a force parallel to the custodial force, except that they supposedly hold allegiance to a higher (but vague) source of authority. Their paternalistic, and often demeaning, treatment of the custodial staff accentuates the arbitrary staff cleavage.

The inmate perceives himself being torn asunder by the two groups that compete for him, or else he is ignored by both camps and falls into the no-man's land that constitutes the schism between treatment and custody. Although the inmate may be wary of long-range hazards resulting from allowing the Therapist to "mess with his mind," the rewards, nonetheless, are substantial. Since the implementation of the medical model of treatment in prison management, the Therapist has become the surest route to parole.

> **WIZARD REINSTATED IN KANSAS JOB**
>
> *Topeka, Kansas*
>
> A psychologist, dismissed from his duties at the Hutchinson (Kansas) Reformatory for practicing witchcraft, was reinstated March 19.
>
> The psychologist, Robert Williams, was awarded full back pay after the Kansas Civil Service Board determined that his practice of the art was not sufficient reason to dismiss him. The board ruled that Williams' use of witchcraft had not affected his credibility with the inmates. [*The Freeworld Times*, March 1974]

Therapists mean well and like to do good. There is a certain satisfaction in curing criminality. Knowledge of the prison horrors tend to fade away and somehow it all seems worthwhile after all. Therapists serve several purposes in the prison. They are a living testimony to the fact that the prison is committed to rehabilitation of the convicts. They are also useful in conducting tours for the occasional pilgrims.

Generally, Therapists are content to play with the inmates (or themselves) and since they avoid being contaminated by association with the guard force (and are never allowed to carry the keys), they pose no threat to the warden or the system. They are viewed by administrators and custodial staff as an annoyance to be tolerated.

The one who resists contamination may become a gadfly within the prison. But his tenure will become shaky and he will leave the system voluntarily or by request. Either way, once again uncompromising ideals are rejected because they are in conflict with the requirements of traditional prison management.

The Curator

The Correctional Curator ("one in charge of a museum or zoo") reaches the top administrative post only after lengthy service and solely from the ranks of the Careerists. The Neophytes are inexperienced, the Therapists are incapable of maintaining order, and the Combatants cannot be controlled by the Diplomat (see the next section).

The function of the Curator is to coordinate the prison subgroups, provide efficient management, and exercise leadership in innovations that will maximize the talents of the prison community. But because he is concerned about continuing in office, the Curator or warden may also resolve the perennial dilemma by performing as expected by his superiors rather than listening to his conscience and exercising his best judgment.

The Curator is King, at least within the walls. It is from him that the Neophyte, Careerist, Warrior, and Therapist, directly or indirectly, derive their power, authority, support, and impetus. He is the chief decision maker who determines the direction the prison will be moved, or if it will be moved at all. The Curator must assume the major responsibility for the presence or absence of prison reform. But, as Professor Korn observes, wardens are not customarily appointed for the purpose of implementing change:

Quiet, economical housekeeping is his safest role. He can be the captain of his ship—so long as no one rocks it and he is content to keep it moored to the dock. So long as he resists the temptation to take it anywhere, he can have a quiet, ceremonious voyage [in port] entertaining visitors at the Captain's table and conducting tours of the staterooms.[5]

Consequently, the Curator's role is one of maintaining equilibrium among the various staff-inmate power blocks. He accomplishes this by limiting the extent to which outside groups can intrude into the prison; serving as the prison's liaison with the free world (the prison press secretary for public relations); and, when necessary, putting down rebellion by the prisoners. The warden sees himself as a full-time Curator, a custodian of captives, keepers, and cages; and only as a part-time leader when forced by conditions to do so. The Curator denies culpability for prison problems and notes that he is "just following orders" from the Diplomat.

The Diplomat

The Correctional Diplomat ("an official representative or messenger") has overall responsibility for the corrections program. In some states, such as Idaho and Mississippi, which have only one institution, the governor can be considered to function as the Diplomat. More commonly, however, comprehensive responsibility is vested in a

---

[5] Richard Korn, "Issues and Strategies of Implementation Pertaining to the Use of Offenders as Manpower Resources in the Administration of Justice," Berkeley, California, March 8, 1968, p. 7.

Director or Commissioner of Corrections. Although the authority of Diplomats varies widely from one jurisdiction to another, they are the chief administrators of corrections programs.

The Diplomat is in a position to remove or circumvent many obstacles that arise with other branches of government, with the public, or between the prison and the governor. His function is to "break trail," develop philosophy, and remove roadblocks that inhibit implementation of his programs. The Diplomat's function is to set broad goals within the framework of the governor's plans. It is his duty to present the corrections budget to the legislative body, establish prison policies, and protect the governor from embarrassment. As Korn states: "The correctional administrator looks to his governor not for direction (which he will not get) but for protection and support."[6]

The Diplomat is basically a bureaucrat who concerns himself with directing a central office staff through a maze of procedures, personnel rules, purchasing regulations, and construction requirements. At best, he is captain of a phantom ship in drydock. He never seems to be available when the Curator requires his support. More often than not, the Diplomat is too busy "putting out fires" to extricate himself from the trap of "management by crisis" in order to respond effectively as the power behind the throne at the propitious moment.

Summary

As noted, all the definable roles are assigned worthy functions within the prison. These roles become eroded only when other considerations are more compelling. Each actor must face his "moment of truth" and make a personal decision in resolving the professional dilemma that must be faced by all in the system at one time or another—even if only momentarily. In general, the three alternative resolutions appear to be (1) to maintain integrity by forging ahead consistently (and risk removal); (2) to resign or be removed from the system (and thus retain little hope for impact on the system); or (3) to convert to another more functional role (for the officer) in the traditional prison (and thus become an accomplice to the travesty).

The subversion of certain roles creates new ones vastly different from their original conceptualization. Thus, regardless of intent, the corruption of power creates static roles that restrict changing

---

[6] Korn, p. 7.

operations and that inhibit, if not thwart, reform of the prison system.

External Roles

In addition to the classic roles within the correctional structure, some clearly defined typologies exist for other actors who are outside the system and yet wield significant influence on it. For purposes of clarity, the emphasis here is on individual activities rather than on the collective pressure of citizens acting in concert.

Those having an impact on the prison system can all be grouped under the classification of consultants. Their services may be solicited or unsolicited; their impact may be direct or indirect; they may or may not be financially compensated for their advice. But since they are all outside the political system, they enjoy an aura of objectivity that often is confused with competence. The three most common typologies are the Oracle, the Prophet, and the Prostitute.

The Oracle

One type of individual who has an effect on the system is the Correctional Oracle ("a person through whom a deity is believed to speak"). Many people accept, as an article of faith, that the universities of our country constitute the genetic repository for the wisdom and knowledge of all mankind. The carrier of the erudition on criminality is the Oracle, who views himself as a sort of cultural chromosome who transmits his omniscience to the unenlightened pagans of penology.

Oracles are most often ensconced behind university walls where they enjoy the sanctuary that affords them all the rights and privileges (but not the responsibilities) of an endangered species. They seem to multiply prolifically and can be observed on rare occasions foraging beyond the ivy walls into the real world in search of a paper tiger to engage in combat. The Oracle, as a "good social scientist," accepts the world as it is and is content to study, observe, and analyze data he diligently collects in the course of his meanderings. He reports profusely on the state of the art of penology and is not too modest to offer "the solution" to criminality.

His research and pronouncements, however, are always within the protocol established by the phenomenon being studied, which is not unlike the accused determining what evidence can be used against him at his trial. Thus the root defects of the prison remain a riddle because practitioners cannot allow any inquiry that might call into question the foundations upon which the House of Penology has been fabricated. the Oracle can be assured continued access to the prison only by accepting these limitations—a fatal flaw in any basic research.

Diplomats, Curators, and most other practitioners scoff (with some justification) at the Oracle as an "armchair penologist" who has little contact with reality. Therefore his effect on the decision makers (who have the power to change the system) is negligible because, for them, the Oracle has little credibility. But the pontification of the Oracle does have a profound impact on the Therapists who act as his priests. The disparity of treatment modes found in the prison are a product of the gamut of diverse theories and/or conflicting research results provided by the Oracle.

> **REFORM RHETORIC**
>
> "We feel it essential to carry out the programs we feel should be carried out."
>
> Louis M. Sowers, Director of Corrections, Alabama. February 25, 1972.

Although the function of the Oracle should be that of casting light into darkness, usually his unintended effect on the system is that of obscuring an already foggy arena.

The Prophet

The Correctional Prophet ("an effective or leading spokesman for a cause") is a part-time advisor, counselor, or consultant to the governor, Diplomat, or Curator. He may or may not be compensated for his services; in fact, his services may not have been solicited. His task (often self-appointed) is to define basic problems, cut through reform rhetoric, suggest realistic solutions, and predict the consequences if his advice goes unheeded. In times of prison crisis, the Prophet may be called on (in desperation) to stand by the Curator's side and interpret the handwriting on the wall.

The Prophet may arise from the ranks of the Warriors (by a circuitous route) or may emerge from other sources not directly involved in penology. The Prophet's "error" is in attempting to engage the prison system and to urge that the structure of the system be modified to bring about rudimentary changes in the prison. His "sin" is the same unpardonable one that is frequently committed by the inmate: he fails to grant respect to those who have forfeited such a right to respect by cheating inmates of their fundamental rights. To

Functional Roles in Prison Reform

this sin are added the derelictions of refusing to compromise and continuing an unrelenting course toward reform with an unshakable belief in the worth of such a venture.

In the event of a major prison scandal that can no longer be contained, the governor may be compelled to "retire" the Diplomat and/or the Curator. If the situation is sufficiently abominable (and especially if there is a paucity of applicants for the beleaguered position), the Prophet may be handed the reins, installed as Curator, and commissioned to "do what needs to be done." At this point, of course, he moves inside the system and becomes the actual, as well as the philosophical, leader of the reform movement. But this dual function is short-lived because from the genesis of his appointment the Prophet is set on a collision course with the appointing authority. He will not survive that collision professionally and will thus be forced to retreat to the position of penological gadfly outside the system. His tour in power may diminish his effectiveness in this capacity as well.

Thus, although the Prophet serves as a catalyst for change of the prison, he may also inadvertently become the agent of abortion of prison reform. His methodology may eventually pose such a threat to the official reformer that the results are the real reformer's removal and loss of the gains.

Like most prophets, he remains "without honor" in his own profession and the impact he has on the system may be less than that of any of the various participants. A pragmatic Prophet will reject the real reformer's role and, not infrequently, become a Charlatan or Prostitute. For after all, there is not much demand for a Prophet who adheres to his principles and refuses to be corrupted by the system.

The true Prophet will be neutralized by one method or another. He finds that (except in times of severe crisis) his advice is not sought. A realistic Prophet may allow his role to degenerate into becoming simply a public relations man for the very system he has been engaged to analyze. He thus forms an unholy (if not immoral) alliance by becoming the prostitute for the system's procurer.

The Prostitute

Some consultants (like others) fail to realize that integrity is an "either–or" entity. They prefer to view this character trait as measurable on a graduated scale. Thus one hears arguments about compromise that contend it is possible to have degrees of integrity. These contentions have been espoused so long that they are now part of our folklore. Those consultants who thus become seduced by the bait of partial integrity risk being referred to by the uncharitable as Prostitutes.

The Correctional Prostitute ("one for hire, devoted to corruption or unworthy purposes") has a major effect on prisons and prison reform. He is a consultant to Diplomats and Curators and has credibility because he was once "one of them." It is not uncommon for retired Curators and Diplomats to become Prostitutes once they retire from the field of battle. Those traits that provided them with upward mobility and acceptance in the professional fraternity will assure these Prostitutes access to the system that the Oracle rarely enjoys.

The Prostitute hires out his *mind* instead of his body. The consultant may fall into this category by refusing to render an independent investigation or recommendations that represent his actual beliefs. Frequently, the Prostitute only recommends those solutions that will be acceptable to the agency that employed him. He becomes an extension of that agency and hence forfeits his "objective" role as a true consultant by becoming an institutionalized part of the commission, committee, or other investigative arm of the government. Therefore, as part of the system he is ineffective in fomenting change. But the Prostitute thus avoids any conflict between himself and the committee and, later, between the committee and the official reformer. One can be assured that his suggestions will be "workable" and will not upset the mock reformer by setting goals beyond the limits of the facade of reform.

REFORMER AWARD

TO: Charles Wolff, Jr., warden, Nebraska Penal Complex, who recently announced the phasing out of tin cups in favor of more homey plastic dinnerware for inmates. The innovative move is part of Wolff's program of rehabilitation through "humanization" of the prison. *[The Freeworld Times]*

Characterizations

Besides these clearly defined correctional roles, there are some that seem more ambiguous. They cannot be equated with specific positions in the organizational structure but tend to cross over personnel classifications and can occur at any level. One such manifestation is the Correctional Eunuch (*eunuch:* "a castrated man employed as a chamberlain in a palace").

Invariably, the Eunuch commences his career in one of the other roles but becomes emasculated by the system over time and is commonly referred to by his colleagues (privately) as one who "has no balls." The officer who has been castrated of his integrity becomes impotent in any real effort to bring about prison reform. He may have the intellectual capacity to know right from wrong. He may suspect, if not know, what will work better than present practices. Once emasculated, he is allowed to roam the sacred harem of the prison unable to achieve any real renovation of the institution because he has been pruned of his potential.

Because the Eunuch represents a modification of some role, he may be referred to in hyphenated terms to describe both his character and his position in the prison hierarchy. Thus we have the Careerist-Eunuch, Curator-Eunuch, Diplomat-Eunuch, and so forth. However, it is grammatically incorrect to refer to an impotent Therapist as a "Witchdoctor-Eunuch" because the words generally are considered to be synonymous.

The Eunuch can be relied on by the Curator to support his prison policies consistently. Although he may not be respected by the inmates, the Eunuch is nonetheless predictable in his behavior and thus there are few surprises to upset the prison routine.

The Correctional Chameleon ("a fickle or changeable person") represents a more difficult problem. The Chameleon cannot be accepted at face value because he appears to be that which he is not. He masquerades as other actors and his deception can be confusing to the Curator and misleading to the inmates. The Chameleon adopts a differential role not through any conversion or change in beliefs but rather as an expedient for his survival in the organization. Thus a Careerist can look like a Warrior at the time a reform-minded warden is appointed. The transformation is almost instantaneous and may seem miraculous to his associates.

Because the Chameleon's true nature is always masked, he cannot be referred to in hyphenated terms. It would be correct, however, to describe his role in parenthetical words. Hence one could correctly describe a worker as a Warrior (Careerist), Careerist (Warrior), or Prophet (Oracle), with the word in parentheses indicating his true nature.

The Chameleon can be counted on by both the mock and the real reformers to carry out their wishes (as long as they are in power) because it is professionally rewarding for him to do so. But the Chameleon constitutes no residual resource as a reform element because he has no real commitment to his adopted role. The Chameleon has no personal integrity and is motivated not by conscience but by greed. He is viewed both by his cohorts and by the inmates as a double agent. He acts out his role as required to please the ones in power but will not hesitate to hedge his bets by simultaneously appeasing the opposition by pretending to be a Clark Kent (see the next section). The result is that the Chameleon is used by all and respected by none.

The Correctional Charlatan ("a pretender, fake, fraud, quack") is the False Prophet of prison reform. He is what the Chameleon only pretends to be. The Clark Kent is a Neophyte or Warrior disguised as a Careerist or Eunuch; the Charlatan is a Careerist or Eunuch disguised as a Warrior or Prophet. The function of the Charlatan is to work within the framework established by the consultant, the commission, and the official reformer to create the impression that reform has been achieved. He sets about his task of change by restricting himself to considerations that only directly affect the prison; he ignores the influence of other agencies on prison management. His dereliction is one of implementing the inhibitive philosophy of the official reformer. He usually has sufficient expertise to recognize the indicators of real reform and to thwart them. He is commissioned to use his knowledge, training, and experience to ensure that real reform does not rear its troublesome head and embarrass the official reformer.

It is the Charlatan who poses the greatest threat to reform efforts. He represents the synthesis of the roles of Prostitute, Curator, Diplomat, and sometimes Oracle. His credentials are impressive. The Charlatan has the right contacts, is in good standing with the professional associations (which recommend him for positions), and has mastered the rhetoric of reform. The tragedy is that the governor may sincerely desire reform but err in appointing this pseudo-reformer.

There may be some temporary panic among the Curators, Careerists, and Eunuchs if they believe the protestations of reform rendered by the Charlatan. Eventually, staff fears will subside when it becomes apparent that the Charlatan intends to do no more than talk about reform. The governor and the public may well believe the system is being reformed. But the inmates will not long be deceived. Inmates' lack of interest in erecting the facade of reform contributes to the decay of reform promises.

The Clark Kent Syndrome

The Clark Kent Syndrome can easily be confused with activities of the Chameleon or the Charlatan. The latter can pretend to be a real reformer while the Chameleon can mask himself and move with equal ease in either direction of the mock-real reform dichotomy. The Clark Kent differs in that he is a real reformer who can only masquerade as a mock reformer.

Most of us resist the necessity of making either-or choices and feel more comfortable in a grey twilight universe. The social philosophers, such as Reichenbach,[7] argue that everything is relative and there are no absolutes. As discussed previously, the Neophyte is discomforted by being presented with only the two suggested alternatives for the idealist: "sell out or get out." Thus the Neophyte finds the Clark Kent route to survival most attractive because it provides him a method of compromising strategy without forfeiting integrity; or so it would seem. He can reject the Careerist and Warrior roles and become a Clark Kent—a *latent* Warrior.

The Neophyte soon realizes that he is ineffective because he lacks power. He rationalizes his failure to take a stand on issues as they arise by deciding to defer action until he attains sufficient power to accomplish the change. He says to himself: "I shall mask my integrity *now* by wearing my Clark Kent suit so no one will know that I am a Warrior until I achieve power. *Then* I'll discard my disguise, abandon the charade, display my Superman uniform, and become a mighty force for justice."

As the disguised Warrior moves upward in the system by dint of his masquerade, other options become available. By the time he reaches the pinnacle of "success," his personal situation may have changed to the extent that he is disposed to consider factors other than the needs of reform. He has acquired a wife (or she a husband), children, a mortgage on the house, and car payments and cannot "at this time" afford to discard the Clark Kent suit. He thus puts a price tag on his integrity that foretells his ultimate destiny in the reform movement.

The latent Warrior may rationalize that he needs more power to become effective, and so he keeps the suit on a bit longer. The difficulty is that it may become quite comfortable and there is a reluctance to discard it. Or it is possible that the Superman costume has disintegrated through years of disuse. It may be that the crusader has become "that which he appeared to be" and is more comfortable in the Clark Kent role than that of Superman. After all, he has not had much experience in leaping over tall buildings and his Superman traits may have atrophied. He never appears in Superman garb, and it

---

[7] See: Hans Reichenbach, *The Rise of Scientific Philosophy* (Berkeley: University of California Press, 1963).

will never be known that all those years a Warrior was a spy in the midst of the enemy camp. But then he posed no real threat anyway.

Another possibility is that the officer will retain his commitment and may one day achieve sufficient power to effect the desired change. He then casts off his Clark Kent suit, stands resplendent in his dingy but recognizable Superman uniform, and prepares to battle the enemy. The initial response to such a revelation is likely to be stunned disbelief followed by incredulous laughter. If the administration accepts Superman at face value, he will be transferred to an ineffectual position or removed from the system; after all, they appointed Clark Kent, not Superman. The job description calls for a Careerist, not a Warrior. Or perhaps the administration will cast one questioning glance at this ridiculous apparition and determine him to be harmless to the system. In fact, such a figure on the payroll would add immeasurably to the image of reform that is in vogue.

But if he is ever allowed to function in his new role, Superman will find himself without power—which he must receive not from Krypton but from staff and inmates. He lacks credibility with reform-minded staff who have not been drawn to him because of the successful masking of his integrity. More importantly, he will have no credibility with the inmates he has allowed to be degraded in order for him to survive and reach a position of power. The atrophy of integrity by suppression results in emasculation of power. And the Clark Kent finds that he is left with neither honor nor power. He will continue to participate as the token reformer on the staff as a Chameleon or put back on his Clark Kent suit and again disappear into the morass of "loyal" Careerists.

As the serpent tempted Eve with the forbidden apple, so the Charlatan deceives the Neophyte with the Clark Kent apple. Much later, the Neophyte may discover that he was sucked into the rhetoric and has been effectively neutralized all these years in the quagmire of pseudo-reform. In one agonizing moment, he may comprehend that he is not now, and never has been, a Warrior but has been seduced into becoming a Prostitute. Although his role is not intended, the result is the same. The Clark Kent holds the unenviable position of becoming a Combatant-Eunuch retaining the knowledge of good and evil. He is doomed to live out his existence knowing that by pursuing a fictional course midway between real and mock reform he defrauded not only the inmates (by thwarting their rising expectations) but, in the process, cheated himself of potential self-fulfillment.

The Clark Kent fails to see that a man's character is the sum of the individual actions he performs daily and not the result of one mighty thrust. Most of us are not privileged to receive the allotment of "one shining hour" to do a great deed. Greatness is an accumulation of just actions in minor, daily confrontations; it is in facing up to "evil" conditions consistently. Some men bypass dens of snakes while searching in vain for the dragon to slay. The tragedy is that at the end of the quest, one realizes that he never encountered a dragon; or, if he did, he was unprepared to joust with it because his sword of truth had rusted in the scabbard. Therefore he is either devoured in the process or forced to relinquish the field of battle in dishonor.

Summary

Various easily defined organizational roles both inside and outside the prison system have been described in functional terms (in relation to maintaining the prison system as it is), as well as in relation to the ramifications of alternative routes that may be taken by the officer. (See the diagram.)

The Neophyte is faced with one of the either-or dilemmas of prison reform: he must choose either to fit the mold of the Careerist and remain within the prison system or to become a Warrior and risk being ejected from the system. The Careerist is confronted with no real dilemma because he accepts his role without question and is assured of tenure and probably upward mobility within the system. The Warrior, on the other hand, immediately faces the same dilemma that confronts the Neophyte: if he maintains his integrity, he will be rejected by the system; yet if he masks his integrity and becomes a Careerist, he will attain tenure and "success" within the system but in the process will forfeit any chance to bring about real reform.

If he is removed from the system, the Warrior may reappear later as a Prophet and may have some indirect influence on Curators and Diplomats. On rare occasions he may reenter the prison system in an internal position as Curator or Diplomat, but unless he disguises his true character, he will once again be relegated to the periphery of the penal arena.

Curators are content to maintain the status quo until they either retire and become consultants or are promoted to Diplomats. Diplomats can also look to retirement as consultants. But normally the route to success as Curator or Diplomat has as a prerequisite emasculation, and the only consultant roles available thereafter are those of Oracle or Prostitute.

A TYPOLOGY OF PENOLOGICAL ROLES AND THEIR INTERRELATIONSHIPS

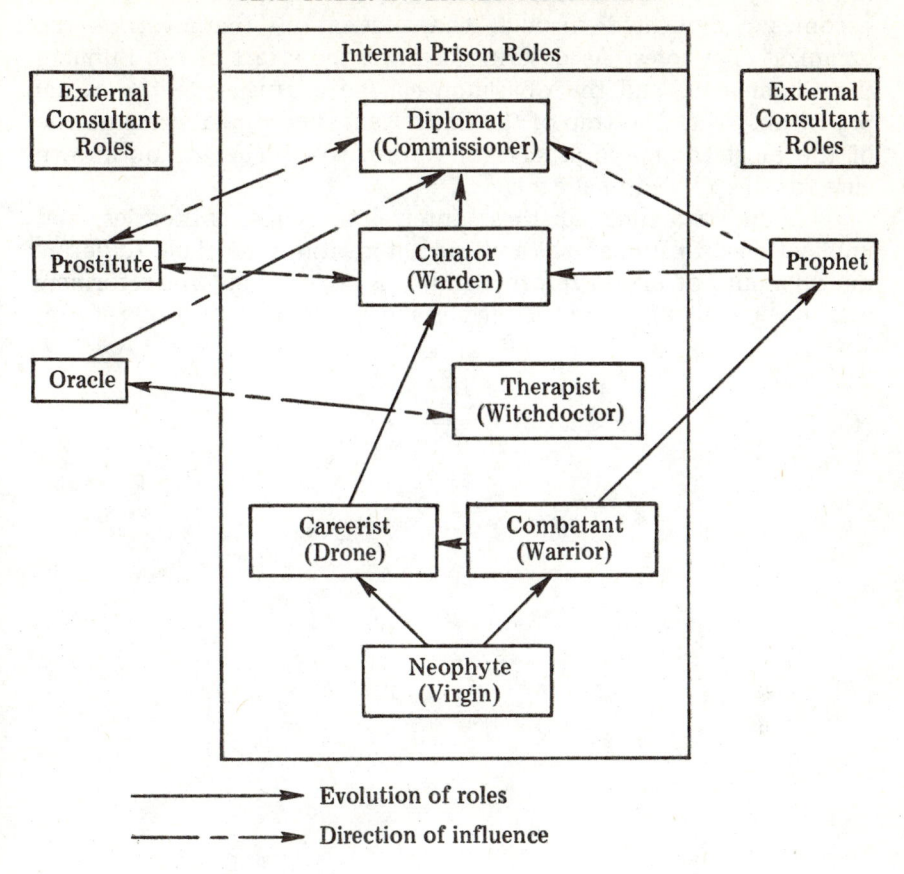

```
                Internal Prison Roles
   External          Diplomat              External
   Consultant       (Commissioner)         Consultant
   Roles                                   Roles

   Prostitute        Curator               Prophet
                     (Warden)

   Oracle            Therapist
                     (Witchdoctor)

                 Careerist   Combatant
                 (Drone)     (Warrior)

                    Neophyte
                    (Virgin)
```

———▶ Evolution of roles
– – –▶ Direction of influence

Oracles have the greatest influence on the Therapists, who have a static position within the prison system. The Therapist's position is not in the progression of promotion within the system; entry and exit are lateral. The disenchanted Therapist can become an Oracle and thus continue to influence other Therapists. The Oracle may also affect the Diplomat, but usually to a much lesser extent because of his lack of credibility with practitioners.

Prostitutes have a direct effect on both the Diplomat and the Curator because the roles may be interchangeable. Also, Prostitutes have high credibility with the practitioners because they emerge from that group.

Functional Roles in Prison Reform

Although the impact and functioning of these various roles are rather easy to understand, the sub-rosa operation of the prison system becomes complicated through characterizations that override the organizational roles. As described earlier, the effect of the Eunuch, the Chameleon, and the Charlatan can be confusing to the casual prison observer. The trap of the Clark Kent syndrome represents one of the most traumatic aspects of reform roles. There is no known cure for this correctional cancer.

An understanding of these interrelationships, intricacies, and implications of various roles and characterizations may help to define the dilemmas of prison reform—and, it is hoped, would-be reformers will thus be able to avoid the pitfalls and quagmires of prison reform.

7

The Spiral Nature of Reform Movements

> The best laid schemes o' mice and men
> Gang aft a-gley;
> And leave us naught but grief and pain
> For promised joy.
> —Robert Burns[1]

The initial efforts of the real reformer to change a prison system may not differ radically from those of the mock reformer. Both will endeavor to abolish physical brutality, corruption and exploitation of inmates as a group. Elimination or reduction of such conditions within the institution on a fragmented basis is met with less enthusiasm by the inmates and, accordingly, less resistance by staff than overall categorical attacks on prison defects.

Reform programs grafted onto existing prison structures consistently fail to survive because they are rejected as foreign organisms. Thus, systems protect themselves from change by neutralizing treatment of the basic illness. It makes no more sense to graft healthy tissue to a totally diseased body than it does to graft diseased tissue to an otherwise healthy body.

Most correctional reformers have an abiding faith that change can come about by infiltrating the sick system and gradually curing it. This theory, of course, ignores the strength of the organism's antibodies which enable it to survive all efforts to change it. Also, this philosophy makes about as much sense as attempting to cure pneumonia of the left foot. It is the whole organism which is sick; it is the entire organism which must be cured.

---

[1] Robert Burns, "To A Mouse," *The Poems of Robert Burns* (New York: George H. Doran Co., 1920), p. 90.

The governor as official reformer is not disturbed about efforts to "clean up the prison situation" that initially consist only of basic legal and humanitarian considerations. But once the prison is under control and headed toward real reform, the official reformer may mistakenly assume that his support is no longer essential and turn his attention to other, more pressing areas of responsibility. By assuming a neutral position, he may unintentionally withold his influence by not exercising his power at the most critical time in the prison revolution. During this period the existing power structure at the prison is being destroyed and the real reformer needs the leverage that can be provided only by the official reformer. Another possibility is that the official reformer's enthusiasm may tend to wane as the prison moves closer to real reform. This can happen for various reasons. One is that the official reformer's understanding of reform quite possibly differed from that of the real reformer at the time of the original agreement, but because of semantic confusion, these differences were not seen.

CAT-O-NINE-TAILS RENOUNCED

With the signing of the Revised Criminal Code bill by Governor Russell Peterson, Delaware has formally renounced use of the cat-o-nine-tails.

In use since the pre-Revolutionary War days, the whipping post was a feature in Delaware corrections until Governor Peterson ordered the post to be put away in the basement of Delaware Correctional center in 1969. The post had served as punishment for a variety of crimes including embezzling, wife beating, robbery, and larceny.

The whipping post was last used in 1952 but candidates and incumbents for office had recently called for maintaining the practice in the name of law and order. [*The Freeworld Times*, August 1972]

The official reformer may begin to have doubts, based on his essential ignorance of prison dynamics, about the direction in which prison reform is moving. Because of his apprehensions, it may even appear that the new regime wishes to carry out some of the same questionable activities conducted by the previous administration. It is precisely at this point that the official reformer may succumb to doing what is necessary to remain in office so that at least some changes are instituted. But by doing so, he forfeits any hope for achieving real reform.

Once he makes the decision to pursue what is politically expedient instead of what is for the benefit of the inmate population, the reformer will lose credibility and the inmates will lose confidence in him. Real reform will be aborted. This failure results because the reformer can only provide the opportunity for reform to emerge; he cannot impose it over the objection, or without the cooperation, of the inmates.

In an attempt to salvage reform efforts, the real reformer will continue to explain both his philosophy and his strategy to the official reformer and others exercising power or influence over the prison system. He will attempt to demonstrate that prison reform is a direction, and if not kept on course, the prison ship will be diverted and drawn back into the usual orbit of failure or mediocrity. Real reform requires a nonstatic situation to move the prison toward this goal.[2] The prison either moves toward reform or away from it; there is no neutral position in a real reform movement.

In the final analysis, it may be necessary for the real reformer to enunciate his position clearly and take a posture of "no compromise" on basic reform measures. As Martin Luther nailed his theses to the door of the Wittenberg chapel and announced "Here I stand," so must the true reformer establish his position of not compromising on principle if he is to maintain his credibility with staff and inmates and continue to guide the prison toward real reform. Although it may be theoretically possible to improve the prison without the support of the official reformer, it is *not* possible to reform it without the support of the inmates. The past two centuries of prison experience amply demonstrate the fallacy of such efforts.

The following case studies of two state prison systems are presented to demonstrate the spiral nature of reform movements. These particular jurisdictions were selected because the systems were significantly different before reform intervention, reform efforts were contemporary (in the 1960s), and documentation is abundant.

The Alaska Division of Corrections

Historically, the administration of Alaska since purchase from Russia in 1867 has been characterized by congressional apathy, judicial neglect, political corruption, and official incompetence. Lack of machinery for self-government, the appointment of absentee

---

[2] Thus plateaus cannot be tolerated in a real reform movement. The equilibrium of power, activities, and routine must be a little off balance at all times if movement is to be sustained. The challenge for the real reformer is to maintain control of the unstable situation without stabilizing it into the stagnation of complacency. It is not unlike controlled fission of a nuclear stockpile to prevent reaching a critical mass that would result in a catastrophic explosion.

officials, and the complexities of a frontier society all contributed to mismanagement of the affairs of Alaska as a territory. The operation of penal institutions did not remain unaffected by these conditions.

Jail administration, as practiced by the United States Marshal, can be described as informal at best. As recently as 1952, few prisoners committed to jail were incarcerated pursuant to a lawful writ. Release procedures were equally casual. Because the deputy marshals in charge of the jails served at the pleasure of the United States Marshal (who was discharged from office with each change in national administration), the quality of institutional management was marginal. The historical record reflects a lack of attention to civil rights of the accused, no classification of prisoners, kangaroo courts, inadequate facilities, and exploitation of inmates.[3] The marshal, out of necessity, assumed a pragmatic approach to the incarceration of adult prisoners and concerned himself less with juvenile offenders or the mentally ill.

The Alaska Jail System

In July 1953, in an effort to upgrade the quality of service to inmates, the United States Bureau of Prisons assumed control over the Alaska territorial jails and created the Alaska Jail System. Federal prison officials were transferred to Alaska to manage and coordinate the various facilities, and efforts were made to extend the United States Constitution to prisoners in Alaska. Under the various superintendents of the system, political patronage was eliminated, civil service[4] personnel were recruited, legal rights of the incarcerated were strictly observed, prisoners were not exploited by staff or inmates, and care and custody of territorial and federal wards were conducted in a respectable manner. The jails soon approached acceptable standards.

But the efforts to reconstitute the penal system in Alaska were directed more toward improvement of the existing system than toward any real reform movement. The quality of service steadily increased, but radical change did not occur until after Alaska was granted statehood in January 1959.

The institutions in Alaska today can easily be traced to their predecessors or to the actual social conditions that spawned them.

---

[3] See: Thomas O. Murton, "The Administration of Criminal Justice in Alaska, 1867–1902," unpublished master's thesis, University of California, Berkeley, June 1965.

[4] There are both positive and negative implications of a civil service system. See p. 236 for further discussion.

The organizational structure of the state and its strong executive form of government was a direct reaction to the federal abuse and exploitation of Alaska as a territory. The correctional system was subsequently constituted between 1960 and 1964 within that framework. The ingredients for development of an advanced system were all present: the organizational structure of the state government eliminated the lethargic managerial boards, and the avoidance of the county subdivision of government agencies eliminated most duplication of effort and conflicting jurisdictional problems. All prosecution of criminal offenders was vested in the Department of Law; all policing outside municipalities (and, in many cases, inside as well) was provided by the Department of Public Safety; and all judges were appointed by the Alaska Court System. There was no prior state correctional system to bequeath a tradition of probation, parole, or institutional treatment. Also, no archaic penal code existed to restrict the developing correctional philosophy. The frontier policy of accepting a man even while recognizing his faults provided a climate among the people, as well as in the legislature, of concern for the criminal offender. Consequently, criminal conviction in Alaska did not generally carry the stigma that accompanies the administration of criminal justice in other more "advanced" societies.

At the time of statehood in 1959, federal facilities became the responsibility of the Alaska Department of Health and Welfare. Choosing to avoid this responsibility as long as possible, the commissioner of that department contracted with local municipalities to operate the jails. Alaska had never had a prison. Customarily, the difficult or long-term offenders were transported outside Alaska to be boarded with the United States Bureau of Prisons in one of its penitentiaries. Under the contractual agreements, the jail operations returned to the low level of performance that had existed under the supervision of the United States Marshal. Evidence of corruption, brutality, exploitation, and malfeasance soon become abundant. Within a few brief months, management of these jails by city police departments quickly resulted in conditions that negated most of the progress achieved by the Bureau of Prisons. In one jail, for example, inmates were fed a "scurvy diet" at a cost of 25¢ per day; in another, juveniles were suspended and handcuffed to bars with their feet barely touching the floor; and, in a third, 16 inmates were confined in a single cell on rations of pilot bread[5] and water.

---

[5] A biscuitlike cracker carried by sailors as a substitute for leavened bread, which molds.

The Youth and Adult Authority

Charles Pfeiffer became the Director of the Division of Corrections (then known as the Youth and Adult Authority) in 1959. He was determined to create a radically different correctional system unencumbered by the traditional concepts that have plagued other jurisdictions. Existing systems were studied in order to avoid factors that inhibited reform and to adopt those that seemed to enhance its realization. As a result, a single agency was created to provide coordinated services to all offenders—juvenile and adult, male and female, misdemeanant and felon. Functions of probation and parole were combined in the same office. The agency directly operated all institutions in Alaska with the exception of local facilities in the city of Anchorage.[6] Hence uniform procedures were established, a single philosophy was instituted, and flexibility of institutions, programs, staff, and inmate utilization became a reality. A civil service system was created to "ensure professionalism."

By the summer of 1963, the experimental Chilkoot Camp had been operating for three years, the Youth Camp had been in operation for four years, and probation and parole offices had been established in all regions of the state. Most of the state institutions were under direct supervision of state officers. The permanent Adult Conservation Camp at Palmer was nearing completion. And, finally, uniform procedures had been implemented statewide in both probation and institutional services. It was anticipated that within a year the remaining contractual jails would be staffed by officers of the Division of Corrections, construction of the Adult Conservation Camp would be finished, and its staffing would be completed. It was also anticipated that upon achieving these goals and reaching a necessary level of correctional philosophy and coordination, it would then be possible to begin real efforts to regenerate the wards of the system.

The Effects of Compromise

Pfeiffer, however, had begun to compromise in programs and philosophy almost from the time of his appointment. He often would say something like: "I want to establish a meaningful rehabilitation program in Alaska. And, if we are going to take this ship anywhere, I must remain at the helm. Because if I am not in the system, I cannot bring about change. Therefore we must be patient and accept temporary setbacks in order to achieve the big picture."[7]

---

[6] In January 1973, this facility was leased to the state for operation.

[7] This was the gist of verbal statements that Pfeiffer made to me on numerous occasions between July 1960 and December 1963.

A familiar refrain, but one in which he sincerely believed and to which he adhered during his entire tenure in Alaska.

Pfeiffer allowed political pressure to affect employment practices (to the detriment of the program). He deferred plans for new facilities to appease the legislature. He endeavored to compensate for unresponsive bureaucratic decisions by the shortcut of extralegal devices. Programs were sacrificed for political considerations; construction of the Adult Camp was not only delayed but nearly aborted. Furthermore, Pfeiffer declined to tell the governor that other state agencies were inhibiting the progress of the Division of Corrections.

The year 1963 was the critical period in the evolution of the correctional system because it was in October of that year that P. L. (Swede) Severson was appointed Chief of Institutional Services. Severson replaced the acting chief of this division for reasons that were less than valid in relation to improvement of the system.[8] He had earned a high school equivalency diploma from the United States Marine Corps, had been Chief of Police in Juneau for several years, and had been a motorcycle officer in Los Angeles. The fact that he did not meet the civil service standards set for the position did not pose any real problem; the standards were simply downgraded by order of Governor William Egan so that Severson could qualify.

Severson's police orientation, belief in the political spoils system, and lack of knowledge in the field of corrections ill-equipped him to cope with daily problems.[9] His insistence on placing the institutions under the state police could only be viewed as a regressive movement. His administration was characterized by improper use of inmates, political hirings, and overt efforts to eliminate the adult minimum-custody camp. He abolished the Chilkoot Camp, which had been a training camp for officers and inmates, suggested transfer of the Youth Camp to the court system, and attempted to purge the system of competent officers.

---

[8] Severson had just been fired as Chief of Police by the Juneau City Council for allegedly misappropriating $20,000 of city funds. He was not accused of stealing this sum but of diverting it from receipts from the state for care of prisoners in the city-operated state jail. It was also rumored that Severson had strong political influence with the incumbent Democratic administration and that Governor Egan was obligated to him for personal favors.

[9] Pfeiffer, unable to prevent Severson's appointment, ordered him to study the Ketchikan Jail for a few weeks before touring other institutions so that, as Pfeiffer hoped, "he will get an idea how a jail is supposed to be run." (Telephone conversation from Pfeiffer to Murton circa October 3, 1963.)

The Spiral Nature of Reform Movements

The prime effort of this new correctional administration was to level off the programs and stabilize the system. The initial planners had recognized that as the correctional system evolved it would require readjustment of other agencies if the objectives were to be achieved. But rather than rock the boat, it was decided in the summer of 1963 that the continued success of the governor's office would be best if there were harmony within the official family of state agencies. The fact that progress was being unnecessarily thwarted was not considered.

One could view Severson's appointment and actions as a way of neutralizing reform because the correctional system was nearing the stage, in both philosophy and programs, of gaining a momentum that would be difficult to control from the outside. The state administration perceived this closeness to reform as a potential threat for reasons that were never stated. Work release programs were stopped; incompetent (but obedient) officers were promoted to managerial positions; manipulation of officers and inmates increased; initiative was stifled; and the first riots in the history of Alaskan institutions began to occur.

Construction of the Adult Conservation Camp was ordered stopped, programs were curtailed, officers were required to pay for their meals and to work overtime with no compensation, and the number of personnel positions was reduced. While the correctional system was degenerating, uniforms, credentials, and forms were all changed. These and other "improvements" served only to destroy morale while modifying the *image* of corrections according to Severson's perception of how to wed "rehabilitation" with political expediencies.

As the momentum of the reform movement was interrupted, further steps were taken to ensure that it would not again occur. The superintendent of the adult camp testified before the state legislature that was inquiring about the failure of the executive branch of government to implement legislative intent in camp construction. He was subsequently fired. Other competent superintendents were also eliminated. In fact, the director himself, Charles Pfeiffer, was ultimately fired after he had been drained of his last ounce of compromise.

Since Pfeiffer's removal in 1967, a juvenile reception and diagnostic center (McLaughlin Youth Center) has been completed. Yet the pattern of institutional administration there reflects no basic change in dealing with juveniles in Alaska. The terms used to describe inmates and facilities have been changed and a new facade has been created, but inmates have been handcuffed to the steam radiators for disciplinary reasons.

The Results of Reform Efforts

The summer of 1963 represented the apex of improvements, the highest point thus far achieved in the cycle of reform efforts in Alaska corrections. The decay of the system thereafter was not due to a single issue or event but was rather the result of an insidious, nearly imperceptible erosion of correctional programs over an extended period of time. We usually do not forfeit our integrity in a single cataclysmic surrender. We only compromise "a little" each day until we realize there is nothing left to compromise—that the compromise of *any* principle may lead ultimately to the forfeiture of *all* principles.

Some observers contended that much more "good" could have been attained if the correctional leadership within the agency had attempted to work within the system and compromised "just a little." The critics hold that larger gains would have been achieved by this method. Unfortunately, a close scrutiny of the history of Alaska corrections does not support such notions. Nor does an examination of "accomplishments" since 1964 reveal any evidence to support the contention that going about things gradually is viable. In contrast, one can point to the substantial, if modest, accomplishments under the brief but radical reform efforts between 1960 and 1964. Brutality toward inmates under the management of city-operated state jails was eliminated, as were grossly incompetent staff people through establishment of minimal standards for correctional personnel. Participatory management—inmates working with staff to run the institution—was implemented at the adult camp. Basic requirements for inmate comforts were instituted; a coordinated correctional system was created; and two minimum-custody institutions were built to lessen the trauma of institutionalization. The development of a reception and diagnostic center (with all its acknowledged deficiencies) provided an improved physical environment for juveniles, and flexible laws were enacted that have at least maintained the potential for achieving the destiny envisioned by the pioneers in the Alaska correctional system. Although these rudimentary accomplishments fell far short of the desired goals, they nonetheless constituted a substantial step in the right direction and significantly exceeded those achievements attained under any other system of correctional philosophy during the 97 years of American rule over Alaska.

During his regime (1959–1966), former Governor William Egan forfeited his chance to sponsor a true renaissance in corrections. As the official reformer, he possessed the power to ensure reform; he chose instead to use that power to inhibit reform. The subsequent administration succeeded only in manifesting the "law and order" movement in corrections. After struggling to become free from the archaic incarceration procedures of territorial days, experiencing the traditional, but advanced, techniques of the United States Bureau of Prisons, and briefly enjoying a few excursions into the uncharted seas of correctional reform, the Alaska Division of Corrections will probably now return to the oblivion of the territorial institutions that were concerned simply with detention of those accused of committing a crime. Alaska had the potential for creating the most advanced correctional system in the United States. It will not now achieve it.

The insurmountable obstacle to reform of the Alaska correctional system came not from the public, not from the trade unions, not from the legislature, not from the judiciary, not from the inmates or staff, nor from any public or private power groups—the ultimate impediment to creation of a model correctional system in Alaska came from the office of Governor William A. Egan after he had been apprised of all facts. The power and strategy in reform movements do not include the wherewithall to overcome the power-giver. The governor will always retain sufficient power to neutralize the correctional system if, in his estimation, it runs amok.

A new feeling of hope was in the air in 1970, however, when a new administration was swept into office. The successful gubernatorial candidate promised an era of progress, integrity in government, and increase in social services. In January 1971 William A. Egan was once again inaugurated governor of Alaska. His first official act in relation to treating the criminal offender in Alaska was to fulfill an objective of his previous administration: he ordered that the construction of Alaska's first prison be completed by the summer of 1972.

Professor LaMar T. Empey of the University of Southern California has served as a consultant for several years to various Alaska institutions. However, his major impact was the conceptualization of the Alaska prison that is euphemistically known as the "South Central Regional Correctional Institution" (also called Eagle River Correctional Center). Fervently adhering to the medical treatment model of rehabilitation, Empey argued, successfully, that Alaska needed a captive situation where officials could intensively do more things to more inmates. Originally, he thought that if inmates were grouped together in units of 13, transformation of the criminal offender would be easier to achieve. But this figure was later changed to ten and became the basic determinant of the structure of the new prison.

In arguing for creation of the facility, proponents pointed out that the average daily number of inmates in adult institutions in

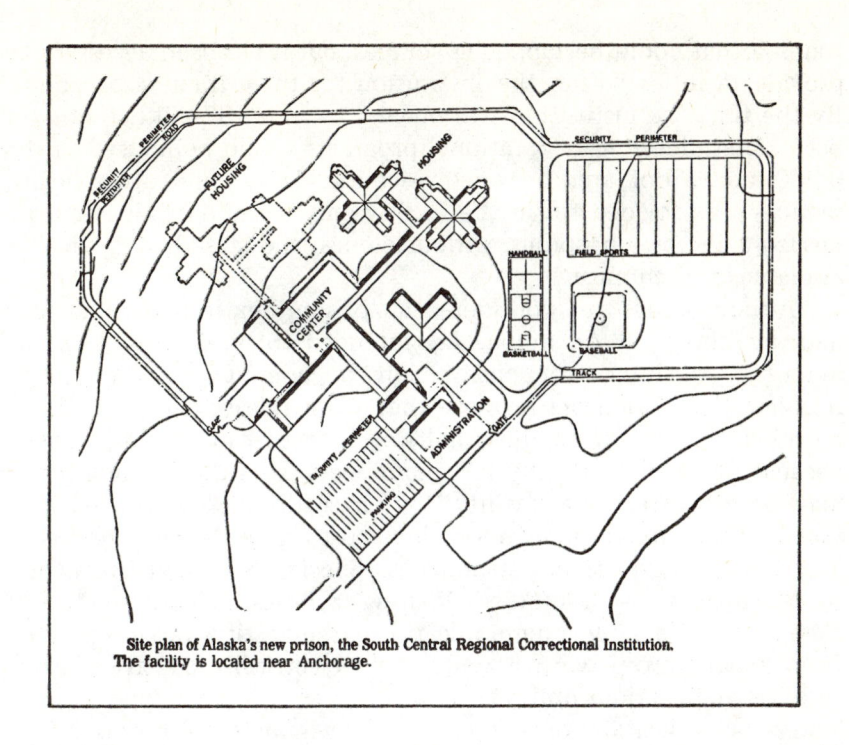

Site plan of Alaska's new prison, the South Central Regional Correctional Institution. The facility is located near Anchorage.

1969 was 330. However, they "overlooked" the fact that the total capacity of existing adult institutions at that time was 427—one-third more than the demand for space.

Convinced that Alaska needed a prison to bring its correctional system up to date, Alaska voters approved a $5.2 million bond issue for construction of this facility. The complex is located on 207 acres in an isolated rural area 13 miles from Anchorage. The first phase of construction provided facilities for a prison population of 100 inmates with the second phase possibly reaching a total of 180. The philosophy of the institution is treatment in group settings. Daily group therapy is programmed. Space has been provided for education and vocational training facilities.

Important questions come to mind regarding this facility, however. Although there are three adult institutions in the United States that are "coeducational," the Alaska facility is for males only. Although the rehabilitation movement in America is toward treatment in the community, the Alaska prison is created as a self-contained community in rural isolation. The availability of higher education and vocational training in the Anchorage community has been ignored. There are two universities and a community college in Anchorage providing both academic and vocational

The Spiral Nature of Reform Movements

training that could be tapped as sources, but it has been necessary to provide facilities within the institution for these training programs. By the time the institution was opened in June 1974, it had not yet been determined what vocational programs would be housed in the 6,000-square-foot area provided. Medical, dental, and other health services are provided for in the facility only because it is located too far from the two hospitals, various clinics, and state health services available in Anchorage.

Although it is not considered a "prison," existing (or planned) halfway houses in Anchorage are intended to be used to ease the inmate's transition from institution to community when he is released. Also, sponsors propose that work release and educational release take place from these halfway houses instead of the prison because of the prison's physical remoteness from the community. It may be a "correctional facility" but it is surrounded by a security fence and contains ten maximum custody cells and ten cells described by corrections personnel as "Special Treatment Units" and by the inmates as "the hole." Visiting facilities include bulletproof glass with telephone communications; the institution is operated from a bulletproof control center; and electrically controlled steel gates separate various units.

As an indication of the concern for inmates, the new prison provides 20,145 square feet of floor space directly related to administrative services; 24,000 square feet for inmate services such as education, training, and therapy; and the remaining 8,400 square feet for inmate living and recreation space. To put it another way, less than 6.3 percent of the space in this facility "for the inmates" is allocated for their direct use. Outside, however, the facility is covered with cedar siding that was used to "avoid the institutional appearance which would result with other materials."

According to Austin MacCormick, who served as a consultant on the project, "The design is excellent, I'd say. There's a feeling here of a small community rather than a big institution. Alaska was lucky. You could have been stuck with upgrading an old penitentiary. Instead, you started from scratch."[10] Some would argue that Alaska could have continued to have no prison and thus have been luckier still.

Apparently there was no difficulty in locating the institution at the wilderness site; local homesteaders saw it as a source of employment. According to Assemblyman Ed Willis, "People here

---

[10] "New Prison at Eagle River," *Anchorage Daily News*, Anchorage, Alaska, October 26, 1972.

have now accepted the fact that there will be a prison in their backyard. The community has even gone a step further. They're thinking of the economic advantages—available jobs, for instance."[11]

Two years after construction of the facility, the local residents were probably thinking of more than employment opportunities. On October 11, 1974, Dennis Ray Anthony was convicted in an Anchorage Superior Court of first degree murder in the contract killing of a Fairbanks resident three years previously. The next day, he was taken from the Anchorage jail to the South Central Regional Correctional Institution by the Alaska State Troopers and was placed in a maximum custody cell at 5 P.M.

Anthony was subsequently released by correctional officers into a yard for exercise, scaled two 14-foot fences, escaped through the woods, broke into the home of a correctional officer, raped the officer's wife, took clothing, and stole his car—all within 78 minutes after his confinement to the facility.

According to Associate Superintendent Roger Endel:

It's a new facility, we've made some blunders in its early operation, and we'll have to take full blame for Anthony's escape.... Since July, we've been getting prisoners who shouldn't be assigned here.... I'm afraid that this whole thing is going to kill the program.[12]

The local grand jury investigated the incident and submitted its report to the presiding judge on November 8. It found, in part:

The Commissioner of Health and Social Services [Frederick McGinnis], the Director [Charles Adams], and Deputy Director [Thomas R. Branton] of the Division of Corrections are strongly criticized for their lack of concern for the safety of the public and their poor leadership as exhibited in the lax operations of the Eagle River Facility [SCRCI].

... We have found that security in the maximum security area of the Eagle River Correctional Center was incredibly lax and the Commissioner and Director were aware of the situation.... We firmly believe the funding of the Eagle River Correctional Center is adequate at the present time. The problems at the center are due to poor and inefficient management, lack of foresight, and negligence in its opera-

---

[11] *Ibid.*

[12] "Escape May Jeopardise Rehab Plans," *Anchorage Daily News*, Anchorage, Alaska, October 14, 1974.

tions. . . . The only work programs at the facility are the food service and system maintenance.

A beautiful, shiny new facility with every physical comfort but lacking in direction and programs has little chance of rehabilitating anyone.[13]

Commissioner McGinnis responded to the court on November 15 by saying:

We do not concur that the leadership of the Department did not stress and has not stressed the function of the protection of the public in the operation of the Eagle River Correctional Center.[14]

As if to emphasize the correctional administrators' lack of culpability, McGinnis informed the press on November 26 that the facility's superintendent, two assistant superintendents, and a correctional officer had been suspended; one officer had been demoted, and another fired, over the incident. (The suspensions were staggered so the entire management staff would not be gone at the same time.)

Judge Occhipinti was not convinced of the quality of leadership in correctional programs and stated that he still had not received a satisfactory explanation for an incident involving another prisoner, Michael L. Alexander. Alexander had been released from the center on a work pass (although the court had ordered that he receive no such privilege) and allegedly raped three women.

As a point of comparison, the Alaska Adult Conservation Camp was built to house 120 inmates. It was designed and built by the inmates and the staff. The total cost of the facility was $79,000—less than the $80,000 planning grant awarded by the Law Enforcement Assistance Administration for the design alone of the present prison. The construction cost of the camp per inmate: $658. The cost of the prison per inmate: $52,000.

The prison idea was sold to the voters because of a lack of detention space inside Alaska and the desirability of keeping offenders in Alaskan facilities rather than sending them to prisons outside Alaska. But Alaska officials have advised that they will continue to contract with the U.S. Bureau of Prisons and that inmates will continue to be sent outside in the future.

---

[13] *Report of the Grand Jury*, Superior Court, Third Judicial District, Anchorage, Alaska, November 8, 1974.

[14] Frederick McGinnis, Letter to the Honorable C. J. Occhipinti, Juneau, Alaska, November 15, 1974.

The new prison may offer employment to local hunters; it may give a boost to the construction industry; it may provide Professor Empey with a laboratory to test his notions; but it will do nothing to provide new, needed services for the inmates—and that, theoretically, is what it's all about.

Through neglect or insight, depending on one's perspective, Alaskans avoided building a prison for 107 years after it came under American control. One would have thought that a century is sufficient time to demonstrate the efficacy of an idea. Not so. Prison reform has had no meaning in Alaska because there has been no prison. Previously, the consultant could not "improve" the Alaska prison because it did not exist. That deficiency has now been solved. And one cycle is complete.[15] (Refer to the diagram.)

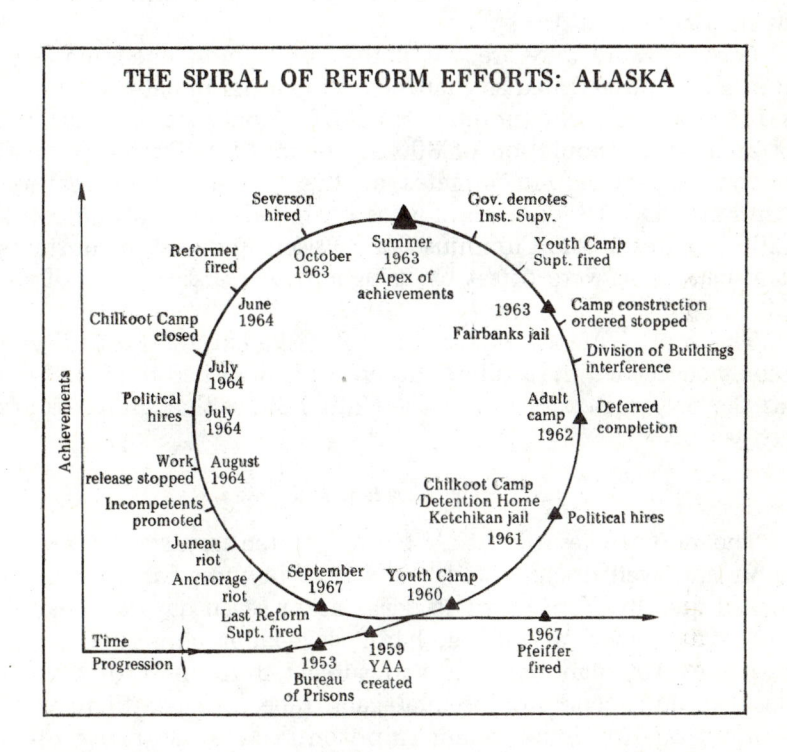

THE SPIRAL OF REFORM EFFORTS: ALASKA

- Severson hired
- Gov. demotes Inst. Supv.
- Reformer fired
- October 1963
- Summer 1963 — Apex of achievements
- Youth Camp Supt. fired
- Chilkoot Camp closed
- June 1964
- 1963 Fairbanks jail
- Camp construction ordered stopped
- July 1964
- Division of Buildings interference
- Political hires
- July 1964
- Adult camp 1962
- Deferred completion
- Work release stopped
- August 1964
- Incompetents promoted
- Chilkoot Camp Detention Home Ketchikan jail 1961
- Political hires
- Juneau riot
- Anchorage riot
- September 1967
- Youth Camp 1960
- Last Reform Supt. fired
- 1953 Bureau of Prisons
- 1959 YAA created
- 1967 Pfeiffer fired

(Axes: Achievements / Time Progression)

---

[15] For further discussion of Alaska corrections, see: Thomas O. Murton, "The Alaska Penal and Correctional Institutions in Transition, 1952–1967," unpublished doctoral dissertation, University of California, Berkeley, June 1968.

The Spiral Nature of Reform Movements

The Arkansas Department of Correction

Although slavery in America may have been abolished at the close of the Civil War, the conditions that created it were not eliminated. The sprawling plantations remained, and it became customary throughout the South to turn to the prison for a cheap source of labor. Arkansas was no different.

In 1897, the legislature authorized the acquisition of land to make the penitentiary self-supporting.[16] Over the next 20 years, the state acquired two parcels of land that prisoners farmed in order to sustain themselves and to return a profit to the State. By 1930, all prisoners had been transferred from the main prison at Little Rock to the Tucker and Cummins prison farms consisting jointly of about 21,000 acres. The Little Rock prison was torn down shortly thereafter to make room for a state police barracks, and no prison has since been built to replace it.

Guard towers were erected at the farms, and some inmates were given guns and assigned as guards over the other inmates. As recently as 1967, a freeworld (noninmate) staff of only six was authorized for an average population of 300 at Tucker State Prison Farm. Five matrons supervised 40 inmates at the Women's Reformatory at Cummins, and 18 paid employees exercised nominal control over 1,200 inmates at the Cummins State Prison Farm. Staff shortages at each institution were offset by using inmate guards—a total of about 250.

The motto of the prison was "Punishment for Profit," and it quickly succeeded in fulfilling this creed: it punished the inmates and was the only prison system in the United States that showed a profit each year.

The Decadent Past

The deficiencies of the Arkansas penitentiary system are both legion and well documented.[17] Inmates in these institutions were worked literally from dawn to dark, six or seven days a week, in all kinds of weather, at menial, hard, slave-labor chores. They were housed in 100-man barracks and subjected to theft of property, abuse, assaults, and homosexual gang rape. Because there was no minimum age for commitment to prison in Arkansas, many 14-year-

---

[16] The Davao Penal Colony in the Philippine Islands has been self-supporting since 1931.

[17] See: Tom Murton and Joe Hyams, *Accomplices to the Crime: The Arkansas Prison Scandal* (New York: Grove Press, 1969).

old boys were housed with older offenders and were therefore vulnerable to almost all conceivable acts of sexual depravity.

No underwear, boots, jackets, or gloves were ever issued; food consisted of watery rice or weevils and beans; meat in the form of hog-head stew was received only annually; milk was never provided.[18] At the time of the police investigation in 1966, the inmates were observed to be at least 40 pounds underweight. In order to survive, some prisoners stole food, others bought it, and some set traps in the fields to catch anything edible.[19]

The lack of supervisory personnel resulted in the inmates operating the institutions. They determined all work assignments, granted special favors, merchandised prison commodities, and provided the entire guard force. Officials explained to curious visitors that one way to distinguish inmates from employees was to realize that "any person carrying a gun in the prison is an *inmate*; freeworld staff traditionally are unarmed."

The structure of extensive exploitation relied on fear rather than respect to maintain any semblance of control. Since a system of fear must be enforced by more than the mere threat of violence, it is understandable that a system of brutality evolved. The Arkansas statutes provided for lashing an inmate ten times a day with the "hide," a five-foot leather strap capable of maiming.[20] This official method of discipline was augmented by such illegal but customary techniques as inserting needles under the fingernails, crushing knuckles and testicles with pliers, hitting the inmate with a club, blackjack, or "anything you can lay your hands on," kicking him in the groin, mouth, or testicles—and, of course, use of the infamous "Tucker Telephone."[21] A logical extension of such a system of brutality is the threat of death. For this threat to be meaningful, it must, from time to time, be carried out.

The Arkansas prison system survived periodic scandals and investigations for 100 years with little modification. It was perpetu-

---

[18] For a discussion of medical services, see: Tom Murton, "Prison Doctors," *The Humanist*, American Humanist Association and American Ethical Union, Buffalo, New York, May–June, 1971.

[19] When goods and services are not provided by the established order, an informal order emerges to fill the void.

[20] On December 10, 1968, the Eighth Circuit Court of Appeals sustained a trial court ruling that the use of the hide constitutes "cruel and unusual punishment" as prohibited by the United States Constitution. Use of the hide was authorized in Mississippi by state statute and was unaffected by this ruling because Mississippi is not in the Eighth Circuit.

[21] See Chapter 4, footnote 10.

ated by those both inside and outside the prison who had a vested financial interest in penal slavery. The state police investigation of 1966 documents corruption or malfeasance of prison officials, prosecutors, the director of the state police, the judiciary, law enforcement personnel, legislators, the governor's office, and businessmen.

Reform Efforts

Governor Winthrop Rockefeller successfully campaigned for prison and other reforms and was inaugurated in January 1967 as the first Republican governor of Arkansas in nearly a century. As the official reformer, he was almost instantly confronted with a crisis at the prison, and as mentioned in Chapter 2, I was appointed to reform the system.

At Tucker, the first things that I tried to do were to abolish corporal punishment, eliminate brutality, stop the rackets, and demonstrate to the people of Arkansas that a prison could be run without torture and violence—a foreign concept at the time. We were able to break the inmate power structure and substitute a form of inmate self-government.[22] Unrest, assaults, and escapes were virtually eliminated. Clothing was purchased, inmates were fed an adequate diet, and the work day was reduced.

Farm management, facilities, and livestock operations were renovated. Schooling, vocational training, and other services were instituted. Condemned prisoners were integrated into the population, an inmate band was created, dances were held, and a new prison community consisting of both inmates and staff came into existence. Tensions and hostility lessened as decision making was shared with the inmates and they became really involved in self-determination.

By the end of 1967, Tucker Prison Farm was stabilized, and I was elevated to the joint appointment as superintendent of Cummins State Prison Farm and as head of all Arkansas institutions. At Cummins, my new administration overcame the opposition of both hostile inmates and staff, and we were able to begin the changes that had been achieved at Tucker.

The first thing we had to cope with was getting the new superintendent (myself) installed despite death threats from some staff and inmates who feared loss of power. Soon, however, the new administration increased the food allotment for inmates, fed the livestock, determined the number of inmates incarcerated, stopped the brutality, moved the inmates back into the prison from their

---

[22] See: Tom Murton, "Inmate Self-Government," *University of San Francisco Law Review*, vol. VI, no. 1 (1971): 87–102.

squatter shacks, and began to interrupt the rackets. We took the women inmates to dances at Tucker, liberalized their living conditions, and allowed one inmate to have her newborn baby with her at the institution. The initial reform efforts were directed toward survival, gaining nominal control, and reversing the dehumanization process of the prison. They were successful; hence they "failed."

On January 28, 1968, about 30 days after my arrival at Cummins, I excavated the remains of three inmates allegedly murdered by officials and inmate guards at the Arkansas prison. Since it was necessary to expose the depravity of the system in order to enlist general support for the reform movement, I went to Bob Scott, Governor Rockefeller's aide for prison affairs, and told him what I intended, and the digging was done with his and the governor's blessing—at the time. The criminal justice system, however, mobilized to focus attention not on how the inmates came to be *exterminated*, but by what authority they had been excavated. Although no one was ever indicted or tried for killing these inmates, I narrowly avoided indictment for "grave robbing" and no doubt subsequent sentencing to the maximum 21 years in the Arkansas prison system.

Over the next few weeks, the state police, the state pathologist, and the grand jury conducted investigations that resulted in the general contention that a "paupers' graveyard" had been uncovered. However, it is not customary to decapitate indigents because they cannot afford the usual burial fee.[23]

It was expected that the installation of the new prison board in 1968 would effect some changes beyond what the superintendent had the power to do. Then, it was believed that the board could audit the effectiveness of the prison management and that the gains made at Tucker and Cummins could be consolidated. At the same time, progressive bills were being prepared for the legislature; a contract was being negotiated with Tennessee authorities for care of female prisoners; and federal funds were pending for construction of new facilities nearer Little Rock. Soon, it was hoped, the inmates would be properly fed and clothed; the Cummins inmate power structure would be broken; and a thorough investigation of the bodies in the mule pasture would be completed.

By March 1968, Tucker was still progressing and Cummins was coming under control. It was the consensus of the new Cummins staff that, left to their own devices, the entire prison would have been reconstituted by the end of that year. After all, the old prison

---

[23] Two of the victims had been decapitated prior to burial.

board had resigned and a new "progressive" board had been selected to assist the reform movement. Yet it was to be this very board that would succeed in stifling reform where all other opponents had uniformly failed. This group of men was destined to deliver the coup de grace to the prison reform venture under the guise, ironically, of "prison reform." The achievements were all within grasp, but the board members, sensing no real support from the governor, did not reach out to seize real prison reform. Instead they chose to undermine every aspect of the work. Governor Rockefeller became frightened on the very threshold of success and deferred to opponents who wished the prison system to remain as it had been for a century. Both his opponents and his advisors convinced him that prison officials were damaging the image of Arkansas and that his continuation in power depended on their immediate removal.[24]

I met the members of the new prison board officially for the first time on March 2, 1968. At that time, they stated that I probably would not be appointed as Commissioner of the Department of Correction, which had come into existence the day before. Five days later, the board met again, and advised that I had been summarily fired and was to be placed under house arrest until departure from the prison three days later.

Regression of Reform

Sixteen of the new staff members were subsequently removed and a general downward spiral of the prison began. The new facilities were never built near Little Rock; promised prison industries never materialized; and no contract with Tennessee was ever signed. It was necessary to sell part of the dairy herd in 1968 and 1969 in order to provide prison operating funds. The audit revealed evidence of official corruption, but the Board of Correction suppressed the report and no action has been taken against the malefactors.[25]

---

[24] According to a statement of Tom Eisele, aide to Governor Rockefeller, telephoned to me on March 5, 1968. Eisele also speculated that if I were left in office I would have more popular support than the governor within another 90 days. A common defect apparently inherent in prison reform efforts is the delusion that essential programs are a function of law instead of personalities. Essentially the same laws and facilities existed under my regime and those of Bruton, Urban, Sarver, and Hutto. Yet there is a demonstrable difference among these administrations and the accomplishments of each.

Making the foregoing erroneous assumption, the official reformer frequently chooses to sacrifice the prison reformer ("for the moment") in order to obtain prison reform legislation. But he does not realize that management of the prison is a manifestation of the personality of the administrator, largely irrespective of the existing laws.

Subsequent superintendents lacked the courage to abolish the prison money system in Cummins. Hence the inmate power structure continued to exist for several years with the related graft, corruption, intimidation, bootlegging, gambling, and killings. There were 22 stabbings and 9 reported deaths during the first 18 months of regression; there were none under the reform administration.

The inmate council and disciplinary and classification committees were abolished. Inmates again work personally for staff. The open press policy was eliminated, and the prison defies scrutiny. Prison officials report an annual 85 percent turnover in staff. There is evidence that the inmates once again engaged in brutality, dispensed medications, and bought and sold jobs. The food returned to the former unpalatable level; clothing was rarely purchased (in 1969 inmates were working in the field barefoot); and the women were again being placed in "the hole" naked, without bedding or toilet facilities.[26] The dances were eliminated, the baby was removed from the prison, work hours were extended, there was a general reversion to the former system. Prison rackets flourished and officials admitted the prevalence of freeworld whiskey, LSD, and an abundance of illegal weapons.[27]

During the first two years after my departure from the prison system, the federal courts in Arkansas ruled three times that specific practices at the prison constituted "cruel and unusual punishment" as proscribed by the United States Constitution. The first ruling involved conditions imposed on the inmates in isolation units; the second, the chaining of inmates to a fence for several days; and, third, the court ruled that shooting inmates sitting in peaceful protest violated their rights.

As discussed previously in Chapter 2, Federal Judge J. Smith Henley condemned the Arkansas prisons in February 1970 and threatened to close them unless state officials could devise an

---

[25] A "reform" prison bookkeeper was accused of selling "good time" and otherwise profiting by exploiting the inmates—in the same manner as did his predecessor under the former system. He was not prosecuted. See further: *Arkansas Democrat*, Little Rock, Arkansas, November 21, 1968; *Daily Log*, Tom Murton, Cummins Prison Farm, Arkansas, 1968; *Minutes of Meeting of the Arkansas State Penitentiary Board*, Little Rock, Arkansas, February 7, 1968, p. 3; and *Transcript of Proceedings: Extradition of Winfred Payne (aka Winfred Walker)*, Chicago, March 7, 1974.

[26] See: Tom Murton, "One Year of Prison Reform," *The Nation*, January 12, 1970, pp. 12–17.

[27] According to Commissioner Sarver as reported in the *Arkansas Democrat*, Little Rock, December 26, 1969.

acceptable plan for reforming them.[28] "It is small comfort to a barracks inmate to know that he may expect to be reasonably safe at some time after July [1970] if that safety depends on his being able to live that long."[29]

On July 13, 1970, Commissioner Robert Sarver, who had been appointed in 1968, admitted that he had been punishing inmates who refused to work by banishing them to a ball diamond. The inmates lived there day and night and were removed only during rainstorms. One inmate "has taken gruel and water there three times a day, bakes in the sun during the day, and sleeps on the ground at night without benefit of a blanket."[30]

On November 2, 1970, armed inmates tried to shoot their way out of the isolation unit at Cummins, and before the event was over, the superintendent, Sarver, and two others were held hostage for a time, under the threat of death unless certain demands were met. It was not by accident that this incident took place the night before the election. Winthrop Rockefeller had been installed as governor of Arkansas in January 1967 with a mandate from the electorate to provide prison (and other) reforms. He had made significant efforts in that direction, but his enthusiasm had begun to wane as the threat of rebellion at the prison lessened. He disappointed those on the prison staff who wished to reform the prison. He deferred to intimidation by the legislature and broke his agreement with the inmates.

Twenty-four hours after the incident began, Dale Bumpers became the victor in the gubernatorial race. One of the major issues of his campaign was that of prison reform. He contended that Rockefeller had not reformed the prison and had thus failed to carry out the mandate from the electorate. Apparently enough people were convinced that Rockefeller had indeed forfeited his opportunity to make a significant contribution to mankind.

Less than three weeks later, the prison was rocked with the first riot ever to take place in the Arkansas prison system. Though the riot, consisting of 40 percent of the prison population, was suppressed, state troopers remained at the prison for several weeks afterward to maintain control.

---

[28] Judge J. Smith Henley, *Opinion: Lawrence J. Holt et al. v. Robert Sarver et al.*, United States District Court, Eastern District of Arkansas, Pine Bluff Division, February 18, 1970, p. 44.

[29] *Arkansas Democrat*, Little Rock, April 15, 1970, p. 1.

[30] *Daily News*, Anchorage, Alaska, July 12, 1970, p. 1. The court subsequently ruled that this practice violated the United States Constitution and ordered Sarver to discontinue the practice.

In January 1971 Sarver obtained a three-year $281,660 grant from the United States Department of Labor to upgrade skills of the prison guards. The five 17-week training programs were designed to develop 100 men into "competent correctional officers." The goal of the programs was to teach "new skills in treatment of inmates and also to enhance their job classification and earn a pay increase." The course ostensibly included "educational training and orientation to the prison philosophy of rehabilitation and prison routine."

The training was conducted by two state police lieutenants from the Arkansas Law Enforcement Training Academy who provided instruction in "the proper use of firearms and the baton and riot control stick." It was reported that: "The men were tested on a firing range for accuracy with an assortment of weapons, including a .38 caliber pistol, a .30-.30 caliber rifle, and shotguns."[31]

In October 1972, project director Jack Grasinger reported that the federal program to recruit and train guards for the state's penal institutions was "a bomb." Of 150 trainees who underwent the training, only 22 remained to work within the prison system. Grasinger claimed it had failed because it made the "mistake of hiring people with hang-ups to work with people with hang-ups."[32] However, Grasinger's predecessor, A. L. Rice, charged that the crux of the problem lay not with the trainees but with the prison administration that allegedly doubted the value of the program and was disinterested in its success.

On May 5, 1971, the Eighth Circuit Court of Appeals in St. Louis, Missouri, affirmed Judge Henley's decision that the Arkansas prison system was unconstitutional. The opinion said, in part:

> *Contemporary conditions in Arkansas do not vary greatly from those condemned in England in the 1700s. The Eighth Amendment prohibiting "cruel and unusual punishment" relates to "evolving standards of decency that mark the progress of a maturing society."*
>
> *The present record reflects the prison system at Cummins Prison Farm to be not only shocking to "standards of decency," but immoral and criminal as well.*
>
> *New buildings and additional guards, although essential for compliance with the court's decree, fall far short of remedying the defilement of individuals and the inhumane treatment of prisoners practiced in the name of the state.*

---

[31] *Pine Bluff Commercial*, Pine Bluff, Arkansas, January 20, 1971.

[32] *The Freeworld Times*, Minneapolis, Minnesota, October 1972.

> *Imprisonment in buildings of newly laid brick with the most rigid security will not alleviate the depravity and criminality which are fostered by the Arkansas prison system.*[33]

Commissioner Sarver steadfastly adhered to his original promise to "work within the system" and to survive. He made daily compromises to the adversaries of prison reform—the legislature, the criminal justice system, the governor's office, and, indeed, the Board of Correction. He chose to appease his enemies as long as he had anything with which to bargain. When it became clear that Sarver had delivered all within his power, the legislature demanded his ouster. Governor Dale Bumpers lacked the authority to remove him. Deferring once again to the wishes of the legislature, Chairman John Haley of the Board of Correction conducted the meeting that resulted in Sarver's dismissal on March 29, 1971.

On June 2, 1971, Terrell Don Hutto of the Texas prison system was appointed Commissioner of Correction for Arkansas. On October 12, he appointed Robert G. Britton superintendent of the Tucker Intermediate Reformatory. Britton was imported from the Texas prison system where he had worked with Hutto. Testimony in federal court later was to reveal that Britton was not the only import from Texas.

Judge J. Smith Henley convened court in mid-November 1971 to continue his function as ex-officio commissioner of the Arkansas Department of Correction. These hearings were the most recent of a series routinely held every few months to determine whether the prison system had reached constitutional standards or whether the facilities should be closed. Some of the testimony was reminiscent of earlier pages in the history of Arkansas penology.

Ten inmates stated they had been subjected to beatings by prison officials and complained of poor living conditions. One inmate testified that he had been stripped naked and placed in a "quiet cell" for 28 days without lighting, mattress, or blankets, and fed a diet of bread, water, and "grue."[34] He also stated that while in the cell he had been approached by several prison officials who handcuffed him and beat him with blackjacks.

Fifteen-year-old inmate Tommy Oliver accused Superintendent Britton of hitting him and kicking him in the back and stomach

---

[33] United States Court of Appeals for the Eighth Circuit, *Appeal from the United States District Court of the Eastern District of Arkansas*, Holt v. Sarver, no. 20. 348, St. Louis, Missouri, May 5, 1971, pp. 12 and 13.

[34] An unpalatable food prepared by baking kitchen scraps that are later cut into four-inch squares and served as a punishment diet; a "contribution" of the Texas prison system.

while another officer held him to the ground. Other inmates complained of having no towels or socks and of having to wear the same underwear for several days. Still others testified that they had been intimidated by Britton, who they accused of attempting to prevent their subsequent testimony in court concerning prison conditions. Britton also was accused of driving a pick-up truck at 40 miles per hour with three inmates draped over the hood; when he suddenly stopped the vehicle, the inmates were catapulted onto the ground. Tucker Chaplain J. F. Cooley testified that he heard Britton say to a black inmate, "Move, nigger." Inmate testimony also contended that Britton required his inmate houseboy to refer to him and his wife as "master" and "madam" respectively. Inmate "Big Jim" Williams summed it up with this observation: "A lack of leadership we got down here."[35]

One of the interesting "innovations" revealed in the course of the hearings was the institution of "Texas TV" as a disciplinary measure at the prison. This treatment program calls for the inmate to stand about two feet from a wall or fence, clasp his hands behind his back, and lean his forehead or nose against the wall or fence. Inmates testified that they were required to assume this position for several hours at a time. Assistant Attorney General Henry Ginger contended the practice "to be of benefit to the inmate rather than a detriment, as would other punishments called for in the situation."[36]

Judge Henley interrupted the proceedings when he was informed that inmates waiting in the hallway to testify in court were at that moment standing in such a position. Henley ordered the United States Marshal to halt the practice immediately. "I don't wish the inmates to get an impression of punishment in advance of their testimony or after the fact. I see it could be easy to get that impression."[37]

Governor Bumpers said that he had personally tried the "Texas TV" position and that "about 30 seconds was all I could take."[38] Bumpers commented that he had hired prison officials from Texas because he had read that Dr. George Beto (then Commissioner of Correction in Texas) had transformed that system from one similar to Arkansas' to one of the finest in the country. Beto testified in court that the Arkansas prison had been improved over the three years

---

[35] *Arkansas Democrat*, Little Rock, November 19, 1971, p. 6A.

[36] *Arkansas Democrat*, Little Rock, November 17, 1971, p. 11A.

[37] *Pine Bluff Commercial*, Pine Bluff, Arkansas, November 17, 1971, p. 3.

[38] *Arkansas Democrat*, Little Rock, November 11, 1971, p. 1A.

since his last visit and endorsed the "Texas TV" disciplinary procedure.

Hutto stated that he tried to teach correctional officers to be "respectful and courteous." In explaining his theory of administration he said there is "a concentrated effort to observe and take some kind of action whenever a problem does develop." In commenting on the gains that had been made under his administration, he observed: "We do have people who have a great interest and have made some great inputs in this total year. . . . I think we're moving in the right direction and making progress every day."[39]

During the course of the hearing, 17-year-old Willie Stewart was committed to the prison for a one-day sentence, which has become part of common judicial practice in the state, in an effort to scare young offenders out of criminal behavior. If there is any merit to such a theory of rehabilitation, certainly the right prison was chosen to implement it. Circuit Court Judge Paul Wolfe estimated that he has sent about 175 youths to the prison for one-day terms since 1969.

> *The people at the penitentiary were quick to grasp the opportunity to let these boys know what they were getting into if they kept up a life of crime. They have tried to do their part to realistically impress these boys with what prison is like—within legal limits.*[40]

As part of the "realistic" treatment program, a freeworld guard shot at the feet of Stewart "to scare him."[41] Commitment to the Arkansas prison is conceded to be a most frightening experience. Stewart was "impressed." He died at the end of the day.

Federal Judge J. Smith Henley ruled in August 1973 that sufficient progress had been made in the prisons to permit him to relinquish jurisdiction at that time. However, inmates appealed the decision to the Eighth Circuit Court of Appeals in St. Louis, arguing that Arkansas prison conditions still did not meet minimal constitutional standards. On October 10, 1974 (fourteen months later), the appellate court held "the firm conviction that the Arkansas correctional system is still unconstitutional."[42]

---

[39] *Arkansas Democrat*, Little Rock, November 25, 1971, p. 4A.

[40] *Pine Bluff Commercial*, Pine Bluff, Arkansas, December 4, 1971, p. 1.

[41] Testimony revealed that this practice had been common since at least March 1971 and was considered routine treatment of the one-day prisoners. Other forms of brutality were also cited.

[42] *Pine Bluff Commercial*, Pine Bluff, Arkansas, October 12, 1974.

The three-judge panel remanded the case to Judge Henley for immediate action "to eliminate the unlawful conditions which now exist in the Arkansas prison system."

As the respondents urge, there is no such thing as a "perfect" prison system but this does not relieve respondents of their duty to make their system a constitutional one in which human dignity of each individual inmate is respected.

We find major constitutional deficiencies particularly at Cummins in housing, lack of medical care, infliction of physical and mental brutality and torture upon individual prisoners, racial discrimination, abuses of solitary confinement, continuing use of trusty guards, abuse of mail regulations, arbitrary work classifications, arbitrary disciplinary procedures, inadequate distribution of food and clothing, and lack of rehabilitation programs.[43]

The court dismissed long-range plans for new inmate housing as being "no satisfactory solution to those who are assaulted and physically harmed today."[44] In spite of a Correction Department policy prohibiting abuse, the court found:

The continued infliction of physical abuse, as well as mental distress, degradation, and humiliation by correctional authorities demonstrates that mere words are no solution.

Such unlawful conduct by correctional personnel is of major significance leading to this court's finding that the present correctional system in Arkansas is still unconstitutional.[45]

Correction Commissioner Terrell Don Hutto said the court's ruling was "untimely and in error." Hutto contended that the decision had been based on the "status of the Arkansas prison system for a period of two to four years ago."[46]

Disagreeing with the Commissioner, 200 inmates at Cummins State Prison Farm refused to report for work on October 14, 1974. According to prison officials, the strike resulted because inmates believed the court ruling absolved them from working for an unconstitutional prison system. However, a spokesman for the

---

[43] *Ibid.*
[44] *Ibid.*
[45] *Ibid.*
[46] *Pine Bluff Commercial*, Pine Bluff, Arkansas, November 5, 1974.

The Spiral Nature of Reform Movements

striking inmates contended that the peaceful protest was over "physical brutality of inmates."

> We asked why [there] were so many Inmates in Isolation with stitches and bandages on their heads. After this an official and 25 to 30 Free World Personnel came to 8 Bks [Barracks] and told us to work or him and the Wardens were going to start busting head and afterwards they were going to take all class and good time earned and place us in isolation.[47]

The Cycle of Hopelessness

The inmates continue to look on the staff with distrust, suspicion, and contempt. Once more they shuffle silently to and from work, trapped in the futile, endless cycle of imprisonment, pondering the hopelessness of their plight and the mystery of how they again have been cheated of the promised emancipation from penal slavery. They will not again believe in reform promises as long as the underlying evil of the prison is not dragged into the sunlight and exposed. An appropriate remedy to the prison problems cannot be prescribed until the basic sickness has been diagnosed.

There is no statute of limitations for the crime of murder.[48] But for the alleged murder of Arkansas prison inmates, no one has been convicted; no one has been indicted; no one has been charged; and, in fact, no complete investigation of the atrocities has ever been undertaken. Yet the nonmurder of inmates is obviously a nonnegotiable element of real reform.

There is ample reason to believe that inmates of the Arkansas State Penitentiary have been murdered under the color of law. Aside from the criminal justice system, the governor of Arkansas and the Board of Correction both have sufficient executive powers to provide a thorough and honest investigation of the alleged incidents. It would seem that one way to refute contentions that inmates have been murdered is to do the obvious: dig up the remaining 200 bodies and demonstrate that they were *not* murdered. But statements attributed to Chairman John Haley nearly two and one-half years after I was fired by him and the Board of Correction indicate that he fears additional excavation of inmate graves might prove that inmates *were* murdered; this is what prevents further digging.

---

[47] Willie Graves, "The Reasons Behind the Cummins Protest," *Pine Bluff Commercial*, Pine Bluff, Arkansas, November 5, 1974.

[48] For other felonies, charges must be filed within seven years of commission of the crime or the offender cannot be prosecuted.

Haley has amassed some interesting figures through the use of the prison's new computer system. Between 1916 and 1950 there were 110 Negroes and 107 whites who were listed as escapees and never recaptured.

These figures seem normal enough on the surface, but currently the comparison of escaping Negroes to whites is about 1 to 20. Today, the Negro prisoner just doesn't try to run off. If he gets a furlough for five days, he is back when he is told to be back.

So what? Well, Haley believes that those 110 Negroes may not have escaped. He said that he believes a lot of them are buried out there in the fields of Cummins Prison Farm and were conveniently listed as having escaped.

This brings up the old argument of former Prison Superintendent Thomas O. Murton and the skeletons he dug up in 1968 to create a national sensation. Murton ended up getting fired, largely over the publicity caused by the skeletons. Now, Haley says, every so often something comes up to back up the buried prisoner stories.[49]

It would also seem that the inmates of the Arkansas prison system, the survivors of the alleged victims, the people of Arkansas, and the world at large have a vested interest in having the following question answered honestly:

Can government wards be exterminated with impunity under the color of law?

The Arkansas inmate asks no more; the freeman must demand no less; or we shall all indeed become "accomplices to the crime."

Sarver did not reform the prison; in fact, he allowed it to regress to such a condition that the federal courts declared the entire system unconstitutional while he was loudly proclaiming, along with the governor, that the prison was on the way to reform. He did succeed in surviving a bit longer than his predecessor, but at the end of his two-and-one-half-year tenure, one is hard pressed to find any evidence of any substantial movement toward real reform.

Sarver failed to demonstrate that by working within the government's framework he achieved either personal success or improved the prison system. In fact, one could argue that the conditions of his employment, the awareness of the Board of Correction of the elements of real reform, and the deference to

---

[49] *Arkansas Democrat*, Little Rock, July 26, 1970.

everyone else in prison management foredoomed his strategy to failure. He neither reformed the prison nor secured his tenure.

And the cycle is complete. (Refer to the diagram.)

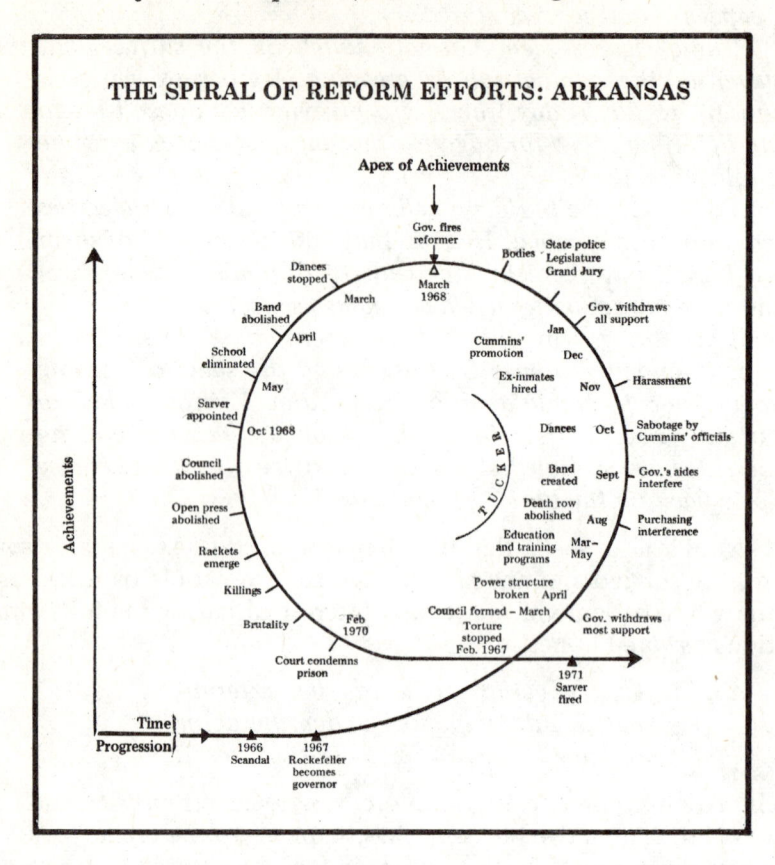

THE SPIRAL OF REFORM EFFORTS: ARKANSAS

Apex of Achievements

- Gov. fires reformer
- Bodies — State police, Legislature, Grand Jury
- Dances stopped — March
- March 1968
- Band abolished — April
- Cummins' promotion — Jan
- Gov. withdraws all support
- School eliminated — May
- Ex-inmates hired — Dec
- Harassment — Nov
- Sarver appointed — Oct 1968
- Dances — Oct
- Sabotage by Cummins' officials
- Council abolished
- Band created — Sept
- Gov.'s aides interfere
- Open press abolished
- Death row abolished — Aug
- Purchasing interference
- Rackets emerge
- Education and training programs — Mar–May
- Killings
- Power structure broken — April
- Brutality — Feb 1970
- Council formed – March
- Torture stopped Feb. 1967
- Gov. withdraws most support
- Court condemns prison
- 1971 Sarver fired
- Time Progression
- 1966 Scandal
- 1967 Rockefeller becomes governor

(TUCKER)

Achievements →

The Spiral of Reform: A Theory

By most measures Alaska and Arkansas are extremely diverse. Alaska, the newest territorial acquisition of the United States, is characterized as the Last Frontier with no long American historical antecedents to correctional practices. On the other hand, Arkansas has a lengthy history of the rural south, the Bible Belt, slavery, and conservatism. A more unlikely pair of states would be hard to find. But penal practices in both jurisdictions had failed to keep pace with general progress in other areas of contemporary living. Although the deficiencies of each system were of varying dimensions, a growing awareness of this decadence gave the impetus for improving the systems. In Alaska, statehood precipitated this awareness; in Arkansas, it was the election of a new governor.

After the intervention of new forces in each case, there was a dramatic and rapid movement to "catch up" in corrections. But while the correctional systems were moving toward real reform, other forces both inside and outside the systems embarked on divergent paths. Political influence guided hiring and firing practices; the goals of corrections were subordinated to political considerations; and, in both cases, the reform movement was stopped just before it achieved the initial objectives.

Although each state had different problems with corrections, the results and the tactics used to suppress reform were quite similar. Both Pfeiffer and Sarver tried to survive within the system by serving the needs of the inmates in a politically expedient way. In the final analysis, it was the governors who exerted their ultimate power to thwart the reform movements.

Both correctional systems are now safely in the hands of Curators who are charged with cleaning the cages, feeding the occupants, and providing a caretaker government until the next administration will be forced to deal with prison problems. The cycle of scandal–investigation–denouncement–promise of reform–reform efforts–regression–scandal suggests at the least a notion if not a theory of the character of reform movements. (See diagram.)

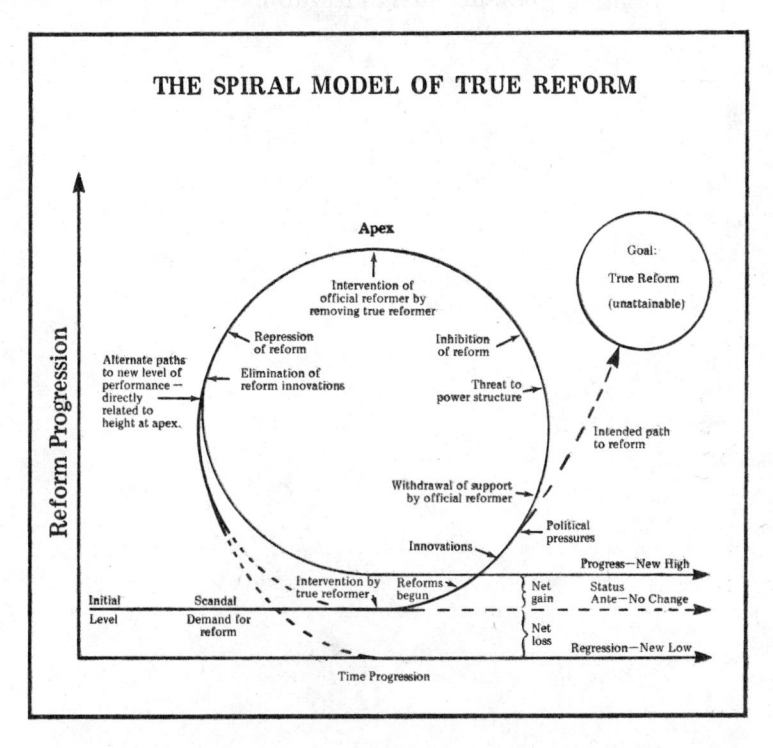

THE SPIRAL MODEL OF TRUE REFORM

The Spiral Nature of Reform Movements

The Spiral of Reform describes the predictable sequence of events that constitute a pattern in reform movements. Reformistic systems eventually become indistinguishable from the decadent systems they replace. Investigations will suppress true conditions; reform efforts will be cosmetic; substantive reform will be annihilated; and the system will be purged of the real reformers by the chief executive. In challenging the rationale of those who argue for "working within the system" it is noteworthy that for all their compromise they, too, are eventually forced to leave the system. Hence, in discussing strategy, one needs to consider the ultimate impact on the individual administrator, who serves as a pseudo-reformer, as well as on the system. His tenure may be longer than the real reformer's, but his demise is just as predictable. In the process of his gradual expiration he has, perhaps unintentionally, participated in his own defeat, as well as in the abortion of reform efforts, the confusion of freeworld observers, and the disenchantment of the inmates.

He who attempts to straddle the picket fence of compromise between right and wrong risks becoming impaled upon his own indecision.

8

The Substance of Real Reform

> It is not the critic who counts, nor the man who points out how the strong man stumbles, or where the doer of deeds could have done better. The credit belongs to the man who is actually in the arena; whose face is marred by dust and sweat; who strives valiantly; who errs and may fail again, because there is no effort without error or shortcoming.
>
> —MAHATMA GANDHI

Real prison reform, as previously defined, is restructuring the institution for both the interim and long-range benefit of the inmates' welfare and thereby, it is hoped, of the free society. It may well be that true reform is a direction and not a destination since it is not unlike the Christian ideal of striving for perfection even while realizing that perfection cannot be attained—at least within the temporal life.

The real reformer approaches his endeavors with a different set of assumptions and loyalties than the pseudo-reformer. The former states that he is "working for the inmates" (in the context set forth above); the latter avows his allegiance to those who appointed him to office. Idealistically, the reformer should be able to do both; that is, he should be able to discharge his obligations to his employer by doing his best for the inmates. But there is a difference.

There comes a time in reform movements when the goals and objectives of the official reformer (the one chosen by the electorate to provide reform) are tangential to the path toward real prison reform. At that time, a decision has to be made by the correctional administrator as to whether he is working for the inmates or the appointing authority. The real reformer will choose the former course; the pseudo-reformer, the latter. If the reformer becomes trapped in the reasoning of the "if-I'm-not-here-I-can't-bring-about-reform" fallacy, his efforts will then be directed toward actions designed to keep his employer and himself in power. As a result, many of the prison activities suggested by the official reformer after he is in office may not be unlike those decried by him during his reform campaign.

It would seem logical that the greatest service the real reformer could render to the official reformer would be to stimulate real prison reform, thereby assuring the continued support of the official reformer by the electorate. But in this case, logic does not prevail. The real reformer is not given the opportunity to complete the assignment because the free society does not really want reform but merely an abatement of brutality and inhuman conditions. Thus their anticipated negative reactions to real reform become determinative and reform is eventually suppressed for political expediency.

The real reformer will handle the day-to-day issues by making policy decisions that reflect his allegiance to the inmates and not necessarily to the system. The pseudo-reformer, however, will do the opposite. For example, work release may not be implemented for fear of arousing the ire of the labor unions. Similarly, coed recreation or training programs, allowing female inmates to keep their babies at the institution, or allowing inmates a legitimate voice in prison management may not be instituted because of assumed objections from the citizenry.[1]

There are three observations that should be made about this suppression of programs. First, if handled properly, such innovations can be brought into existence with no, or minimal, resistance. Second, there may in fact never be (or have been) any resistance. And, finally, as mentioned previously, it is an abdication of leadership to defer to uninformed laymen in determining the course of prison management even when there is actual and formidable

---

[1] A high school physics teacher once related a personal story about the counterproductivity of operating on a fact not in evidence. As a young man, he had worked in a power plant where he had been given the task (among others) of periodically removing the accumulation of grease on an electric generator to avoid a fire hazard. He was carefully cautioned against ever touching the generator because of the output of 30,000 volts that would be lethal to him. He was given a dry stick to use in conjunction with a rag for this time-consuming cleaning process.

In an idle moment one day, he applied the voltage formula to the known watts and ohms, which resulted in his conclusion that the output of the generator was in reality *30* volts; not 30,000! Consequently, he threw away the stick and proceeded to clean the machine daily by hand with the rag, thus saving considerable time and concern.

He reported that the previous method of cleaning had been in existence for decades because of an erroneous supposition—and because no one had ever questioned the basic assumption.

The Substance of Real Reform

opposition. The real reformer must cautiously assess the significance of each issue to determine whether it is essential to real reform or whether it is a luxury that can be postponed without undue adverse effect on the reform movement. The criteria for assessing the issues are these: (1) Is it an essential element of reform? (2) Is its primary function the reelection of the official reformer? (3) Does it coincide with the objectives of the real reformer for the inmate body? And (4) can it serve all these functions?[2] The latter is the ideal, but as the real reformer moves the prison ship out of the safe harbor of Traditionalism toward Real Reform the voyage becomes more difficult. It is possible to chart a course for two ports sequentially, but not simultaneously—at least, not with a single vessel nor with one captain.

Assumptions

The real reformer can be identified initially by the different set of assumptions with which he approaches his task. The first of these is the belief that there is little correlation between the danger posed by the offender when at large in the freeworld community and his physical threat to the inmates or staff in the prison community. Murderers, for example, are the most feared of all offenders by the public. Yet prison administrators uniformly agree that murderers, as a class of inmates, constitute no threat inside the prison and become dependable, trusted prisoners.

Second, the inmate may or may not be in need of behavior modification. Not all inmates are sent to prison for "rehabilitation"; some are confined simply for punishment. Al Capone, Billy Sol Estes, Jimmie Hoffa, and Mickey Cohen are examples of prisoners for whom rehabilitation is probably never even considered by the court or correctional authorities. Imprisonment for punishment alone is a justifiable action on the part of the larger society. Concomitant with the state's right to punish should be the inmate's right to nontreatment; that is, among the choices offered the inmate to "rehabilitate" himself should be the option of selecting *no* program at all.

Third, the authoritarian (dictatorial) model is not only dysfunctional for, but also antithetical to, preparing the inmate for

---

[2] That is, there are some real reform ventures that do not jeopardize reelection of the official reformer, and there are other activities designed to enhance reelection possibilities that are not antithetical to the reform movement. For example, a governor can get political mileage from stopping brutality and corruption within the prison while at the same time advancing prison reform.

acceptable social adjustment in a democratic society on release from prison. One could argue, dispassionately, that a despotic model *is* functional in a totalitarian form of government such as Nazi Germany or any other dictatorship. Although such a model might not be acceptable to the humanist, it nonetheless provides relevant training for conformity to the established order to which the inmate will return in that country. (Excluded from consideration here is the question of whether that form of government *should* exist.) The prison trains for social conformity and not for political activism.

Fourth, the medical model of treatment must be rejected. Although it may not be certain what combination of factors is actually necessary to accelerate or bring about positive behavior modification, it is apparent that use of the medical model has not brought about the desired results and should, therefore, be discontinued. If such a thing as "rehabilitation" exists, its discrete components have not yet been discovered. Even assuming that the ingredients of positive change can be identified, isolated, and encapsuled, the notion that a shot of "rehabilitation" can be injected into the patient-inmate as an antidote for criminality is pure nonsense. The master can no more impose rehabilitation on the slave than the teacher can inflict "education" upon the student. The most that can be achieved in either process is only the outward manifestation that is presumed to indicate a more fundamental change in human behavior.

Fifth, prison staffs, *as now constituted*, are probably not the best means for bringing about positive change of attitudes because prison officials, as well as inmates, are greatly affected by the negative, exploitive prison community. The prison paranoia (distrust of everyone), the obsession with security considerations, and the selection and training processes of the staff all tend to reinforce the inmate concept of the guard force as "the enemy." Yet treatment presupposes trust between the treater and the treatee. The inmate, understandably, looks with suspicion on any act of "benevolence" proffered by one he has been conditioned to view as an opponent.

Sixth, an adversary relationship now exists between staff and inmates. Because of the foregoing conditions—creation of the prison as a despotic environment, adoption of the medical model, and the official belief system of staff—a classic example of the "we-they" syndrome has become institutionalized. Although it has been suggested that both staff and inmates have the same objectives for the inmate body, the actual methods used to achieve these objectives have polarized these groups. Both inmates and staff perceive "rehabilitation" as the result of ideas imposed by the combined efforts of the prison and the freeworld power structures—collectively known to the inmates as "the system."

Seventh, inmates participate in the management of all institutions. Inmate impact on prison operations may be covert as demonstrated in the more sophisticated prison systems where control is exercised by means of subtle indirect pressure (see Chapter 3). Or it may be an overt exercise of legal, but illegitimate, power as in the prison systems of Arkansas, Louisana, and Mississippi where the armed inmate guards have had official life and death control over the other inmates as well as controlling, to a large extent, the classification, assignment, and management of inmates in general.

As Ray Page, former warden of the Oklahoma State Penitentiary, observed: "If twenty-five percent less of our inmates returned to the prison, we couldn't run them."[3] He is correct. Warden Page was no doubt referring primarily to the dependence on inmates, not so much for management, but for performing the housekeeping chores of the institution.[4] Because of the traditional lack of sufficient funds to employ additional staff, the philosophy that inmates should "earn their keep" and the tendency to accept assistance from the inmate,[5] prison systems have come to rely quite entensively on inmates to provide the services required to operate the prison community. Traditionally, inmates take care of the laundry, dry-cleaning, sewing, making of uniforms, and preparation of the food; they repair and maintain the institution; they issue clothing and other supplies; they operate the commissary, library, barbershops, and movies; they keep institutional records of all sorts; and they assist in whatever "treatment" programs are provided. In fact, they even frequently provide dental, medical, and pharmaceutical services.

When decision making is granted to the inmates, and the prison administrators begin to rely on them to keep the machine running, inmate power is a reality. Denial of this obvious (to some) fact by prison administrators does not obviate its existence. A thing is or it is not, irrespective of the belief system of the observer. It is true that it may not exist *for him* if he does not perceive it, but he nonetheless will have to deal with the reality of its being whether he chooses to acknowledge it or not.

---

[3] Statement made at a meeting of the Wardens' Association of America on October 16, 1970, at Cincinnati, Ohio.

[4] At Tucker State Prison Farm in Arkansas during 1967, approximately 60 percent of the population was engaged in such activities.

[5] Such assistance is not gratuitous but implies a contractual relationship. The result is an accommodation between staff and inmate based not on mutual trust and respect but on reciprocal fear and intimidation. Such relationships erode any sincere efforts to eliminate exploitation.

> **DO WORK STRIKES WORK?**
>
> *[Excerpted from The Prisoners Free Press, Philadelphia, Pennsylvania, March–April 1973.]*
>
> Yes, they do!
>
> All prisons function on the labor of the prisoners. The state depends upon the labor of prisoners. What does this mean?
>
> It means that prisoners, if united, can completely bring the entire state's penal system to its knees. It means that prisoners can control the prisons.
>
> A good example of this can be seen in the sit-down strike that took place at the Western (Pennsylvania) Penitentiary around February of 1970.
>
> What the prisoners at the Western Pen did was close down the "tag shop" in protest to the prison officials' banning their prison newspaper, VIBRATIONS, on the basis that the paper did not meet *their* qualifications.
>
> Though the strike turned out to be a failure, due to the lack of unity amongst the prisoners, the point is that it did succeed in setting back the entire state in the production of license tags, which affected every car-owner in the state of Pennsylvania.
>
> Had the prisoners been united, better organized, they could have attained all, or any, demands.

As Harold Cardwell, former warden of Ohio Penitentiary, has stated:

> *It is a well known fact to prison administrators that prisons actually are run by the inmates and they will riot any time they feel conditions are intolerable. We keep order by the consent of the convicts—just as this country is governed by the consent of the governed.*[6]

The question "Should inmate power exist?" is academic. A more proper question might be: "Since inmate power exists, how can it be used as a positive force for change?" To elicit the most profitable response, one must ask the correct question at the right time—and, I suspect, most importantly, address it to the one most likely to provide insight.

---

[6] *Statement of Harold Cardwell*, Warden, Ohio Penitentiary, before the Senate Subcommittee to Investigate Juvenile Delinquency, Washington, D.C., September 28, 1970, pp. 5–6.

The Substance of Real Reform

Postulates

The false dichotomy of treatment and custody results from the confusion brought about by assigning different attributes to two aspects of a single phenomenon in an effort to explain the constant dispute between the two, as well as the relative merits of one over the other. Sociological literature deals extensively with the conflict between the treatment and custody staffs.[7] The thesis is postulated that one group is charged with *keeping* the inmates (custody) and the other is charged with *treating* them (the "professional staff"). Yet most observers generally agree that the inmate is most likely to be influenced, positively or negatively, by the guard with whom he comes in daily contact. Therefore, both the explanations and the justifications regarding the relative merits of treatment over custody, or vice versa, in an institutional setting beg the question. What both adversaries fail to recognize, or admit, is that custody *is* treatment. Whether they realize it or not, all staff are involved in treatment of the inmate; the ideological conflict is not between so-called treatment and custody staffs, but over the definition of what actually constitutes "treatment."

There is no "typical" correctional officer. Because the offender population is a cross section of personalities, the guard force should also represent a cross section in order to enhance understanding between inmates and staff. The best tower guard would probably not possess the attributes necessary to supervise a crew of inmates in a minimum-custody setting. The best counselor would probably fail as a tower guard. Certain functions of the prison require specific qualities. To train, or select, for the prototype "ideal officer" who is all things to all men (and consequently nothing to anyone) would be impossible—not only would it cause the prison to cease functioning, but there would be no way to provide the variety of personalities necessary so that the inmate might find an officer with whom he could relate.

One might speculate that little difference exists between staff and inmates. Studies indicate that guards tend to have many of the characteristics of hostility, resentment of authority, and aggressiveness commonly found in the inmate population. One could argue that the basic difference is that the guard, by circumstances not

---

[7] See: Donald Clemmer, *The Prison Community* (New York: Holt, Rinehart and Winston, 1958); Erving Goffman, *Asylums* (Garden City, N.Y.: Doubleday and Company, 1961); Donald Cressey, *The Prison* (New York: Holt, Rinehart and Winston, 1961).

available to the inmate, managed to escape or elude the criminal justice system, and were it not for the badge and uniform, it would be difficult to distinguish between the two.

A Rhode Island study of psychological characteristics of correctional officer candidates, conducted in 1971, produced some interesting findings. Officer candidates deemed acceptable for employment through civil service procedures were tested psychologically to determine final eligibility. A representative group of inmates was also administered the Minnesota Multi-Phasic Personality Inventory (MMPI). The researchers then contrasted these two groups with data from previous studies and came up with the following results:

> *Comparison of the mean profile of officer candidates along with the mean profile of the inmate group, and the typical 4—9 profile of Marks and Seaman (1963) reveals that the curvature of the three profiles is almost identical, but there are differences in elevation.*
>
> *The similarity between the profiles of correctional candidates of the Prison Inmate population occurs most vividly on Scales 4 (Psychopathic Deviate) and 9 (Hypomanic). This would indicate that correctional officer candidates, like inmates, show emotional shallowness, alienation from social customs, and relative inability to profit from social sanctions.*
>
> *[T]hey profess poise and confidence and deny social estrangement [but] indicate tendencies toward uncontrollable temper outbursts, improductive overactivity, and general unreliability of goal-directed behavior.... [T]hey lack control of impulses, frequent acting-out, incapability of close personal relationships, excitability, irritability and self-centeredness.*
>
> *...Both the officer candidates and the inmates seem to be about equal in their feelings of aggressiveness, hostility, resentment, suspicion and desire to act out assaultively.... In both cases, for officer candidates and inmates, profiles show consistently high negative ratios, indicating strong attempts to "look good" and answer in socially desirable ways.*
>
> *...While it is apparent from the present results that officer candidates and inmates have similar aggressive tendencies, similar hostility and resentment, and similar inner desires to be rebellious, it cannot be determined from the*

MMPI profiles what the probability is that a person will act out more or less blatantly on these impulses.[8]

Philosophy

The true potential of the inmate as a person participating in his own "rehabilitation" has never been fully explored. Pupils can become teachers; patients can become medical practitioners; but prisoners are prohibited from becoming penologists. Imprisonment is probably the only course of training from which students graduate with the foreknowledge that they will not be allowed to use their expertise.

The alarming tactic of proclaiming the ludicrousness of "letting the lunatics run the asylum" serves only to divert attention from the basic objection to involving the inmate in his own destiny. (The assumption implied in such a statement is that the inmates do not *now* run the institution.) Furthermore, the administration finds the idea personally threatening. If, as some of us suspect, the inmates are more qualified to bring about change than the professionals, then the implications are, of course, quite threatening to those in power.

Sharing decision making with the inmate implies that he has something to contribute to his "cure"; it calls into question the validity of the medical model and the contention that treatment is the private domain of the staff. If the patient can heal, then the role of the healer must be reexamined. The ramifications of such a venture include the possibility that the professional is not really equipped to impose treatment, and it follows that the academic preparation for correctional work must be reassessed. Realizing that the inmate may be more qualified than the professional to bring about positive change in inmate attitudes also calls into question the validity of the certificate hanging in the gold frame in the professional's office. If the concept of the inmate as healer becomes a reality to the penologist (be he a custodian or treater), and if he is sincere and committed to doing what is right, he must realize that he has perhaps wasted much time in formal training and must reconstitute his recruiting procedures and training programs.

Furloughs from the Walla Walla penitentiary in the state of Washington are processed in the traditional manner. Behavior reports prepared by the custody staff are evaluated by the caseworkers who

---

[8] Allan Berman, *MMPI Characteristics of Correctional Officers*, paper presented to the Eastern Psychological Association meeting, New York, April 16, 1971.

determine which inmates will be granted parole. Under that system it was reported in March 1972 that of 292 inmates released on furlough, 26 escaped, 28 were late in returning, and 17 violated the law while on the outside. Of the total 594 leaves granted, 12.1 percent resulted in a violation of one sort or another.

Because of an armed robbery and the killing of a state trooper by inmates on furlough, the policies were reevaluated. About 98 percent of the Walla Walla inmates signed a petition urging the administration to appoint five inmates to a screening committee.

We know the people. We're with them 24 hours a day. An inmate might look good on paper but we know the goofups. The inmates have to accept the responsibility of turning someone down. It's the only way we can protect our program.[9]

In support of their argument that the inmates could do a better job of predicting success on furlough, they cited the "Take a Lifer to Dinner" program. In this program, inmates serving a life sentence (usually murderers) are allowed out for eight hours for a visit in the community. No professional staff is involved in the screening for this leave; only other lifers make decisions. There has been only one violation in "several hundred" of such leaves.

One can readily observe that such an apparently modest suggestion as involving the inmate in his own destiny carries with it the virus that may in fact contain the potential destruction of the prison order. A revolution is portended. There is nothing more frightening to the traditionalist than a new idea. One can eliminate the prophet who expounds the idea, but the prophecy lingers on in the minds of the oppressed and may lie dormant until the time is right for the idea to bear fruit. It is that day which the correctional administrator fears the most. And this partially explains the fanaticism with which the seeds of discontent are attacked. The essence of the problem is that the ego of the prison official is challenged because he must admit to his subjects that he is not omnipotent—an admission he equates with psychological suicide or self-castration.

---

[9] "Prison Furloughs," *The Freeworld Times*, March 1972, pp. 6, 7.

The real reformer begins with some rather modest postulates that are fundamental to his reform efforts. Without addressing himself to the question "Should prisons exist?" (a legitimate inquiry), he focuses on dealing with the reality that the prison *does* exist. Then he attempts to accomplish what has been espoused throughout the past century of "prison reform."

Reform of the prison *must* precede any plan to reform the inmate. Appending the accoutrements of reform to the existing prison world is no more productive than "putting a $100 saddle on a $5 horse." A work release inmate certainly has many advantages: the benefits of associating with freeworld people, of taking part in a useful work experience, of earning some money, of a chance to demonstrate responsibility, and of a brief absence from the prison environment. Yet if he returns to the prison after a full day's respite only to be homosexually assaulted, gang-raped, intimidated, and otherwise exploited, there is little likelihood that his attitude toward himself, his fellow man, or the society that has subjected him to this punishment will be substantially enhanced.

It may well be that it is necessary to reform the "reformers" before one can reform the prison in order to reform the inmate. Nonetheless, whatever "rehabilitation" is, it is a process that takes place within the individual and is a function of the quality of interpersonal relationships among staff and inmates.

Characteristics

The real reform model may have some of the outward manifestations of the facade of reform, thereby confusing the casual observer peering through a remote telescope. The difference is that in real reform the inmate service programs are suggested by the inmates, are relevant to the freeworld situation, and are realistic. A distinction is made between production and training; prison industries are recognized for what they are: a method of reducing the costs of incarceration. Institutional maintenance is not confused with vocational training programs.

The real reformer distinguishes his administration from that of his predecessors by allowing an open press policy. This policy is instituted to educate the community, to gain support from the media for the difficult times ahead, and to establish a tradition of making the prisons available to the scrutiny of the freeworld, which has a vested interest in their operation.[10]

A reorganization of the prison has other benefits. The activity of reorganization engages the inmates in an essentially productive venture that diverts their attention from disruptive activities and tends to direct their concern outward instead of inward. Indulging in self-pity may be comforting to the individual but does not contribute to the healthy mental approach that is required for reform.

Another benefit is that the keepers and the kept are no longer enemies, but cohorts in the reform venture. The traditional tactic, by design or accident, has been one of "divide and conquer." Inmates contend, for example, that the racial conflict in prison is fostered by the staff on the theory that as long as the inmates are fighting one another they are less likely to be fighting the staff. A more productive approach would be for the administration to eliminate the conditions that foster and perpetuate the adversary role of these two groups.

A contemporary "reform" effort that is gaining wide support from lay groups concerned about prison conditions is the prisoners' union. Major efforts to establish such unions inside prisons have been made, primarily in California, in some New England states, and in Minnesota. Unions, of course, like any other program, can only exist

---

[10] One of the hazards of real reform may be inherent in an open press policy. The real reformer does not attempt to manipulate the press or manage the news. Instead he believes that complete candor with the media will enhance his credibility with both inmates and the freeworld. Also, when his tactics later come under attack, the representatives of the news media will be operating from a frame of reference that trusts the prison administrator and are less likely to join in the attack.

Under my regime at Tucker and Cummins in the Arkansas prison system in 1967 and 1968, we had such a policy. Newsmen were allowed to come to the prison at any time and talk privately to any inmate. Such activities provided a forum for acquainting the freeworld with improvements at the prison that reflected positively on the administration.

But it was the same policy that later revealed to the public (prematurely from my point of view) that we had dances at the prison for staff and inmates, black and white, male and female; that two inmates from death row were regularly playing in the prison band *outside* the prison, under the escort of an unarmed, ex-inmate; and that a female inmate was allowed to keep her baby at the Women's Reformatory.

Any attempt to be selective in determining areas of an "open press" policy is as futile as discussing degrees of pregnancy. My experience has been that newsmen, in general, are not easily deceived and will tend to balance the good with the bad of the reform administration. In any event, a relationship of trust and mutual respect between the prison officials and the press can only be achieved by this method. And this relationship is essential to a real reform movement.

in the prison with the approval of the warden. The proponents of organizing prisoners into a union concede that the right to strike will not be demanded in the prison setting, and it is unrealistic to believe that any warden would be likely to grant power to the inmates to strike and thus effectively shut down the institution. Yet without the right to strike, the major negotiating weapon of arbitration is denied the inmates.

Advocates argue that to counteract the abuse of power by the prison management, a semblance of equal power must be granted to the inmates as the prison labor force. They view prison conditions as the result of classic labor—management disputes. Prison union proponents recognize the nonproductive and oppressive use of prison power as being negative; yet they advocate not *elimination* of that form of power but *creation* of another power base with all the coercive ingredients of the power structure they seek to neutralize. Consequently, prison unionization may appear to be an improvement in existing conditions but may, in fact, create more problems than it solves.

Prisoner unions are conceived on the premise that resolution of conflicts is best brought about as a result of a balance of power between two adversary groups through the process of intimidation and coercion. But I would argue to the contrary and state that prison unionization is counterproductive to developing a coalition of power, that it is the antithesis of developing a federation of trust, and that it will only polarize further the present staff and inmate adversary groups in the prison community.

If one adheres to the thesis that an escalation of force to meet force is in the long range productive, the prison unions make sense in a prison reform movement. But the present balance of terror in the nuclear arms race probably could be traced to the first Cro-Magnon man who picked up a club to overpower an assailant attacking him with his fist. Some of us believe there must be another way; perhaps by one of us first laying down the club.

In the traditional model, the energies of each group are dissipated on the other in this internal conflict, and that precludes any chance of real reform ever being reached. As long as the passengers are in mutiny against the crew, it is unlikely that the prison space ship will ever engage the real enemy; or, in fact, even embark for the planet of Real Reform.

Methodology

The first commandment of real reform is "Never lie to an inmate" (or to anyone else). Since the inmate has been conditioned through experience not to believe what he has been told by the prison officials, the real reformer will have to prove that he is different; that he speaks the truth. Actions will be compared with statements to determine whether there is a positive correlation. The inmate judges the reformer, as he does everyone else, by what he *does* and not by what he *says he will do*.

A comment by an inmate editor of a prison newspaper illustrates the point:

Is it too much for the body convict to ask for a fair shake? Nothing more is expected. Anything less is hypocrisy. What else can you call it, gentlemen, when you speak to us on one hand about honesty and fair play and righteousness, and then unceremoniously rip us off with the other?[11]

The priorities set by the warden provide a significant cue for the inmates in terms of his sincerity and desire to develop trust. A staff–inmate council at the Adult Conservation Camp in Alaska discussed problems at the first meeting. The first one the superintendent dealt with was the installation of a heat lamp above the toilet seat in the outhouse. To the inmates, something had to be done because of the extreme cold temperatures and the accompanying discomfort.

At the first farm council meeting in Arkansas, one of many problems cited was the fact that the buildings had never been painted and the inmate quarters were thus very gloomy. The housing for staff and the administrative area of the institution were in the same state of ill-repair. The superintendent ordered the barracks painted first, then the staff quarters. By his actions, the administrator clearly announces what he considers the important issues to be and whether he sees himself working for the betterment of the population or for the convenience of staff and freeworld people.

The attempt to develop a mutual feeling of trust between staff and inmates requires great courage on the part of the reformer because in establishing trust he must take a greater risk than the inmate. Any real innovation includes the possibility of failure; and failure is considered intolerable by the correctional administrator. Inherent in the true chance of success is the chance of failure.

Most administrators are not willing to risk the possibility of failure (by staff or inmate) as a means of achieving success. But the

---

[11] "Inmate Welfare Fund Rip Off Called Outrageous," *The Prison Mirror*, State Prison, Stillwater, Minnesota, May 24, 1974, p. 3.

warden must be willing to take the risks in order to succeed in taking the prison in a new direction. As Korn has observed, the safest course is circling the harbor in calm waters rather than facing the open seas. The voyage will be smoother but, of course, the ship will never reach a destination.

The traditional warden may roam the halls of his institution and be confronted by an inmate "buried" in a cell. When this happens the following typical dialogue is likely to occur:

WARDEN: *"What's your name?"*

INMATE: *"Lee Taylor, 48715."*

WARDEN: *"How are you getting along?"*

INMATE: *"I'm doing O.K. warden, but I sure would like to get out and go back to work. Sitting in a cell is pullin' hard time."*

WARDEN: *"Well, we'll let you out as soon as we're convinced that your attitude has changed and that you can act responsibly."*

INMATE: *"I realize you've got a lot of problems in a difficult job like running the prison, so you probably don't realize I've been here seven months now. I think reports from the guard will show that I haven't caused him any trouble."*

WARDEN: *"Well, that's true. I don't recall reviewing any disciplinary reports from the cell block concerning you. But you must realize, of course, that the reason your behavior has changed here is that you are under close supervision and strict control. There's not really too much you can do to cause trouble except rattle your cage. So how do we know if your basic attitude has changed and that you will not cause us problems if we put you back into the population?"*

INMATE: *"That's a good point, warden. Maybe you can fix it so I can get out of my cell for a few hours each day. I can clean the corridor, issue soap and toilet paper, and act as a runner for the guard, and this way you can use the trusty in some other assignment. This way I can show you that I can be trusted."*

WARDEN: *"But how can I risk letting you out if I don't know I can trust you first?"*

INMATE: *"How can I prove you can trust me if you don't let me out?"*

WARDEN: *"Well, I think you need to demonstrate you can*

accept responsibility before we can take the risk. Remember that privileges are earned. We cannot give you a privilege first and expect you to earn it later. How can I trust you if you don't first demonstrate trust?"

INMATE: *"How can I demonstrate trust if you don't trust me?"*

Having "resolved" the issue the warden moves down the cell block, bestowing his benevolent smile and concern on other unfortunates.

This interaction demonstrates how the inmate is locked into the system and the difficulty he experiences in breaking out of the cellular thinking of the penologist. Reminiscent of the irreconcilable conflict presented in *Catch-22*,[12] the foregoing exchange represents one of the real dilemmas of prison reform: the option of relief from a negative situation is offered by assigning impossible prerequisites that can only be demonstrated *after* the relief. The lesson should be obvious if not palatable to the traditionalist. He must take the first step in establishing trust.

Under Illinois' "sexually dangerous person" law, the prisoner is held in the penitentiary until a judge decides he is no longer a threat to society. Ronald Cross, a University of Illinois graduate, was committed to the Menard State Penitentiary for sexual assaults on four university women during a short period of time.

In the fall of 1973, a hearing was held before Circuit Judge Frederick S. Green to determine whether Cross was ready to be released from prison. The court testimony emphasizes the conflict presented by the statute in protection of the rights of both society and the inmate:

The real testing has to take place where there is a risk. (psychologist)

The only way for me to demonstrate that I am safe is to be released. (inmate)

---

[12] "There was only one catch and that was Catch-22, which specified that a concern for one's own safety in the face of dangers that were real and immediate was the process of a rational mind. Orr was crazy and could be grounded. All he had to do was ask; and as soon as he did, he would no longer be crazy and would have to fly more missions. Orr would be crazy to fly more missions and sane if he didn't, but if he was sane he had to fly them. If he flew them, he was crazy and didn't have to; but if he didn't want to he was sane and had to. Yosarrian was moved very deeply by the absolute simplicity of this clause of Catch-22 and let out a respectful whistle." Joseph Heller, *Catch-22*, (New York: Simon & Schuster, 1955), p. 46.

We're being told to teach this man to swim, but not to let him go into the water. He needs to be put in the water. (psychiatrist)[13]

Judge Green refused to release Cross until such time as his attorney can devise a real test of Cross's safeness while still inside the prison. At such time, the judge agreed to let Cross "paddle around in the water." Since there are no women to rape inside Menard, a real test is impossible. Cross's attorney observed that his client "may be a very old man before he is allowed to leave the penitentiary."[14]

Increased responsibility must be an ongoing program until the time of release. As the inmate is able to demonstrate that he can act responsibly in small things, he must be granted increasing responsibility rather than be encouraged to level off at a plateau of satisfactory performance. Additional opportunities to demonstrate responsibility may include participating in heterosexual experiences, involvement in planning his own program within the institution, increased decision making affecting himself and his peers (and possibly his keepers), and increased responsibility in management of the institution.

Ramifications

Out of the foregoing efforts, the first thing that will become evident is a change in the inmate's conception of both himself and staff. As the relationships change and are reinforced through positive daily contacts, the inmate will gradually develop a different self-image. If man in general tends to define himself and to react in the terms in which he is addressed, those inmates treated as human beings could be expected to respond as human beings; just as it has been demonstrated that those inmates treated as animals have tended to respond as animals. When the inmate achieves some awareness of dignity as a human being, only then can one rightfully be concerned about more formal efforts to "rehabilitate" him.

The inmate then must be offered hope in lieu of despair. Hope is the sustaining force that will amalgamate the new prison community. As the inmates see "the light at the end of the tunnel," it will not require much motivation to encourage them to take part in the process of collective decision making for the benefit of the total prison community. Such a process, of course, requires the inmates to

---

[13] "Prisoner's 'Test' May Set Precedent," *News Gazette*, Champaign, Illinois, November 5, 1973.

[14] *Ibid.*

become organized; it also requires a new (quasi-democratic) form of government to replace the exploitive autocratic model. Skill must be used at this time to ensure that the change is not in name only. Otherwise, one will have only succeeded in substituting a bureaucratic form of exploitation for the dictatorial one.

As in other reform efforts, this idea must arise from the inmate body itself. The role of the reformer is to create an environment wherein such a change is possible. This method reinforces the new (to the inmate) notion that he does, in fact, have something to contribute. By substituting a cycle of success for the usual cycle of failure, the inmate is thus encouraged to exercise his desire to improve his lot and, thereby, the lot of his fellow citizens in this new community and, ultimately, to improve the very nature of the institution.

Time is probably the most crucial element in real reform endeavors. The real reformer knows that it is far more important to consider *when* to implement an innovation than to consider *what* it will be. The traditional gradualist, however, concentrates on the content of the change (and the political ramifications) and tends to ignore timeliness. He adheres to the adage that "Everything comes to him who waits."

To the uninitiated, just posing the question appears to clarify the dilemma: When is the "right" time to free the slaves? The "right" time to stop the brutality? The logical answer is implied in the question: At that time when prisoners are discovered to be enslaved; at that time when brutality is recognized.

Using the inmate as a "change agent" is a major departure from the modus operandi of the pseudo-reformer. Another major departure is the acknowledgment that there can be no continued movement toward real reform without engaging the total matrix of the social, political, and economic structures that impinge on the prison system. Any real movement of the prison will result in a corresponding change in relationships between it and the other agencies. If prison reform movements result in no change in these relationships and the matrix remains stable, one can rightly infer that the movement has been in a circle and not toward prison reform.

The Gradualism Theory

The governmental system has been in existence for such a long time that equilibrium has been established between the various component branches, agencies, and departments, and the all-consuming efforts of officeholders are to keep their operations under control. It is presumed to be better to preserve the status quo than to undertake innovations that, while possibly improving the agency, might place professional careers in jeopardy. Within such a context, a reformer is commissioned to go to the offending prison and "solve the problems." The reformer is advised that he can do anything he wishes with the prison *as long as he does not try to change the balance of power between the institution and other agencies.*

THE OTHER WORLD   by DRUMMOND

"WE JUST CAN'T RUSH INTO THESE THINGS... WE MUST GO ONE STEP AT A TIME...."

Reprinted from the Penal Digest International

For centuries prison reform efforts have met with uniform failure. The reformer always ventures to the inhospitable prison with the notion of imposing a "revolutionary" philosophy in the hostile environment. He soon realizes, however, that the foreign atmosphere does not support the reforms desired (if any at all), and his efforts at renovation are nonproductive because the essential ingredients to sustain a reform movement are not contained within the prison. Thus he quickly determines that he cannot really hope to reform the prison as long as it remains in the same position relative to the other agencies (see the diagram).

The Substance of Real Reform

**THE PLANETARY MODEL OF REAL REFORM EFFORTS:
THE PRISON AS A PLANET**

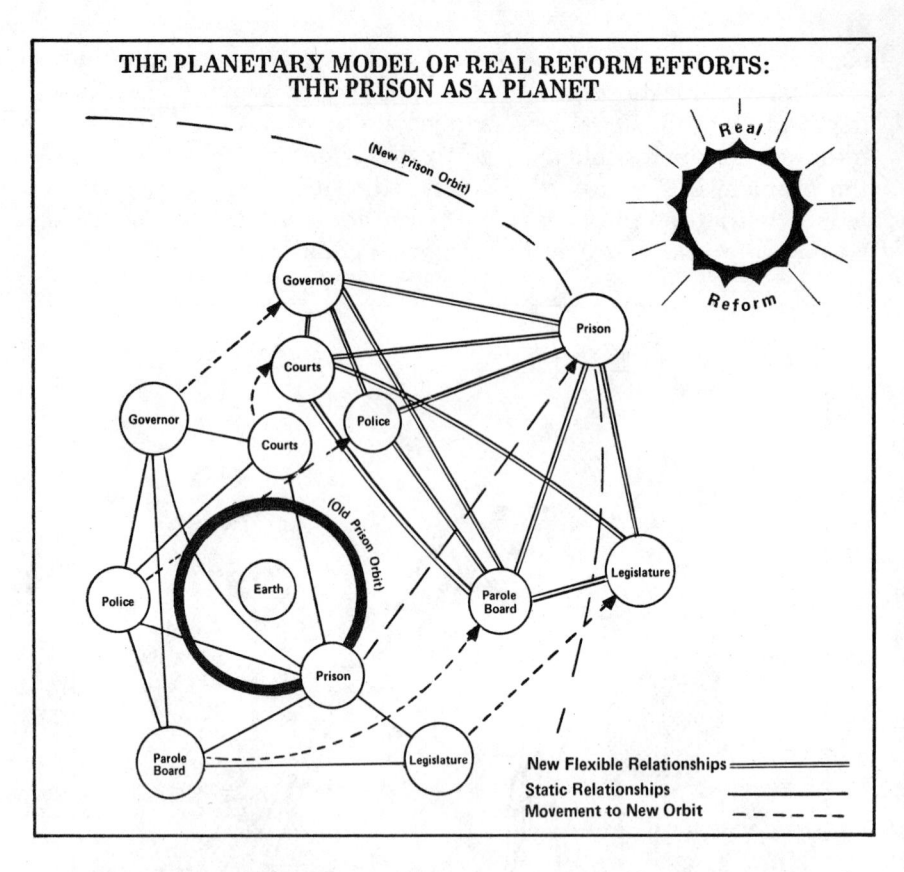

The basic problem with the prison—that real reform cannot be achieved solely from within the prison—is not addressed. The fact that the mock reformer "cannot get there from here" is ignored. No one has ever improved the environment of a prison by leaving it in its traditional framework. It may become somewhat more hospitable, but it is no more viable.

The mock reformer finds solace in the belief that if he applies techniques accepted in the free society with diligence and fervent prayer, his righteousness will eventually bear fruit and the objective of real reform will be achieved. Professor Korn demonstrates the illogic of this gradualism theory of prison reform:

> *One of the abiding doctrines of evolutionary social theory is that radical change is illusory and therefore fruitless to attempt; what appears new or "revolutionary" is actually the slow result of gradual, imperceptible movements, hardly noticed when they occur. The doctrine offers much comfort to the patient and the temperate and has great appeal to*

The Substance of Real Reform

those who consider themselves realists. It suffers from only one embarrassment as a general principle: when applied to the major inventions of mankind, it is wrong. If it were true, one could have confidently predicted that gradual improvements in the sailing ship would have eventually produced the steamboat, that progressive refinement of the gas lamp would have resulted in electric light, and that ultimate refinement of hydroelectric power would have produced atomic power.

The doctrine of evolutionary gradualism, though inadequate as an explanation for major technical inventions, still remains persuasive to many who rely on it for major improvements in the social realm. [15]

Results

Radical change of the prison is proscribed in the reformer's initial plan of action. The reformer subsequently rationalizes his reform efforts by trying to work within the imposed limitations, even as he realizes that they may be futile. He says to himself, in a familiar refrain, "If I am not in the system I cannot change it. Otherwise my power line, which depends on the official reformer, will be severed and I will suffer professional exile."

Although not granted permission to really change the prison, the mock reformer sets about to convince those who endorsed his mission that he really is nonetheless changing the conditions. After all, how can he establish his qualifications as a prison reformer if people are not convinced that he reforms prisons? So he unpacks his "prison reform kit" and busies himself and his staff with the task of creating the impression that reform is taking place. He erects two-dimensional artifacts that, when viewed by the remote public (the only view he will tolerate of the prison ship), give the appearance of three-dimensional structures with substance and depth. He well knows that few can afford the time or trouble to make a pilgrimage to the prison; most will be satisfied with his interpretation of what change has taken place. Any misinterpretation of actual events, if ever discovered by a real reformer who chances upon the institution, will be explained by the traditionalists as distortion by the media that conveyed the image of the reform movement. Negative reports from prisoners returning to society will be equally discounted as unreliable.

---

[15] Richard Korn, "A Review," *Crime and Delinquency*, National Council on Crime and Delinquency, New York, October 1970, p. 446.

The mock reformer, having completed his task of creating the facade of reform, emerges periodically from the prison to receive the accolades, medals, and commendations for a "job well done." With the same strategy, he then moves on to "reform" another prison. If it later becomes apparent that there has been no real disruption of interrelations within the political system and that the prison continues to perpetuate negative phenomena within the system, the mock reformer quickly explains that it is due to the basic evil of prisons, the degenerate inhabitants, or a "lack of funds."

The real reformer, on the other hand, makes every effort to change the essence of the prison. He realizes that efforts directed solely toward improving creature comforts without creating a receptive environment which will sustain real reform are meaningless gestures—given, of course, that he is motivated by basic desires to make significant innovations. He will therefore elicit a promise from the power giver that the prison can be moved into different relationships with other agencies. This permission is usually given in desperation only after the prison is in rebellion and no other reformers are standing in line for the position.

The official reformer initially does not realize that any real change of the prison will result in a realignment of the other agencies in the system. Thus prison reform must be preceded by an agreement of such realignment prior to efforts to bring about the change. Any such movement without a plan for reorienting the other agencies could result in chaos. The difficulty with such a plan is that it will not find ready acceptance by those offices currently enjoying a closer, more profitable relationship with the governor. The principle of sacrificing a few for the good of the many is not particularly palatable to the greedy.

Instead of reform, the command becomes "Preserve the status quo" or, more commonly, "Don't rock the boat." Hence we find that those who are selected to reform the hostile prison and provide an atmosphere that will benefit the entire system are not commissioned to reform but, rather, to perpetuate the system that provides preferential treatment for the few. One difficulty is that because the mock reformer must maintain his contact and relationships with the official reformer, he will not try to develop an independent power base in the community.

The real reformer, on the other hand, can develop a new power base by forming a revolutionary government at the prison and joining forces with the inmates, staff, and citizenry to move in a new direction. Unfortunately, the real reformer never can become totally self-reliant in the new environment because he, too, must rely on the official reformer, not only to provide support to sustain himself but also to grant the power necessary to change the entire system.

Less than a new dimension the real reformer cannot accept. An impasse results, the power giver withdraws his support, a mock reformer is dispatched on the next airplane to repair the "damage" of reform, destroy the three-dimensional models, and erect his facade of reform.

As Korn observes: "The critics of gradualism suggest . . . that the difficulty with most of our social innovations is that they are neither radical nor rapid enough, and that the essential function of gradualism is not to achieve basic change but to prevent it."[16] In fact, it may be the function of the mock reformer to stabilize an erratic equilibriuum of the prison rather than attempt to move it in the direction of real reform. Maybe, as it has been suggested, "We are not the doctors; we are the disease."

The Impact of Real Reform

Real reform efforts have a considerable impact on those involved with the prison system, and the implications of reform movements should not be considered lightly.

The Official Reformer

Once convinced by his palace guard that real reform is antithetical to his own personal goals and objectives, the official reformer becomes dismayed, experiences disaffection with the real reformer, and withdraws support. Ultimately, he will not only fail to support the reform effort but will take overt action to prevent real prison reform from being attained. It is at this point that he implements the art of nonreform that may result in the facade of reform.

The impact on the official reformer may be no more than a brief flurry of consternation from irate supporters of prison reform. The power of the official reformer is usually quite adequate to neutralize the adverse effects of a reform movement, and he is usually skillful enough to convince the majority that he is still committed to reform. If not, he may be challenged at the next election to justify his failure.

---

[16] Korn, p. 447.

The Staff

The notion of joining forces with the "enemy" inmate population to bring about reform is not only a frightening idea to the staff but one which they quickly reject. The warden, for example, lists his prison experience as a qualifier for a prison post yet denies the same privilege to the inmate.

Because real reform efforts that engage the inmates in self-determination pose a threat to the staff member's self-concept and his belief system, he must either reject real reform or reject himself. If he has sufficient ego strengths, he may become "converted" and modify his concepts to tolerate and accept involvement of the inmate in his own destiny. But, more often than not, he will choose to remain in the security afforded by the traditional perception of his role. Thus he will resist reform efforts with the utmost of his personal and professional power and persuasion (and that of the professional associations) to prevent any incursion into "his" domain by either the "radical" reformer or the inmates.

The Inmates

Under the reform system, the inmate is given hope through promises of real reform and begins to view himself once more, or perhaps for the first time, as a human being. Being exposed to real reform ventures for a brief time is perhaps a disservice to the inmate who, having once tasted freedom, is never again satisfied to plod hopelessly through the prison catacombs. The inmate's frustration increases when his expectations are not realized. Had he continued in ignorance he would not seek freedom from tyranny so vigorously.

The concept of the dignity of men, which may be the only remnant of the reform movement, may serve further to increase the hopelessness, despair, and frustration of the inmate as regression of the prison takes place. The awareness of this ramification of aborted reform continues to haunt the real reformer as he is forced from the system.

The real reformer watches as the innovations are removed, and he takes some comfort in the observation that his greatest contribution—an idea—can never be eliminated. Ironically, it is this very ingredient of real reform that constitutes the central threat to the opponents of reform. This most crucial element of real reform will lie dormant until, it is hoped, fertile conditions and the passage of time will once again spawn a rebirth.

*Killing the prophet may serve only to
enhance the prophecy.*

The Substance of Real Reform

The Real Reformer

The real reformer must anticipate ridicule, banishment from the professional community, rejection by his colleagues, personal humiliation, and severe financial difficulties while seeking solace in the notion that he did what needed to be done. Although not achieving the goals of real reform, he may have made a contribution by demonstrating an idea and raising the prison to a higher plateau. And then again it may be, as the traditionalists contend, only a rationalization by the reformer to justify his "failure."

One aspect of aborted reform is that a condition is created analogous to the unintentional development of a DDT-resistant variety of flies. The real reformer succeeds initially because he is considered an "expert." It is not known what he plans to do nor is it apparent that his actions may constitute a threat to the official reformer. But in the process of the reform movement, the real reformer inadvertently identifies the ingredients of real reform to the official reformer. He polarizes the prison and freeworld community by revealing the secrets of reform to the officials. Excessive dosages of real reform result in a residual strain of administrators who have survived such ventures in the past. They know enough about real reform to recognize the embryonic development, the indicators and cues that, if ignored, may result in real reform.

The System

Real reform constitutes a foreign body, and efforts to graft it onto an existing sick system will only result in rejection by the organism. The traditionalists, the insecure, the corrupt, and the frightened will all rally around the flag to ward off the enemy. The individual responses will become manifest in a collective reaction toward real reform.

Prime resistance to change of the prison comes not from the inmates, as might be presumed, but rather from the staff. Because real reform requires that the system change in essence and be reconstituted, staff are required to make major changes. For decades, the inmates have been required to accommodate to the system; to suggest that the process be reversed is inconceivable to staff. Hence, either through action or inaction, they constitute a force to be reckoned with as an inhibitor of real reform.

The response of the system is not unlike the reaction of the staff. It differs in that it forms an umbrella of discontent and operates as a coalition of dissidents who, for disparate reasons, join forces to overthrow the common enemy. Such mobilization not only interferes with current reform movements but also provides valuable experience to prevent future intervention by real reformers.

Thus equipped, the nonreformist administration successfully anticipates every strategy, if not every tactic, in the process of reform and is able to thwart it. Thus it may be, as John Haley contended, that aborted real reform is antithetical to real reform. The real reformer must be aware of these secondary ramifications of reform efforts. He must carefully calculate the risks of inadvertently not only contributing to his own demise but aiding the opponents of reform by alerting them to strategy that will assist in repressing future reform efforts. This consideration is one of the dilemmas of prison reform.

9

Participatory Government: An Alternative Prison Managerial Model

> Some men see things as they are
> and say "why?"
> I dream of things that never were
> and say "why not?"
> — ROBERT F. KENNEDY[1]

One can hardly refute the contention of scholars and the admission of prison administrators that the prison, as far as rehabilitation of inmates goes, has been an abject failure. Obvious evidence of this failure is the fact that we continue to build *more* prisons to accommodate *repeat* offenders. The past two centuries of prison experience have certainly demonstrated that the usual approaches to rehabilitation do *not* work. As a result, many people, both inside and outside the walls of penology, have become disenchanted with the prison and its various "treatment" attempts and have begun to despair over the absence of any real renovation of the system. For these people, the slogan "tear down the walls" is becoming a rallying cry. Although it is possible that the prison, as now constituted, may indeed one day be abolished, a pragmatic view makes clear that our society may not yet be sufficiently advanced to cope with such an innovation.

It may well be that one day society will devise another system of degradation sufficient to identify, label, and ostracize the "deviants." Perhaps a "stocks and pillory" psychological ceremony could serve the needs of the dominant "in-group" and at the same time not carry

---

[1] As attributed by Edward Kennedy in "A Tribute to Robert F. Kennedy," *Representative American Speeches*, vol. 40, no. 5 (New York: H. W. Wilson Co., 1968), p. 178.

with it either the trauma of treatment and institutionalization or the continuing stigma of the ex-convict as part of the "out-group."[2]

If an alternative system is ever to be successful, it must be recognized and supported by the deviants. That is, as long as the inmate's confession of his "deficiency" is required as a prerequisite of treatment, the inmate or offender must sincerely accept both the diagnosis and the efficacy of the treatment. The confessional must then be followed by a realistic scheme to restore the individual to the free society, a scheme that will allow his rebirth and reentry into the society that created him.

It is conceivable that such a plan could take place without an institution. Current use of probation by the courts represents such a direction; yet the ritual of the court trial, the stigma of being a convicted felon, and the haunting supervision that the probationer must undergo all constitute a continuing imposition of power that reinforces the artificial caste distinction between the treaters and the treatees. Although a possibility exists for new dimensions in dealing with deviance, it remains speculative at this time. It appears unlikely that an era of "law and order" will spawn demands for either more liberal or radically different modes of prison reform and management of the criminal, or for the development of a new definition of deviance. Neither is it feasible to urge abandonment of the monumental facilities now in existence, especially in view of the considerable financial investment made in them and the psychological comfort they afford the freeworld. Hence, although eliminating the prison as a method of social control may remain a dream for reformers, the belief that the prison will soon be replaced by more humane, effective means appears to be unrealistic. Even were it possible, few would dispute that there will always be some people who will require detention because they constitute a real, physical threat to the free society. In this regard, one can also argue that the function of punishment should not be entirely discounted.

With these ideas in mind, then, one can justify efforts to reform the prison as an *interim* venture undertaken to tame the monster while simultaneously attempting to destroy it. An alternative model to the present prison is therefore suggested—one that can be instituted within existing facilities, expanded with the creation of new facilities, and, quite possibly, aid in developing new methods for dealing with criminality.

---

[2] See: Howard Becker, *Outsiders: The Sociology of Deviance* (New York: The Free Press, 1966).

A New Prison Community

The traditional definition of the prison community (in other words, inmates of an institution) must be rejected. A new prison community is created by forming a coalition between staff and inmates to combine power and expertise in changing the prison to a mutually beneficial environment; refer to the diagram. This new concept of the prison community does not come about spontaneously; it must be nurtured and developed. In effect, staff members say to the inmates: "Come, let us join hands and climb the mountain together." The substitution of legitimate power is being suggested for the current illegitimate one. This new dimension in prison administration requires some courage, and a great deal of perception, on the part of the reformer. To turn the prison in a creative direction, to allow the formation of a new society within it, requires both skill and intuition.

**The Coalition of Staff and Inmates
in a Concerted Effort at Prison Reform**

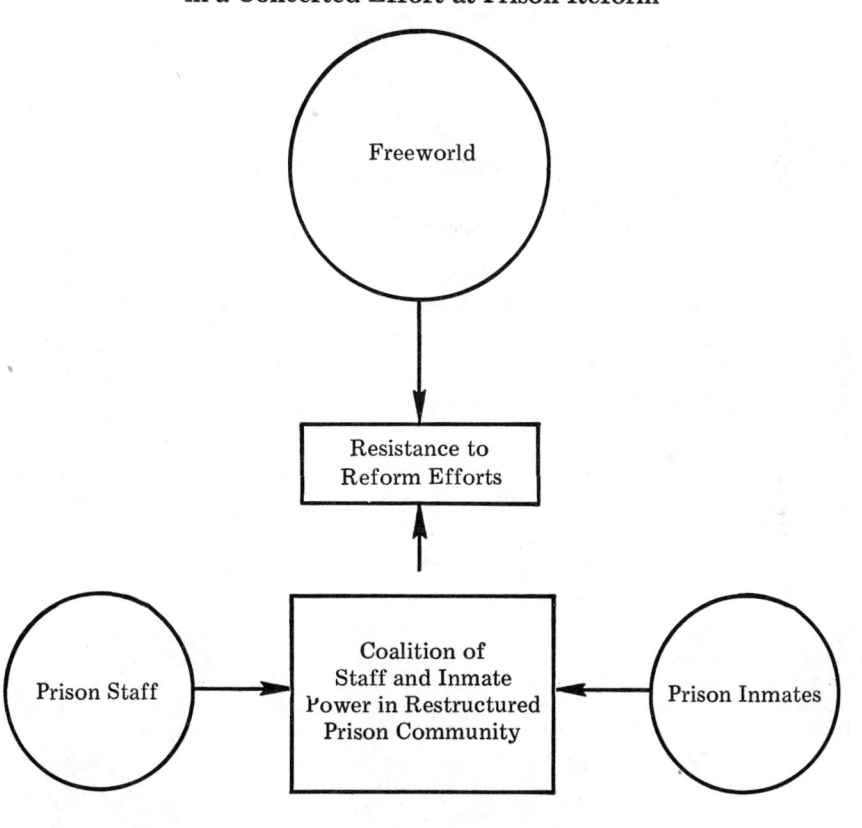

Participatory Government

> **LION TAMER OR PROPHET?**
>
> "If the beast who sleeps in man could be held down by threats—any kind of threat, whether jail or retribution after death—then the highest emblem of humanity would be the lion tamer in the circus with his whip, not the Prophet who sacrificed himself."
>
> —*Boris Pasternak*

Before the inmates can be constructively involved in self-determination, it is essential that they have a vested interest in keeping the warden in office. Otherwise their decisions may be directed toward immediate rewards for themselves and may not take into consideration the long-range gains that need to be made. Conversely, once the inmates as a group believe that the continued tenure of the warden is to their ultimate benefit, their decisions will take into account possible impact on his administration.[3]

The notion of allowing inmates to assist in governing themselves is not particularly new. In varying degrees, inmates have exercised some form of control over other inmates either as an expediency or from some belief by the proponent that this experience would have a therapeutic effect on the criminal offender.

Inmate Guards

Mordecai Plummer introduced the use of inmate guards in the New Castle Workhouse in Delaware in 1920. This "Plummer System" was abandoned in 1933 because of exploitation by the inmate guards.[4] The system was adopted by the states of Arkansas, Mississippi, and Louisiana and resulted in the same negative aspects experienced in Delaware.

The Nazis used the "Kapos" in managing concentration camps during World War II. The option was offered to some Jews either to be gassed or to assist in gassing their fellow men. Some chose the latter with the promise of one more day of life.

---

[3] There is an unstated aspect of allowing the inmates to participate in self-determination. If the warden is willing to share decision making with the inmates, then the inmates must be willing to share responsibility with the warden for the decisions made. By this method, a by-product is that inmate hostility is redirected away from the warden back to the inmate group.

[4] See: Harry Barnes and Negley Teeters, *New Horizons in Criminology* (New York: Prentice-Hall, 1947), pp. 746–798.

But none of these examples reflects a particularly new concept in managing prisoners. Even the Bible records an early account of such an event. Joseph had been sold into slavery in Egypt and became a prisoner of Potiphar, an officer serving Pharoah as well as being captain of the guard. Joseph worked as a servant in Potiphar's house until he was accused (falsely) of having an affair with Potiphar's wife. This charge resulted in his confinement in the king's prison.

> *But the Lord was with Joseph, and showed him mercy, and gave him favour in the sight of the keeper of the prison.*
>
> *And the keeper of the prison committed to Joseph's hand all the prisoners that were in the prison; and whatsoever they did there, he was the doer of it.*[5]

The foregoing examples deal primarily with the use of inmates in controlling institutions. Other, more sophisticated efforts to establish inmate government based on concepts of rehabilitation have also been used.

The Soviet Union established the Bolshevo Colony for youthful offenders in 1924 outside Moscow. There was a staff of only five for a population that at one time reached 2,000. There were no armed guards, there was complete self-government, and the inmates could have their wives with them.

There have been a few glimmers of hope in the bleak field of penology when an occasional heretic has emerged to light a candle, briefly illuminating a possible pathway out of the abyss of traditionalism. This chapter discusses some classic examples of efforts to involve the inmate in the decision-making process and thereby in self-determination. Excluded from consideration are those prisons, such as in Arkansas, Mississippi, and Louisiana, where inmates exercise illegitimate power to exploit their fellow inmates. Also excluded from this discussion is the omnipresent Inmate Advisory Council[6] that is proudly displayed by the warden as an example of "involvement" of the inmate in his destiny. Since these councils do not perform any decison-making functions, they are impotent. Such councils hold meetings, write proposals for change,

---

[5] Genesis 39:21, 22.

[6] The traditional inmate councils common in many institutions are excluded from any consideration here because they are in reality part of the facade of reform. The traditional councils are allowed only to make recommendations to the administration concerning prison management. Their true decision-making power is usually limited to voting on the admission of Red China to the United Nations and what color to choose for painting the latrine. Notable exceptions are the Scandinavian prison systems wherein inmates are given extensive authority to govern their own affairs.

and make recommendations—but they cannot implement the desired change. A classic example of the foregoing is the Resident Governmental Council (RGC) of the Washington State Penitentiary at Walla Walla. It has been in existence since December 1970, but even two years later neither the warden nor the inmates were able to cite a single decision that had been made by the RGC, and it was subsequently abolished in March 1975.

Participatory Management[7]

Four case studies have been selected that demonstrate historical efforts to involve the inmate in prison management.

Alexander Maconochie (1787-1860)

Norfolk Island was established as a penal colony in 1788. A long succession of commandants (including the notorious Captain William Bligh) supervised the colony with varying degrees of harshness until it was abandoned in 1814. Ten years later, the colony was re-established for the worst offenders in the colonial penal system. "[T]he felon who is sent there is forever excluded from all hope of return."[8]

Captain Alexander Maconochie of the Royal Navy departed London in 1836 to serve as private secretary to Sir John Franklin, who had just been appointed Lieutenant Governor of Van Diemen's Land (Tasmania) off the southern coast of Australia. Prior to leaving, Maconochie had been commissioned by the London Society for the Improvement of Prison Discipline to investigate the convict system in those colonies. His report to the society and his subsequent writings, speeches, and commentaries reflect his then-radical departure from accepted principles of penology:

> *The essential and obvious error in this system is its total neglect of moral reasoning and influence, and its exclusive reliance, in every relation of life, on mere physical coercion.*
>
> *I am inclined to question the right which society has assumed to itself of framing its laws so as intentionally to punish its erring members in reference, not to themselves, or*

---

[7] This material originally appeared as a chapter titled "Shared Decision-Making in Prison Management: A Survey of Demonstrations Involving the Inmate in Participatory Government," co-authored with Phyllis Jo Baunach, *Prisoners' Rights Source Book* (New York: Clark Boardman Company, 1973), pp. 541–573).

[8] John Vincent Barry, *Alexander Maconochie of Norfolk Island*, (London: Oxford University Press, 1958), p. 90.

> to the abstract quality of their own crimes, but to the impression that may be so made on others.
>
> This appears to me a sacrifice of their rights and interests to ours, which would be very difficult to reconcile with any abstract Christian principle; for we may not do evil even that good may come; and in truth, so little real good ever does come from our attempting to seek it through evil, that we may almost draw an inference from this against the fact of our deriving any material advantage from acting on a principle, manifestly unjust in its very basis. *[Emphasis added.]* [9]

Maconochie's theories gained some acceptance in London, and in 1839 he was offered the superintendency of Norfolk Island. Although Norfolk was not suited to implementation of his plan for resocializing the convict because of its remoteness, he accepted the position and landed on the island in March 1840 to assume his duties. The principle that was to guide his innovations is probably best summarized in Maconochie's own words: "The first object of prison discipline should be to reform prisoners and thus prepare them to separate [from prison] with advantage both to themselves and to society after their discharge."[10]

The essence of Maconochie's social management theory was the "Mark System"—the convict could make restitution for his crime by paying off his "debt" to society by earning marks through daily work. When he had accumulated a sufficient number, the convict was released on parole.

Manocochie rejected the arbitrary, punitive, and debasing nature of the traditional prison: "Man is a social being; his duties are social; and only in society, as I think, can he be trained for it."[11]

> It is very interesting also to see social impulses strictly reciprocal, action and reaction equal, and the oppressor injured, both in character and in circumstances, by the result of his oppression.
>
> It shows enlightened benevolence to be true practical wisdom, and cruelty or indifference to be folly as well as crime.

---

[9] Alexander Maconochie, *Australiana: Thoughts on Convict Management* (London: John W. Parker, 1839), pp. 7, 8, 114.

[10] Barry, p. x.

[11] Barry, p. 68.

> *The justice administered may be called poetical; but its sphere is amid the most ordinary realities of social life.*[12]

In retrospect it would appear that Maconochie had a specific strategy to bring his reform system into existence. His first efforts were addressed toward restoring some dignity to the convicts. He provided markers for the graves of deceased convicts whereas previously only the graves of freemen were entitled to headstones. He allowed inmates to keep their earnings in their possession.

> *Those among the men who by any means accumulated money I used to encourage to keep it themselves, for I wished to extend the presence of temptation, and the practice of resisting it, in the body, and it was extraordinary how few losses were thus ever sustained; but on extraordinary occasions, when men were near the period of their final departure, I would receive their little hoards, and give them orders on Sydney for their amount, that they might be sure to retain and receive them when they would be most useful to them.*[13]

Maconochie was taking into consideration both the impact of self-concept and the development of trust between the administration and the inmates. The significance of this act can easily be overlooked. The essence of developing responsibility involves creating experiences wherein the inmate has the opportunity to *fail.* Thus when success occurs, it is real and self-reinforcing.

Maconochie took many other steps to develop trust between the inmates and himself. Not only did he make himself readily available to the inmates by walking and riding among them almost daily and encouraging all to approach him with their problems, but he opened the courts to inmate attendance and, in cases of great import, actually held court in the prison yard. Although he was not able to fully implement his plan to utilize inmate jurors (because of legal restrictions), he did seek and consider inmate testimony and advice in matters before his court. He appointed inmates as legal counsel for the less sophisticated inmates with orders to provide the best possible defense. He also prohibited the defense counsel from revealing any confidence. After hearing the case, Maconochie would then wait 24 hours to deliberate his decision in order to allow time for further reflection.

---

[12] Maconochie, pp. 94, 95.
[13] Barry, p. 117.

Maconochie used trust as a basis for leading to responsibility. He chose trusted inmates from the population and placed them outside the prison camps in the bush, where they lived, worked, and played together under the supervision of an inmate overseer.

> *This distribution of men necessitated a greater employment of prisoner overseers and sub-overseers, and I was otherwise most favorable to this. In conducting a coercive system it often leads to tyranny and abuse, but in a reforming one it is most beneficial. It encourages the best men, increases their influence with others, and makes these aspire to similar trusts. The very possession of such trust is also a reformatory agent. I saw many instances of originally very indifferent men, thus, and thus almost alone, rendered trustworthy.*[14]

The self-fulfilling prophecy of negative labeling is a reality. It could be argued that positive labeling might also lead to self-fulfillment. That is, granting an inmate trust through responsibility may encourage him, in fact, to attempt to live up to that trust and demonstrate responsibility.

Another technique Maconochie tried was to have the inmates assign themselves to small groups of six men who would be held mutually responsible for each other until they had earned a cumulative total of 12,000 marks for the group. As Maconochie stated, "Superiors may be partial or deceived, but not equals."[15] It was assumed that, through common earnings and common forfeiture, peer pressure would tend to reinforce desired behavior. According to Maconochie, there was considerable resistance to the plan among the inmates because it allowed the innocent to be punished along with the guilty. He later modified the plan so that changes in the group composition could occur. Whatever shortcomings this method had, these minimum-custody camps served as one of the prerelease stages in his plan to ease the transition from the prison to the free community.

Maconochie even appointed an inmate police force that worked under the supervision of two free officers. They patrolled the island day and night and provided general law enforcement functions. This unusual delegation of power to inmates apparently was successful:

> *I was four years in charge of Norfolk Island, with from 1500 to 2000 prisoners on it [but] I never had more than 160 soliders and I never once called on (them) for other than*

---

[14] Barry, p. 113.

[15] Barry, p. 19.

> *routine duty. I had only five inferior free officers... instead of from forty to fifty who have since been attached to it. And my Police [force] was composed of men selected by me from the general body of prisoners, furnished only with short staves—instead of a large free and probationer force armed with cutlasses, and in some cases pistols, that has since been maintained.*
>
> *If, then, with this inferior physical force I was able to preserve perfect order, submission, and tranquility, it seems to me to follow incontestably—either that my measures were most singularly adapted to attain their end—or, as a general proposition, that restraints founded on self-interest, persuasion, exhortation, and other sources of moral influence, are in every case more stringent than those of brute force, even in dealing with the worst of men.*[16]

In addition to the personal relations he developed with the inmates, Maconochie attempted to implement other portions of his master plan of 1840. He built a Roman Catholic and a Protestant church, obtained funds to hire churchmen, and conducted services himself in the bush camps. Each congregation was encouraged to form a band and a choir. The ministry was even extended to the jail, which consisted of 12 separate cells. In the roof of each was a sliding panel to provide the inmate with the option of leaving it open, to hear religious readings from the room above, or of closing it.

To deal with training, Maconochie established schools to provide basic instruction for the inmates. Since each man was to be released to the agricultural community of New South Wales, the principal training was in agriculture. Each convict on the island was given a plot of ground to raise a garden. Men in the bush camps had larger plots of ground and were allowed to raise products for sale to the staff.

> *I thus sought to distribute property among them, and from its possession acquire a sense and value for its rights; and the success of this policy was even extraordinary, petty theft becoming among the most unpopular of all offenses.*[17]

Because of mutual trust and a chance to demonstrate responsibility, the inmates as a group did act responsibly both in prison and on release. An interesting example is cited by Maconochie wherein

---

[16] Barry, p. 166.
[17] Barry, p. 115.

several inmates secured the release from prison of another inmate convicted of assault on a convict. They were so sure of his reformation that they posted a bond in marks to be forfeited should he commit further crimes after release. One of the inmates posting security for his release was the victim of the original assault.

Probably the most dramatic proof of the validity of Maconochie's system of trust occurred only 90 days after his appointment. One of Maconochie's biographers describes a most extraordinary celebration of the Queen's birthday at Norfolk:

Never was Norfolk Island so gay, or its inhabitants so joyful as on 25 May 1840. A proclamation had been issued by Maconochie, describing the pleasures and festivities he contemplated. On this occasion he resolved to forget the distinction between good and bad [inmates], and to make no exception from the general indulgence; but he entreated the men to remember that on the success of this experiment this confidence would greatly depend; he warned them to suppress the first tokens of disorder, and by retiring to their quarters at the sound of the bugle, prove that they might be trusted with safety.

On the morning of the day, the signal colours floated from the staff, crowned with the union jack; twenty-one guns, collected from the vessels and from the government house, were mounted on the top of a hill, and fired a royal salute.

The gates were thrown open, and eighteen hundred prisoners were set free, and joined in various amusements, of which Captain Maconochie was a frequent spectator. Eighteen hundred prisoners sat down to dinner and at its close, having received each a small quantity of spirits with water, they drank health to the Queen and Maconochie—three times three for Victoria and the captain rent the air.

They then renewed their sports, or attended a theatrical performance. New scenery, dresses, music and songs contributed to the hilarity of the party....

At the termination, no accident had occurred; the gaol was completely unoccupied; no theft or disorder had disgraced the day; and thus the notion of Maconochie seemed to be illustrated by the experiment.[18]

---

[18] Barry, pp. 104, 105.

Participatory Government

Of the 1,450 prisoners discharged under Maconochie's system, less than 3 percent were ever reconvicted of a crime; of 920 doubly convicted convicts, only 2 percent are known to have been reconvicted. During Maconochie's four-year tenure, there was only one killing, four escapes, and no uprisings. Even the Secretary of State for the Colonies attested to the value of Maconochie's system—in his letter ordering Maconochie's dismissal!

> *I gladly acknowledge that his efforts appear to have been rewarded by the decline of crimes of violence and outrage, and by the growth of humane and kindly feelings in the minds of the persons under his charge.* [19]

In reading the writings of Maconochie and his contemporaries, one is impressed with the philosophy, strategy, and grasp of the dynamics of reformation that underscored his administration. It is clear not only that he understood the basic evil of the prison, but also that he understood how that evil could be rectified. The records attest to the fact that Maconochie's system was successful insofar as the inmate population and the reduction of crime were concerned. However, he "failed" to secure his continued tenure and was fired at the height of his experiment in February 1844.

Maconochie's major impact on the penal colony is best summarized in his own words:

> *I found the island a turbulent, brutal hell, and left it a peaceful, well-ordered community . . . the most complete security alike for person and property prevailed. Officers, women and children traversed the island everywhere without fear. [To which Judge John Vincent Barry, an Australian Supreme Court Justice, added: "All reliable evidence confirms his statement."]* [20]

Thomas Mott Osborne (1859–1926)

On June 13, 1913, the Westchester County grand jury condemned Sing Sing prison and recommended to the governor of New York the construction of a new prison to replace it. Shortly thereafter, following a series of riots and fires, the warden of Sing Sing was forced to resign under charges of malfeasance. Governor Glynn offered the post to Thomas Mott Osborne, who initially declined.

---

[19] Barry, p. 147.
[20] Barry, p. 167.

Osborne, a prominent citizen of Auburn, New York, his lifelong home, was deeply concerned with the issues of prison reform. His career as mayor of Auburn and as Democratic leader of upstate New York had acquainted him with the problems of crime and criminals. For 15 years he had served as chairman of the board of directors of the George Junior Republic, an institution for juvenile offenders in which the inmates participated in community organization to develop a sense of responsibility. Osborne's experience with this institution laid the groundwork for his later reforms.

In the summer of 1913, Governor William Sulzer appointed Osborne chairman of the New York Prison Commission. Osborne focused his investigations on Auburn prison, interviewing staff and inmates and observing obvious shortcomings. He decided to subject himself to one week of voluntary incarceration at Auburn prison to ascertain for himself the nature of prison discipline. On Sunday, September 28, 1913, he informed 1,400 inmates assembled in the chapel of his plan. Although he realized that his perception of the prison would vary considerably from that of a regular inmate, he sincerely believed the experience would be valuable in his understanding of the prison system:

> I have the feeling that after I have really lived among you, marched in your lines, shared your food, gone to the same cells at night, and in the morning looked out at the piece of God's sunlight through the same iron bars—that then, and not until then, can I feel the knowledge which will break down the barriers between my soul and the soul of my brothers.[21]

Osborne's experience as a prisoner gained him the respect and trust of the inmates and, later, their cooperation in implementing his reforms.

Superintendent of Prisons John B. Riley would not accept Osborne's initial refusal to consider the post of warden of Sing Sing prison and insisted that he come to Albany for an interview. In response, Osborne gathered a group of 25 of his best friends from among the inmates at Auburn prison and discussed the matter with them. After a day and a half of debate, the inmates voted 18 to 7 in favor of his accepting the position. At the same time, Osborne received word from a trusted inmate at Sing Sing that the inmates there had signed a petition endorsing his appointment as warden. Prior to his acceptance of the post, Osborne had an interview with

---

[21] Frank Tannenbaum, *Osborne of Sing Sing* (Chapel Hill: University of North Carolina Press, 1933), p. 65.

the newly elected governor, Charles S. Whitman, and was promised support. With the assurance of official support and confidence in the inmates' cooperation, Osborne finally accepted the position on November 19, 1914.

Osborne rejected the contemporary theories of criminality which postulated that crime was a disease or a function of physical or mental deficiencies. He accepted the disease theory only as a metaphor. Criminals were neither physically nor mentally ill, but spiritually ill: "[I]ll of selfishness, of a peculiar form of civic egotism which causes [them] to be indifferent to the social rights of other men."[22] He rejected the notion of a "criminal type" because he believed that environment and training, as well as heredity, influenced behavior. He argued, however, that there was a "prison type" commonly mistaken for the "criminal type." The lockstep, shaved heads, and striped clothing were hideous signs of degradation used to break the prisoner's spirit and crush his individuality. The "prison type" was the final product of the prison system:

> *[L]arge numbers of men, broken in health and spirit, white-faced with the "prison pallor," husky in voice—hoarse from disuse, with restlessness, shifty eyes and the timidity of beaten dogs . . . are creatures whom we ourselves have fashioned.*[23]

In an address before the National Prison Association in 1904, Osborne attacked the evils of the prison system and enunciated his principles for the true foundation of prison reform:

> *First—The law must decree not punishment, but temporary exile from society until the offender has proven by his conduct that he is fit to return.*
>
> *Second—Society must brand no man a criminal, but aim solely to reform the mental conditions under which a criminal act has been committed.*
>
> *Third—The prison must be an institution where every inmate must have the largest practicable amount of freedom, because "it is liberty alone that fits men for liberty."*[24]

---

[22] Thomas Mott Osborne, *Society and Prisons* (New Haven: Yale University Press, 1917), p. 32.

[23] Osborne, p. 28.

[24] Quoted in Jack M. Holl, *Juvenile Reform in the Progressive Era* (Ithaca, N.Y.: Cornell University Press, 1971), p. 277.

Osborne's approach was "anti-institutional"[25] in that he freed the inmates from the inflexible, uniform discipline of the old prison system and stressed their active participation in their own reformation. He was firmly convinced that the inmates' permanent reformation would occur only if they were trusted to exercise meaningful decision-making powers in the institution. Thus his efforts as warden at Sing Sing were directed toward creating an atmosphere in which the inmates could develop a sense of responsibility through self-determination.

Osborne's first task as warden was the reorganization of the Brotherhood of the Golden Rule, an inmate council created by his predecessor. Although the brotherhood had an elaborate constitution and bylaws, it was a sham for two reasons. First, inmates had been granted privileges without earning them:

> *The rewards were given out before they had been earned; the privileges enjoyed without the responsibility which alone made the exercise of such privileges valuable... prisoners were not being exercised in the bearing of responsibility; they were being bribed to be good.*[26]

The inmates played Sunday baseball and watched movies, but they had no power to make or enforce the rules. They passively followed the lead of the administration. Second, the administration had imposed the council on the inmates. Since the inmates had not taken the initiative to form the council, they had no vested interest in it; the council belonged to the administration, not to the inmates:

> *If a plan of self-government was to work at all, it must be worked by them; and they would certainly work their plan better than they could some outside plan—no matter how perfect... The only self-government that would be successful in prison was the self-government which the prisoners would bring about—their own self-government.*[27]

Osborne reorganized the council around the principles of self-determination embodied in the Mutual Welfare League that had evolved from his voluntary incarceration at Auburn. The league was simple. Every inmate was eligible for membership. Two delegates from each shop were elected by secret ballot every six months. The board of delegates selected an executive board, who in turn selected

---

[25] Holl, p. 243.
[26] Osborne, pp. 204–205.
[27] Osborne, p. 159.

a clerk and sergeant-at-arms. League members received privileges in return for self-discipline and loyalty to the administration. Discipline was handled through a judiciary board; infractions of the rules resulted in suspension of league privileges.

On the evening of his first day in office, Osborne met with the executive committee of the brotherhood and *asked them* to draft a plan for a judiciary board. The inmates' proposal suggested that the judiciary board examine all minor cases of discipline. Osborne responded by turning over *all* cases of discipline to the judiciary board with the right of appeal to the warden's court, consisting of the warden, principal keeper, and prison doctor. In addition, Osborne granted 15 specific requests to change the prison rules within a week after he had assumed office. In so doing, he extended meaningful decision-making powers to the inmates, assured himself of their continued support, and encouraged their initiative.

Inmates traditionally marched to and from work under the watchful eye of the armed guards. Three days after Christmas, Osborne announced to the workers of the knit shop—"the most turbulent shop in the prison"—that henceforth they would march under their own elected delegates instead of armed guards.

> [T]he whole prison population watched the strange sight of the worst company in the prison coming in from work under the leadership of their two delegates, one marching in front, one in the rear of the company. And such marching was never seen in Sing Sing before.[28]

Pleased with their performance, the following day Osborne removed the guards from the shop and left only the civilian foreman and elected delegates in charge. Thereafter, the disciplinary problems in the knit shop were minimal:

> There has never since that time been any serious trouble in handling the discipline of the knit shop; although under the old system they used to have as high as ten or twelve cases of punishment a day, and many serious and bloody assaults a day.[29]

Shortly thereafter, the inmates initiated the move to march the men from all the shops under elected delegates and to remove the guards from the mess hall:

---

[28] Tannenbaum, p. 119.

[29] Osborne, p. 208.

As the noon whistle blew and the men came marching out of their shops there was not a prison guard in sight. The nearly 1,600 men came swinging down the prison yard under their own elected delegates, all prisoners. And when they had turned into the mess hall ... not a single guard was to be seen. The men were eating their noonday meal, all in one big room and not a single guard in sight, only the elected sergeant-at-arms and his assistants. [30]

Osborne eventually placed all the shops under the charge of the civilian workshops, "like any workshop outside."[31] The removal of the guards improved the morale of the inmates and extended the new responsibilities to the prison delegates. In addition to developing a sense of responsibility among the inmates, Osborne endeavored to develop a community spirit. He encouraged the growth of a knitting class, a choral society, a band, and an education unit.

The education unit, called the Mutual Welfare Institute, was initiated by an inmate who succeeded in enrolling between 80 and 90 percent of the inmates. Subject matter was limitless: if a prisoner could teach the desired subject to another who wished it, the class was authorized. The students erected a special school building to house the overflow of classes. The school staff met regularly to discuss educational policy and methods. The staff enjoyed the privileges of serving the inmate community:

All employees of the Mutual Welfare Institute perform their duties in connection with work for the State in addition to the time we give to the school. We consider it an honor to be connected with the school, and welcome the privilege of being permitted to serve our fellow inmates in this way. [32]

Permanent standing committees supervised every aspect of life in the prison:

... sanitation, athletics, entertainment, dietary, kitchen, finances, ways and means, reception of visitors, religious services, reception of new prisoners, employment, fire company, prison graveyard, a bank, a parole board. [33]

---

[30] Tannenbaum, p. 120.
[31] Osborne, p. 207.
[32] Quoted in Tannenbaum, p. 129.
[33] Tannenbaum, p. 130.

Osborne laid the foundation for inmate compensation with a system of token coins, although he left the prison before this plan was firmly established. The plan was to convert the token money into real money donated by the public. Each inmate received $9 a week from which he was expected to pay for his cell, his food, and his clothing. Before long the inmates petitioned for a bank:

> *The bank was chartered and soon in active operation. Money was drawn out and deposited when needed; the depositors supplied with pass books; men were taught the use of saving institutions and how to economize.*[34]

By May 2, 1916, after seven months of operation, there were 1,030 depositors and total deposits of $31,424.41, or an average of $30.50 credited to each depositor.

But the greatest impact of Osborne's reforms was on the inmates' attitudes toward themselves and the prison community:

> *Since the League started, these men find it easier to be law-abiding; they find their self-respect restored as their belief in their own essential manhood grows stronger; they feel responsible for the acts of the community as well as for their own individual acts.*[35]

Some of the prisoners formed an outside branch of the Mutual Welfare League. They met once or twice a year to give Osborne a public dinner and relate their successes and failures. They even tried to involve New York City Police Chief Colonel Arthur Woods in helping ex-inmates readjust to the street.

During the three years prior to Osborne's administration in Sing Sing, the prison hospital treated an average of 373 wounds per 1,450 inmates. After Osborne took office, the prison population increased to 1,600, but the number of wounds treated dropped to 155. An average of 35 inmates were committed to Dannemora State Hospital in each of the three years prior to Osborne's administration. During Osborne's entire administration only 19 inmates were transferred to Dannemora. Industrial production increased 21 percent.

The record for escapes indicates that in the first 13 months of his administration there were three escapes. In previous years there had been ten escapes in 1913; six in 1912; four in 1911; seventeen in 1910; and nineteen in 1909.[36] Some escapees returned voluntarily

---

[34] Quoted in Tannenbaum, p. 134.

[35] Osborne, p. 230.

[36] Tannenbaum, p. 146.

upon learning that their behavior had dishonored Osborne and the league. Judge William H. Wadhams of the Court of General Sessions in New York City observed that he had not had one recidivist from Sing Sing since the creation of the league.

Osborne's tenure was short-lived. On December 28, 1915, he was indicted by the Westchester County grand jury for perjury and neglect of duty. He took a leave of absence to prepare his case. Because of the questionable evidence on which the case was based, however, the court dismissed the charges.

Osborne resumed his position as warden on July 16, 1916, but resigned three months later. His resignation stemmed from an order by the Superintendent of Prisons that long-term convicts were forbidden outside prison walls. Trusties working in the administration building would have to be dismissed. Osborne interpreted this order as an effort to reduce the effectiveness of his programs, since Sing Sing was the only prison with administrative offices located outside the walls.

Although Osborne correctly surmised that it would take many years to gain widespread acceptance for his true principles of inmate government, he nonetheless demonstrated that inmates can govern themselves responsibly if given the opportunity:

> *In Auburn Prison for more than two years, in Sing Sing Prison for more than a year the new system has been in operation and* the thing works. *The truth of that fact no reluctant official and no stupid politician can argue out of existence. It is a rock which affords a solid foundation for the future of prison reform.*[37]

Howard B. Gill (b. 1889)

In 1923, a special legislative committee was appointed to study relocation of the Massachusetts prison at Charlestown. The selected site was part of 1,170 acres set aside in 1912 for a dipsomaniac hospital located about 25 miles from Boston in the Norfolk Township. A group of buildings known as the Oval and about 1,000 acres of land were transferred to the Department of Corrections in 1927. Construction of a wall around 37 acres to enclose the proposed new institution began in August 1927.

Howard B. Gill was graduated from the Harvard Business School and worked for ten years in industrial and commercial research. He became a private business consultant in 1924 and thereafter studied

---

[37] Osborne, pp. 222–223.

prison industries in federal and state systems. He later worked as purchasing agent for the United States Bureau of Prisons and was responsible for developing prison industries.

When offered the Norfolk superintendency by Commissioner Sanford Bates, Gill protested that he was not qualified because he had neither the training nor the experience to operate a prison. Bates informed Gill that that was the precise reason he had been chosen to develop the new institution. On November 10, 1927, Gill was appointed superintendent of the new facility and was given a free hand in establishing a new prison community. Gill proposed the combination of a community-type physical plant with the maximum opportunity for the inmates to develop a sense of responsibility through inmate participation. In this endeavor, he was influenced by his personal contact with Thomas Mott Osborne in 1925.

Gill contrasted his philosophy of prison management with the prevalent one:

> *The attitude of most people toward prisons is that the warden should be a despot and that the inmates should be noted for their docility. Nothing could be farther from the philosophy of Norfolk or the philosophy of modern penology... These men are here because they could not take this responsibility in a free community. We need to reverse the old principle of the bastille prisons, which was that every man should be treated like every other man. We are apt to confuse uniformity with equality.*[38]

Gill's oft-quoted basic rules consisted solely of "no escapes; no contraband." He did not believe in the use of stool pigeons because he despised and distrusted them. He refused to adopt the traditional system of informers, but listened to any prisoner who wanted sincerely to inform him about prison problems. The essential difference between the two systems is that traditionally an inmate "snitches" on his fellow inmates to achieve some personal gain. This gain can be favors from the administration or revenge for a personal grievance. But in the new prison community of which Gill spoke, the inmates and staff had common goals and, consequently, common responsibilities. Hence information provided to the warden by inmates was not a manifestation of desire for direct personal gain but rather a demonstration of responsibility in support of common prison goals.

---

[38] Carl R. Doering, ed., *Report on the Development of Penological Treatment at Norfolk Prison Colony in Massachusetts* (New York: Bureau of Social Hygiene, 1940), p. 77.

One observer commented:

Suffice it to say that through the ramifications of the work and the spirit caught up in the granting of inmate responsibility, many an inmate had learned the rudiments of community living which opened his eyes to the duties of good citizenship in the community. What some of the men needed for their social adjustment was exactly this sense of responsibility, not from official pressure, but of their own volition.[39]

Gill's first reform was rejection of the traditional prison planned to be built at Norfolk. He was granted permission to design and build his "community prison." Gill believed that the needs of the inmates must take precedence over institutional needs and that changes, to be effective, must involve the inmate body. When a flurry of escapes occurred or construction work faltered, Gill called on inmate leaders (as well as staff) to help him solve such problems.

His criteria for staff selection were that the candidates must be "close to the earth, humane and willing to learn." Ultimately, he set two criteria for prison personnel: (1) like a shaggy dog (care for others); and (2) make something out of nothing (be innovative and creative).

He established an open press policy as "public institutions publicly administered." Casework was vested in social workers who were hired to supplement the traditional guards. The staff was dichotomized deliberately; the police force performed strictly custodial functions. Correctional officers had charge of the living units and shops as treatment staff and dealt with inmates' personal problems.

Classic evaluation and classification systems were established. These were later abandoned, however, in favor of what Gill called "problem solving" and "acculturation." In keeping with the philosophy of community, the inmates were housed in small units not exceeding 50 men and 2 officers. The housing officer was required to live and eat with the inmates while on duty. Meals were partially prepared and eaten in each unit (as a family) rather than in a centralized dining room. The "small-group principle" was applied to physical exercise and to all other activities such as school, medical care, and industries. Each group developed subunits including both security and treatment.

---

[39] Doering, p. 87.

An outstanding feature of the institution emerged in the form of an Inmate Council. Patterned after Osborne's Mutual Welfare League, the inmates met as a group to pose problems or to suggest solutions to the warden. The staff was not involved initially. Gill did not envision the council as a form of "self-government" but rather as a form of "inmate participation." In contrast to Osborne's league, the council had advisory powers only and did not handle inmate discipline. But the joint committees, if approved by staff and council, carried out the activities of the prison.

> *Like the early Christian church which was truest and noblest in the days of its adversity, the council system of Norfolk was at its best when it was diligently forging the new plan, and the men involved in its creation were called upon to make sacrifices.*[40]

The principle of joint participation and joint responsibility was adopted. The work of the council and the staff was divided among twelve committees (and numerous house committees) made up of 60 inmates and 30 officers. After some disrupters took over the council a couple of times, it was decided that the candidates for office had to be approved in advance by the administration (although the number of candidates was not limited). Gill appealed to the prison population as a whole and the current council was recalled. Staff members were thereafter included in all sessions of the council and were also assigned to committees.

The Inmate Council, which continued to evolve from 1928, developed into a coalition between staff and inmates who shared responsibilities and decisions. The seeds of this coalition were planted in the spring of 1928 with the development of the Joint Committee on Construction. Thus, in the new facility behind the walls, the housing officers became an integral part of the council system.

> *[T]he real and most crucial accomplishments of the council system lay in the intangibles. It was a spirit of armistice where the two factions of social warfare forgot the gun and the instruments of vengeance to live together in amity to think out and put into practice a plan that would reduce the need for these conflicts.*[41]

---

[40] Doering, p. 86.
[41] Doering, p. 86.

Adding staff to the Inmate Council was neither by accident nor by coercion but was a deliberate effort by Gill to modify Osborne's plan. The Mutual Welfare League was like a pyramid turned upside down. The warden and the inmates got together and then told the guards what to do. According to Gill, resistance by the guards to this method proved to be a major factor in lessening the effectiveness of the league.

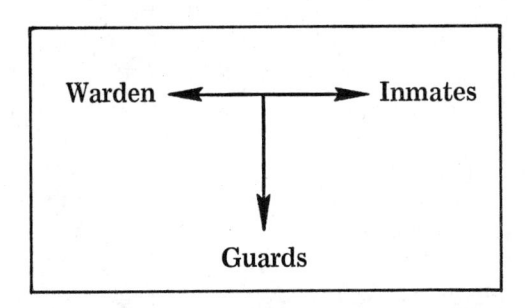

```
          Warden ◄────────► Inmates
                     │
                     ▼
                  Guards
```

Gill reversed this arrangement and set the pyramid on its base: the guards and inmates got together and told the warden what to do—with his consent. As the Norfolk council evolved, Gill recognized the defect in Osborne's plans and so modified the structure to include both guards and inmates in a common effort at problem solving. Thereafter, as Gill says, "It worked!"

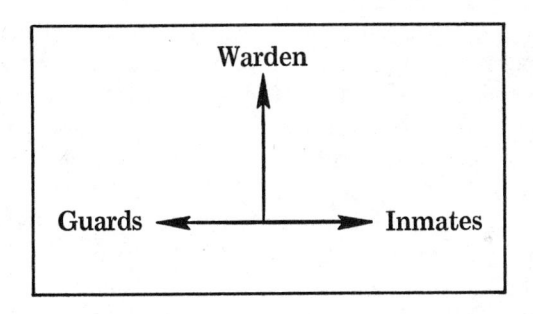

```
                  Warden
                     ▲
                     │
          Guards ◄───┴───► Inmates
```

Construction doubled after a joint committee of staff and inmates was involved in supervision and weekly planning of projects. During the five years of construction, 698 inmates were transferred to Norfolk. Of these, only 35 ran away, although both the minimum-custody section in the Oval and the Farm Colony outside the wall where 100 inmates were housed had no security perimeter.

Participatory Government

During the initial stages of construction, there had been a mutual sense of responsibility in the Oval. Staff members were an integral part of the system. But rapid expansion of the population and the staff and the absorption of other prisoners following the opening of the Wall destroyed the homey atmosphere that had prevailed in the Oval and resulted in both inmate and staff problems. The nostalgic attitude toward the "good old days" in the Oval was characteristic of a few old-timers among the inmates who felt the loss of personal contact with the superintendent who had had to delegate such contacts to subordinates, many of whom were new to prison work and to the Gill philosophy.

Gill's greatest initial impact was no doubt on the tractable, cooperative prisoners transferred from the state prison to Norfolk where, with a few exceptions, they uniformly demonstrated the ability to act responsibly when offered the opportunity of self-determination. The discovery that only tractable, cooperative prisoners could carry on at Norfolk was vital to the success of the Norfolk plan. Gill believed that some other plan would be needed in dealing with intractable and "defective" prisoners.

Gill's charisma enabled a highly qualified staff, imbued with the missionary zeal of the warden, to work together. Gill points with pride to the subsequent achievement of those who experienced the Norfolk experiment.

There is no statistical evidence regarding recidivism (reconviction) at Norfolk, but then that was never an objective of the plan. Gill's goal was merely to change prisoners' behavior. He rejected recidivism as a measure of the effectiveness of prison programs because of the many societal variables that influence failure after release from prison. Nonetheless, Gill demonstrated rather forcefully that the notion of a community prison can work with increased production, less tension, and a reduced number of institutional incidents. Unfortunately, the plan was cut short before further evaluation could resolve some of the questions that naturally developed with the experiment. Gill's own words serve best to sum up his ideas about the effectiveness of inmate participation in prison management:

> *Instead of letting it become the means whereby men can achieve anything they want, it is to be the means of teaching them what they should have. We have got to have certain standards of decency, order, quietness, industriousness, and patience which we must insist be the standards of the meanest, the most undesirable men in the place.*

On the other hand, with the proper plans, I think it has been demonstrated that the whole tone of an institution can be raised by this kind of participation, of exchange of ideas, of expression as contrasted with repression. We see men's faces light up and become normal, and that very atmosphere becomes a part of our therapy, because unless we meet that normal human feeling on the part of our men, we cannot do good casework with them. We cannot do the thing which we have set out to do—that is, to help them to help themselves.[42]

Gill was fired on April 5, 1934, after a political fight that lasted five months. He was simultaneously removed as director of research to evaluate the effects of his experiment.

Thomas O. Murton (b. 1928)

Winthrop Rockefeller became a candidate for governor of Arkansas in 1966. He expressed understandable indignation over a state police report, prepared in August of that year, which catalogued the cruelty practiced in the Arkansas prison system. He campaigned on a reform ticket and won election with a mandate from the electorate to end a century of decadence in Arkansas government.

Rockefeller took office in January 1967 and was promptly forced to deal with the prison issue. To avoid a revolt at Tucker prison farm, Rockefeller fired the superintendent (who had been threatening the inmates with a submachine gun) and three other staff members. This action left only 2 paid staff members and 48 inmate guards under the nominal control of a state police detachment in charge of this institution, which consisted of 300 inmates and occupied 4,500 acres of land. The state police were not allowed by the inmate guards to carry their weapons. By February 1967 there was a stalemate between the state administration and the inmates. The population agreed to nominal control by the police detachment but threatened to burn the prison to the ground and escape en masse if Governor Rockefeller did not keep his promise to reform the prison. More specifically, the inmates demanded the appointment of a reform warden.

A member of the faculty of Southern Illinois University at that time, I was called to Arkansas as a consultant to evaluate what was going on at Tucker. After investigation, my report to the governor

---

[42] Doering, p. 182.

noted the explosiveness of the situation, the total depravity of the system, and steps that could be taken for reform.

The challenge of the apparently impossible task to reform an archaic prison intrigued me, and I decided to apply for the job as superintendent. Since there were no other applicants and because Rockefeller needed to fulfill his campaign promise to "hire a professional penologist," my appointment to the position came in mid-February 1967.

My background included degrees from universities in Oklahoma, Alaska, and California in animal husbandry, education, and criminology respectively. Ironically, it was the former degree and not the latter that assured my appointment, because the superintendent at Tucker was responsible for extensive agriculture operations.

Since I was not interested in simply improving a decadent prison through traditional, evolutionary methods, I rejected the basic concept of the prison as an autocracy and set about to revolutionize it. As I later wrote:

> *Placing a man in prison to train him for a democratic society is as ridiculous as sending him to the moon to learn how to live on earth. The master can no more impose "rehabilitation" upon the slave than a teacher can inflict "education" upon the student.*
>
> *What is being suggested here is the substitution of legitimate power for the present illegitimate one. This new dimension in prison administration requires some courage and a great deal of perception by the reformer. To turn the prison around requires some skill and intuitive action which allows the formation of a new society. A new prison community must be brought into existence which is unique in that it is a coalition between the staff and inmates as opposed to the traditional adversary relationship. This new community cannot emerge spontaneously; it must be developed and nurtured.*
>
> *Truth is the cornerstone for mutual trust between staff and inmates which precedes change. The greater risk lies with the administrator because he must take the first step in establishing trust. In order to be meaningful, the opportunity to demonstrate responsibility must also include the possibility of demonstrating irresponsibility. Inherent in a true chance to succeed is the chance to fail.*[43]

---

[43] Tom Murton, "Inmate Self-Government," *University of San Francisco Law Review*, vol. VI, no. 1 (1971): 88-90.

As reported in Chapter 7, the first things my administration did were to abolish corporal punishment, eliminate torture, and remove sadistic guards.

> My sole authority was that granted by the Governor. Nevertheless, we were able in a few months to feed and clothe the inmates, hire competent staff, upgrade the agricultural programs, establish educational and vocational training programs, provide rational religious counseling service (to replace forced church attendance under the gun), eliminate corruption, move the trusties into the barracks, and practically eliminate the rapes and other homosexual attacks.[44]

Death row inmates were integrated into all activities of the institution including the new prison band. Dances were held at the prison, which were attended by Tucker inmates, their wives or girl friends, and the freeworld staff. Thus the first interracial dances held in Arkansas probably occurred at the Tucker prison farm.

The band even left the prison to play for patients at the state mental hospital. They were allowed to leave the prison escorted by an unarmed, ex-inmate who had been hired as a freeworld guard. Two members of the band were men from death row.

> By Christmas of 1967, a woman supervisor was able to work at the prison laundry, female employees ate in the prison dining hall, female teachers conducted classes inside the institution with no guard present, and the staff and their families attended programs, sitting with the general inmate population.[45]

These efforts were neither reckless nor foolhardy. They were all part of a plan to convey to the inmate some notion of self-worth. My observation was that "mutual degradation fosters mutual empathy," and I proceeded to integrate the black inmates from death row into the activities of the all-white Tucker population without incident. The dances, the female supervisors, and the female employees eating in the inmate dining room were all part of a plan to introduce a legitimate heterosexual element into the prison. The purpose of requiring staff (and the prison board) to eat on the mainline was to

---

[44] Tom Murton, "One Year of Prison Reform," *The Nation,* January 12, 1970, p. 13.

[45] Murton, *The Nation,* p. 14.

demonstrate that there would be no caste distinction between freeworld people and prisoners. The same purpose was served in hiring ex-convicts to work at the prison.

All these activities included the element of trust. It was essential that the administration first trust the inmates before they could be expected to demonstrate responsibility. Allowing condemned inmates to accompany the band outside the prison was a classic example of this trust. A warden cannot say "I trust you" and then, by refusing a request, demonstrate the opposite—at least, not for long.

The operation of the prison was carried out in the context of an open press policy. This was done to inform the public about the needs and benefits of reform, to eliminate suspicion of prison reform activities, and, as was hoped, to enable the press to ensure that the atrocities of the past would not occur again.

After gaining nominal control of the prison in the first few weeks, I sent out a request for assistance from staff I had worked with previously. The criteria for selection were "simply" that the individual must (1) have integrity, (2) have empathy for other people, and (3) subordinate his personal welfare to that of the inmates. To these factors was added one note: "It helps to have been fired before." The reasoning behind this qualification was that the person would thus have demonstrated the quality of his commitment by having been tested "at the wall."

Former staff came from Missouri, California, Alaska, and Australia. They did not come to Arkansas for the climate or the meager pay. And I am sure they did not come because they thought I was easy to work with. They came because they knew there was a challenge that, while appearing impossible, needed to be faced. Perhaps, too, they needed to feel needed.

At the critical point in our efforts to gain control of Tucker, several inmates with whom I had established confidence suggested using inmates to curtail the rash of escapes. The result was the immediate institution of the position of Inmate Sheriff as the chief law enforcement officer over the trusty guard force. More carefully, efforts were made to capitalize on inmate resources through representative government. Without advance notice, the entire population was moved into the auditorium where the election process and purposes were explained.

> [T]he 9th of March marked the first election for an Inmate Council at this institution. I had spent about two weeks in various contact with the inmates, telling them what the council could do, what the purpose of it is, what its functions

would be, and the type of men who should get on it. That is, those who would stand up to me and not bow down to my desires; those who would truly represent the men. They should not be operators but those sincerely interested in trying to see what they could do to improve the lot of the prison.

This is in furtherance of my stated assumption that "we," meaning inmates as well as the staff, need to combine efforts in order to improve the situation here.[46]

Although the creation of the farm council was the objective at that time, it was my feeling that "the process was more important than the product." Extraordinary precautions were taken in the time-consuming process of democratic action. It would have been simpler to have appointed the first council members. But as I later contended:

This process would have made all subsequent decisions suspect, and there was no assurance that the superintendent could select the proper inmates. Moreover, such a method would have negated an essential ingredient of the council: the inmates had to become involved personally in the process if they were to have any commitment to the outcome. Finally, since the representatives were chosen by the inmates, they had credibility, were accountable to the inmate body, and indirectly the general population was thus required to share the responsibility for managerial errors in the future.[47]

The creation of a farm council in Arkansas did not "just happen." As with other reforms at Tucker, it was a planned ingredient of reform that was encouraged at the time the idea "originated" with the inmates. I had been superintendent of five other institutions before going to Arkansas, and my notions about inmate involvement in managing the institution grew out of these experiences.

The Tucker farm council followed the usual pattern of dealing first with housekeeping problems and then moving to weightier issues. When a rash of escapes occurred during my third month as superintendent, the problem was taken to the council. Even though the escape of guards was a sign that the inmate power structure was being broken, the public became alarmed nonetheless.

---

[46] *Daily Log*, Tucker Prison Farm, Arkansas, March 10, 1967, pp. 35, 36.

[47] Murton, *San Francisco Law Review*, p. 94.

The inmates on the council suggested many changes in security procedures, including removal of some of the inmate guards from critical posts and a change in procedures that had become dysfunctional over the years. With a desire to change the prison and a belief in the superintendent, the council members had a vested interest in perpetuating the new administration. And the inmates had information not available to the administration. Consequently, they devised more appropriate rules for punishment in lieu of the then-abolished strap.

Within a month, it became apparent that most functions of the council centered around classification and discipline of inmates. To make the operation more efficient, the council was split in half. One inmate from each barracks and myself as superintendent constituted the Classification Committee, and the other three inmates and myself made up the Disciplinary Committee. In each case, as on the larger farm council, I retained the right to veto—but it was never used.

The Classification Committee concerned itself primarily with changing the inmate's custody grade or job assignment, which included deciding which inmates would become guards and carry rifles, shotguns, and pistols.

> *We did make some good assignments today, I believe, and I'm well pleased with the contributions of the Classification Committee. These inmate members know the man, can make valid recommendations, and I think that we are on the road to success in the area of control of the institution. If we can get adequate classification and adequate disciplinary measures taken, we can perhaps get control eventually. The fact that this is being done by inmates would send a chill down the back of any penologist but this is something that I want to experiment with here.*[48]

One request for a job and custody change appeared to be a good choice to me, but it was voted down unanimously by the inmate members of the committee. They explained that the inmate's mother had visited him the previous Sunday and had informed him that his wife was shacking up with his neighbor. Hence he wished to be reassigned to a position from which he could easily escape and solve his domestic problems. Such information is common knowledge among the inmates but is kept a secret from staff. By using such information through the council members, similar potential errors in classification were thereafter avoided.

---

[48] *Daily Log,* April 13, 1967, pp. 76–77.

The Disciplinary Committee met weekly to hear cases of infractions of the institutional rules. In many instances, inmates were found not guilty by reason of insufficient evidence or lack of intent. No distinction was made between complaints filed by freeworld staff or inmate staff members.

Committee members took personal interest in many of the cases. A 16-year-old inmate continued to act irresponsibly and was in constant difficulty with the administration. One committee member suggested that the recalcitrant inmate be placed on "parole" to him. I was initially opposed to the plan, but the committeeman argued that he had had some of the same problems when he was that age and thought he could change the boy's attitude. The committee voted to parole the inmate from the "hole" to the committeeman after the latter agreed to forfeit his job as barracks orderly if the plan did not work. The committeeman thus had a vested interest in the success of the parole plan. As I contended, "The quality of commitment is directly related to the amount of personal jeopardy." That was the last time the young inmate came before the Disciplinary Committee. He subsequently became a model prisoner, attained promotions in the prison, eventually was paroled, and has remained out of prison.

In spite of the fears expressed about the formation of the Farm Council, after it was fully operational there were no assaults, no fights, and only one escape during the last five months of my tenure at Tucker. (There had been 38 escapes during the first five months.) The single escape was a runaway from a forced homosexual advance.

No inmate classified minimum custody by the inmates ever escaped; no condemned prisoner ever attempted to escape even when outside the prison; no woman was ever assaulted, attacked, or insulted inside the prison; the illegitimate power structure was destroyed; no inmate in whom trust was placed ever violated that trust—as long as I was superintendent; freeworld staff, women, and children were free to mingle with the "convicts" without fear.

But "the most significant change was in the attitude of the inmates. Fear had disappeared, a new community had been created, and despair had been replaced by hope."[49]

The Tucker Farm Council could have been organized crime in lieu of the dictatorship previously in operation. Councilmen could have been elected through intimidation. They could have sold jobs and privileges to their fellow inmates. They could have manipulated the institution and the superintendent for their personal gain. All of

---

[49] Murton, *The Nation*, p. 14.

these things could have happened—but they did not. I later summarized the council experiment as follows:

> *In review, it should be noted that the first requisite for change was that the superintendent did not consider himself omnipotent. Second, the idea for change had to emerge from the inmates. Time was devoted to really involving the inmates in a legitimate self-help effort. Success fostered success and confidence. A by-product of the farm council was the redirection of traditional hostility from the superintendent to the inmate body. The sharing of decision making with the inmates carried with it the implicit collective responsibility for the decision made.*
>
> *Confidence was established through meticulous procedures and credibility. Flexibility was the custom. I did not last long enough to test the final phase wherein the superintendent becomes an advisor and relinquishes the veto power. The true success of inmate government can only thus be validated. The correlation with recidivism would require additional experimentation beyond the institution.*
>
> *What success we had in gaining control of the Tucker Prison Farm and revolutionizing it was the direct result of the efforts of inmates who dared to believe and make a commitment to reform the prison. The whole key is that it was done "with" them and not "to" them nor "for" them.*[50]

Because of the successful implementation of the reform plan at Tucker, I was promoted on January 1, 1968, to the superintendency of the larger institution at Cummins and placed in charge of the entire prison system. Five days later John Haley, chairman of the Prison Board, gave me notice of dismissal and 24 hours to vacate the farm.[51]

Summary

Several common threads characterized the few real reform efforts discussed here. Some would say that these men possessed integrity, empathy, and courage. Firmly committed to the welfare of the inmates, they jeopardized their positions and tenure. They were fair

---

[50] Murton, *San Francisco Law Review*, p. 101.

[51] Ellis MacDougall, then Commissioner of Correction for Connecticut and President of the American Correctional Association, commented: "If Merton [sic] were good, he would have stayed in Arkansas and introduced changes." *Arkansas Democrat*, March 17, 1969.

yet firm in their dealings with the inmates, and they were able to capture the faith and trust of the inmates with whom they developed many lasting relationships.

They shared a common philosophy that was strangely similar in many ways, although Maconochie and Osborne obviously could not have had any familiarity with the work or writings of Gill and myself. Gill was influenced by Osborne, but in 1968 I was only vaguely aware of the work of any of the three reformers. The common view was that the inmate is a human being with certain rights that should not be violated. Further, all believed that reformation cannot be imposed from the top but must emanate from within. The individual must come to have self-respect, confidence, and belief in his own worth. To this end, the iron hand of the prison dictatorship's discipline was rejected and replaced with an environment conducive to the development of responsibility.

These men subscribed to the thesis that man is more easily led than driven. They believed that fairness and honesty lead to mutual trust, which is the basis for developing responsibility. In this effort, the warden must take the first step. From trust comes respect and credibility and a vested interest in keeping the warden in power.

The prison was seen as a place to modify behavior, but only if it approximated the freeworld. That is, experience in meaningful decision making must be available in the prison if the inmate is to become involved in self-determination. In this respect, the warden must risk the possibility that the inmates will act irresponsibly in learning to act responsibly. Involving the inmates in the decision-making process forces them to share the responsibility for the decision made. Collective decision making results in meaningful participation and a coalition of interests toward common goals.

The reformers I have described each aggressively pursued an intuitive master plan to implement his "radical" innovations. The sequence, time lapse, and particulars of the plan were not rigid. Flexibility was a common characteristic that enabled the administrator to adjust to the changing situation as the need arose.

Each also demonstrated that "it works." At the very least, there was a reduction of tension, assaults, and escapes. At the best, there was a reduction in the recidivism rate. Each reformer momentarily succeeded in alleviating the oppressiveness of a brutal system and therein unwittingly sowed the seed of his personal failure.

It should be fairly clear that historical penology has provided us with at least a clue to the valid techniques of modifying the attitudes and behavior of the criminal offender. If so, why then have the appropriate programs not been put into effect?

Perhaps the answer to this question may be found in considering the fundamental issues involved in the dilemma of true prison reform: Is it not a peculiar logic which dictates that those institutional programs successful in achieving the stated objectives of the prison are doomed to fail, whereas those programs that fail in relation to the needs of the inmates tend to succeed in attaining longevity? Perhaps it is not a logic at all.

Reason would dictate that regardless of the treatment methods to be used, the democratic model would more likely be successful in preparing offenders for their ultimate return to a democratic society than the present totalitarian regime. But implicit in that statement is the inference that logic plays a predominant part in the correctional process. One example should suffice to raise some doubts.

We know that as a class, offenders sent to prison on a homicide conviction become model prisoners in the institution, their presence creates no problems, and they are the group least likely to recidivate. Yet we also know that they are the least likely to obtain parole and are most likely to serve more time than other offenders. They are not released simply because of an assumed negative reaction from a public that continues to fear the murderer.

A 1967 study of 1,303 persons convicted of willful homicide demonstrated that paroled murderers "actually present some of the best parole risks."[52] During the first year of parole, 91.25 percent had a favorable performance and 98.31 percent had no new major offense convictions.

A 1972 research project conducted by the National Council on Crime and Delinquency evaluated a five-year follow-up on parole behavior (between 1965 and 1969) of 6,908 convicted murderers. During the first year, 98.23 percent of the murderers were "successful" as compared to 91.01 percent of those convicted of all other offenses (see Tables 9-1 and 9-2). Nonetheless, the researchers observe:

> *Because, from the viewpoint of the general public, the murderer is perceived as the most dangerous type of offender, it might be supposed that murderers as a group present the worst risk on parole. In fact, this is simply not the case.*[53]

---

[52] *Uniform Parole Reports Newsletter,* NCCD, New York, December, 1972. See further: "Study Shows Paroled Murderers Succeed," *The Freeworld Times,* October 1973, p. 11.

[53] *Ibid.*

Rather than educate the public by demonstrating the lack of recidivism (and danger) by those convicted of willful homicide, correctional authorities defer to political expedience instead of the welfare of the inmate. It would appear logical from the evidence to release the murderer at an early date, but this does not happen. Therefore one must assume that although the process of keeping him locked up may be rational in a politically biased system, it is nonetheless illogical when considered in the light of the actual threat to the public.

Councils do not generally exist after the fashion of Tucker,[54] because such a notion is antithetical to the self-concept of the prison administrator and constitutes heresy in the annals of penology. The fact that it "works" and could become a forerunner for rejection of the medical treatment model and establishment of a more appropriate training institute for the freeworld is apparently immaterial. The primary concern of prison officials is personal and professional survival. And one way to assure it is to suppress freedom of expression.

Those factors that inhibit movements such as participatory management, in addition to those already listed, are the obstructionism of the professional associations, tokenism, and concern with creating the facade of reform. It is not possible to implement participatory management in one part of an institution as a "pilot project." The sickness of the prison is pervasive and permeates the entire organism. The cure must consequently deal with the whole prison. To do otherwise is to assure that the innovative program will be "swallowed" and effectively neutralized by the larger body.

Each community has its deviants. One can easily predict that if the world's population suddenly were reduced to two human beings, the master-slave relationship would still exist; one would seek to improve his lot by exploiting the other; and one would eventually succeed in declaring the other deviant. The prison community is no different. By dealing with deviance within the prison complex, the inmates can gain insight into the perplexities faced in the freeworld, gain empathy for the adjudicators, and, it is hoped, determine more effective means of controlling criminal behavior in themselves if not in others. At the very least, a realistic and humane philosophy brought to life in appropriate structures could create an atmosphere supportive of self-determination by the prison population. Previous experiments at self-government by inmates have all demonstrated

---

[54] This system was abolished at Tucker at the time of my dismissal in 1968.

TABLE 9-1. NEW MAJOR CONVICTIONS OR ALLEGATIONS WITH PRISON RETURN DURING THE FIRST YEAR AFTER PAROLE OF PERSONS IMPRISONED FOR WILLFUL HOMICIDE*

New Major Offense Conviction	Number	Percent
NONE	6,786	98.23
Willful Homicide	21	.30
Negligent Manslaughter	0	.00
Armed Robbery	12	.17
Unarmed Robbery	1	.01
Aggravated Assault	29	.42
Burglary	18	.26
Theft or Larceny, except Car	7	.10
Vehicle Theft	7	.10
Forgery, Fraud, Larceny by Check	3	.04
Other Fraud	0	.00
Forcible Rape	2	.03
Statutory Rape	1	.01
Other Sex Offenses, Juveniles	2	.03
Prostitution and Pandering	0	.00
Other Sex Offenses, not Juveniles	3	.04
Narcotics Violations	6	.09
Alcohol	2	.03
All Other Offenses	8	.12
TOTAL NEW MAJOR OFFENSE CONVICTIONS OR ALLEGATIONS	122	1.77
TOTAL	6,908	100.00

*This table gives a breakdown of the 122 cases who failed on parole and shows the offenses committed. Included in this table are persons who were convicted of new major offenses and persons who were returned to prison as technical violators in lieu of prosecution for a major offense (allegations).

positive results—a far better basis for a theory than a belief system based on mythology. Or is it possible, as stated by Patrick Davis[55] in the fall of 1970, that "there is no categorical proof that treating a person like a human being will help."

---

[55] Associate Superintendent of the Women's Reformatory, Shakopee, Minnesota.
   In a similar vein, Leslie Wilkins argues that there is no empirical evidence that flogging is not effective in reducing crime. See: Richard Korn, "Reflections on Flogging: An Essay Review of the Work of Leslie Wilkins and Tom Murton," *Issues in Criminology*, University of California, Berkeley, vol. 6, no. 2 (1971): 95.

Participatory Government

TABLE 9-2. NEW MAJOR CONVICTIONS OR ALLEGATIONS WITH PRISON RETURN DURING THE FIRST YEAR AFTER PAROLE OF PERSONS IMPRISONED FOR ALL OTHER OFFENSES*

New Major Offense Conviction	Number	Percent
NONE	72,192	91.01
Willful Homicide	106	.13
Negligent Manslaughter	26	.03
Armed Robbery	782	.99
Unarmed Robbery	237	.30
Aggravated Assault	351	.44
Burglary	2,268	2.86
Theft or Larceny, except Car	627	.79
Vehicle Theft	708	.89
Forgery, Fraud, Larceny by Check	852	1.07
Other Fraud	50	.06
Forcible Rape	129	.16
Statutory Rape	27	.03
Other Sex Offenses, Juveniles	65	.08
Prostitution and Pandering	0	.00
Other Sex Offenses, not Juveniles	44	.06
Narcotics Violations	356	.45
Alcohol	24	.03
All Other Offenses	478	.60
TOTAL NEW MAJOR OFFENSE CONVICTIONS OR ALLEGATIONS	7,159	9.03
TOTAL	79,322	100.00

*Major offense convictions with return to prison during the first year after release on parole of persons imprisoned for all offenses other than willful homicide amounted to 5,238 parolees out of the study population of 79,322, or 6.73 percent. For willful homicide parolees, the results came to 82 persons convicted of a new major offense during this same period out of a total willful homicide study population of 6,908, or a new major conviction rate of 1.19 percent.

10

An Alternative Correctional Regime

> Far best is he who knows all things.
> Good, he who hearkens when men counsel right.
> But, he who neither knows, nor lays to heart
>   another's wisdom,
> Is a useless wight.
>   —ARISTOTLE

An alternative for the current penology system must reflect a real change in policies as well as in physical structures. In fact, a philosophical renaissance in penological thought must *precede* innovations in structural changes if the behavior of offenders is to be modified positively. The following principles justify that a radical change of the prison must take place in order to make it harmonious with the democratic model of the free society. Although many of these principles are neither radical nor revolutionary in concept, they quickly become so when contrasted with the penological philosophy at the root of current prison practices and traditions.

1. *The Gradualism Theory.* This theory of prison reform must be relegated to its rightful place in mythology and must be replaced with revolutionary concepts, facilities, and strategies.

2. *The Medical-Dictatorial Model.* Since regeneration emerges only from within the individual and cannot be imposed by the "regenerators" on the "regeneratees," the traditional medical and totalitarian models for reforming human behavior must be abandoned as being inherently erroneous in conceptualization as well as in application.

3. *The "Criminal" Type.* Under the present criminal justice system,[1] any realistic conceptualization of the criminal offender must be predicated on the awareness that the institutional population probably does not differ significantly in psychological typology from a cross section of the larger free society.

4. *The Right to Dignity.* An individual convicted by the criminal courts and sentenced to a correctional or penal institution should not ipso facto lose his identity as a human being. Although the courts and the prison have a legal right to strip an offender of his freedom, this does not morally justify the parallel practice of stripping him of his dignity as a person.

5. *Correctional Priorities.* Correctional treatment, to be effective, must (*a*) take precedence over the requirements for inmates to reduce the cost of incarceration by producing goods and services; (*b*) discontinue the master-slave relationship that perpetuates the existing system; and (*c*) become the motivation and justification for all acts done in the name of regeneration.

6. *The Goal of Regeneration.* Through the use of appropriate techniques (possibly not yet defined), restoring the criminal offender to society as a productive, functional member can be achieved in the majority of cases. It is a mutually beneficial goal for both society and the offender and, therefore, justifies revolutionizing the prison and the criminal justice system.[2]

7. *The Responsibility Model.* The democratic model must be substituted for the present despotic one in prison management. This is an essential consideration in order for the inmate to be used as an agent of change. With rare but notable exceptions, his potential energy has lain dormant from time immemorial, yet this energy can be released if he is trusted to act responsibly.

---

[1] Concerning our current method of dealing with deviance, most citizens probably would agree that it does not constitute a "system"; many would contend that it does not provide "justice"; and some would even suggest that it *is* "criminal."

[2] It may be functional to train the offender in "survival techniques," such as methods of avoiding conflict with the criminal justice system, when modification of behavior proves to be neither feasible nor attainable. Perhaps it is justifiable to help him define a satisfactory, attainable role in the free society, explain routes to success, and provide tools that will equip him to conform to the free society.

Admittedly this approach does not deal with issues involving change of society, which is beyond the scope of the responsibility or, indeed, the power of the institution. Yet it is justified if it enables the ex-offender to evade further criminal sanctions. Societal changes, although needed, must be addressed as a separate issue within the global efforts to bring about universal change.

> **ON CRUELTY**
> "Cruel punishments have an inevitable tendency to produce cruelty in the people."
> —*Samuel Romilly*

Personnel

The first consideration in reforming the prison must be directed toward personnel selection instead of new building construction. This first radical departure from custom will immediately come into conflict with the traditional explanation for the failure of prisons to rehabilitate—that is, lack of adequate facilities.

The major criteria for personnel selection designed to foster a positive change in inmate behavior include (1) personal integrity, (2) concern for others, and (3) real commitment. Integrity is the glue that binds the substance of reform movements together. Without it, otherwise noble and meaningful programs and activities become nothing more than insignificant gestures. Genuine compassion, empathy, and concern for the inmates are necessary to provide a positive motivational context for, and explanation of, officer actions. As Paul wrote to the church at Corinth: "Though I speak with the tongues of men and of angels, and have not love, I am become as sounding brass, or a tinkling cymbal."[3] And finally, a deep, personal commitment to the reform movement allows no compromise of integrity. In addition, it requires a willingness on the part of the officer to subordinate personal goals of tenure, promotion, retirement, recognition, and other indicators of professional "success" for the welfare of the inmates and thus for the larger society as well.

Unfortunately, the reality is that personal goals *do* take precedence over inmate welfare for the overwhelming majority of correctional workers. This sad fact was corroborated by Warden Raymond Gaffney of the Kansas State Penitentiary:

MURTON: *You're not going to change a guy's integrity by giving him more money.*

GAFFNEY: *What an asinine statement! There's only one motivation [for going into prison work], unless you're a*

---

[3] I Corinthians 13:1.

> *missionary, and that is to support your family—dollars and cents.*[4]

Warden Gaffney inadvertently hit upon an essential ingredient of real prison reform movements (dedication) while also revealing a prime motive for entering the field of penology (income). The participants in real reform must view their work as a *missionary* endeavor. If they accept the position for reasons other than doing what needs to be done for the welfare of the inmates, then they have placed a price tag on integrity and have indicated they are deficient in that area.

> *Commitment without personal jeopardy is a meaningless intellectual exercise.*

Personal jeopardy becomes the single factor that assures credibility with the inmate population. The reformer must be willing to risk failure in order to achieve success. He who attempts to be all things to all men succeeds only in becoming nothing to anyone. The correctional administrator who views himself as a mediator between dissidents who hold disparate views of "reform" is destined for professional oblivion while also aborting the reform movement.

Any thorough study of the history of reform movements in penology suggests that those programs which succeed in relation to the inmates' welfare are destined to fail because they pose a threat to personnel. On the other hand, programs designed to assure the continued tenure of the pseudo-reformer apparently fail in relation to inmates. The traditional operation of the prison is antithetical to the institution's stated goals and purposes. The Bible contends that one cannot serve both God and man; neither can the reformer serve both the official reformer and the inmates. The criteria for "success" defined by each group are mutually exclusive, and one presumably inhibits the other's goals.

One might conjecture that "success" (in the traditional sense) ultimately leads to "failure." And those programs that "fail" (from the power structure's point of view) succeed when evaluated from the inmates' perspective. Thus success is gained through failure, and failure is achieved through success.[5]

---

[4] Commentary of Warden Raymond J. Gaffney of the Kansas State Penitentiary in response to statement of Tom Murton. *Wichita Eagle*, Wichita, Kansas, November 30, 1971.

[5] Christ could have reasoned, "If I pursue my present ideology, I am doomed because I am on a collision course with the official power structure. Perhaps I should compromise by remaining silent on those matters that pose a

Success is assured as long as failure is not considered a possible alternative.

To understand this apparent paradox, the real reformer must redefine his terminology. He defines personal "success" as maximum use of his intellect, training, and courage to correct an intolerable wrong. "Failure," then, is seen as falling short of making a total commitment toward this end. Tenure, wealth, recognition, promotion, and retirement thus become irrelevant. Personal integrity must be the primary consideration.

Further, personnel must really believe in and practice the religious ethic of service to others, and this belief must take priority over service to self. It is only through demonstrating morality that credibility, rapport, and trust can be established between staff and inmates—the basic foundation on which reform efforts are erected. If the staff does not possess these attributes, formal education, in-service training, staff meetings, manuals, organization charts, brochures, programs, institutes, activities, and facilities are irrelevant considerations. In fact, such considerations may actually inhibit real reform even under ideal conditions. As others have observed, positive programs can exist apart from structure of any kind.[6] It does not necessarily follow that moving a program into a "better" structure will enhance its potency.

Programs are more a product of personnel than of property.

The officer who demonstrated the most consistent success in assisting the positive changes of the attitudes of inmates, in my experience, is one who never completed the fourth grade, could barely read, and had some difficulty writing his name. Yet he was able to develop meaningful interpersonal relationships with the majority of inmates, and these are the relationships that are fundamental to any overall prison reformation.

---

threat to the established order. Thus I can succeed in forming a religious reform movement within the system and one day we will achieve peace on earth. Because if I am not here on earth, I cannot change conditions."

Had he fallen victim to such fallacious reasoning, he no doubt would have founded some form of earthly kingdom as his followers envisioned. Yet I suspect that in the process he would have "lost" in the long run because he would have forfeited his long-range mission for temporary gains. And it is likely that even those modest accomplishments would have been neutralized by the emperor.

From the perspective of Christianity, it was essential that he "fail" (to save his own life) in order that he "succeed" (in expiating the sins of man).

[6] Austin MacCormick of the Osborne Association contends that "you can have a good program in an old barn."

Although one cannot generalize that illiteracy is a prerequisite for becoming a "treater," it can be suggested that there may be little correlation between education and treatment effectiveness. Going further, one could argue that education may only deepen the schism already existing between the convict world and the "treatment" world of the "professional" staff.

If interpersonal relationships and communication are the heartbeat of real reform, it is not difficult to see that the diploma on the wall, the desk barricade, the white shirt and tie, the use of social science jargon, and the other artificial artifacts (which only reinforce the caste system, the medical model, and the ego of the treater) can quite effectively, if unintentionally, block any meaningful rapport between counselor and inmate.

Organizational Structure

In focusing on the importance of human attitudes and relationships it is not my intent to view the prison in a vacuum and pretend that personnel are all that is significant in achieving prison reform. Nor is it my intent to discount the importance of broader considerations for bringing about social changes. Certainly the democratic prison model can flourish only within the context of a larger, coordinated correctional system that provides a supportive environment. The philosophy of that environment must be to emphasize continuity of treatment along with a variety of correctional alternatives.[7]

Apart from the main facility described in a subsequent section, some of these correctional alternatives could include other regional facilities, intermediate institutions, farms, and camps. They could provide a variety of services as the reorganized corrections agency makes the transition to private control. County jurisdictions could be required to contract with the state correctional system to care for inmates from lower courts.[8] This procedure would eliminate a dual system of institutions and the attendant deficiencies of county work farms, such as inadequate medical, food, and other services, as well as a lack of useful activities. Facilities could provide agricultural training in regions where men will be returning to the farm. The products of the enterprise would be used for food consumption at other institutions.

---

[7] That is, the coordination of probation, institutional, and parole services in a statewide, single agency with a consistent (but flexible) correctional philosophy and policy.

[8] Both Connecticut and Alaska corrections agencies operate state jails.

Other components could be residential units for released inmates in the freeworld community when no other facilities are available. These could be operated by ex-offenders and, whenever possible, the offender could be expected to pay for the service. This would help to increase his interest in becoming self-supporting, as well as enhance his commitment in making his new life actually work. There is some merit in the concept that the effect of treatment is certainly enhanced if the client has both an emotional and a financial investment in the success of the program.

Such an alternative system can be envisioned as one that exercises control only as necessary for it to function. The services provided within the correctional agency would not only be modifications of the presently accepted ones of probation and parole, but would also include many other community institutions. It would also supervise all state correctional or penal institutions and support local innovative programs. Institutionalization would generally be a last resort and would provide a wider environmental flexibility, such as treating male, female, juvenile, and adult within the same facility. The option of contracting with private business for care and custody of state wards would be available.

An Alternative Correctional System

The advantages of a privately operated correctional system are readily apparent, numerous, and significant. As Professor Korn contends,[9] the rich have always had an alternative criminal justice system available to them. He cites the advertisements in the *New York Times* for "summer camps" and military academies as examples of treatment facilities for the wayward youth of the well-to-do. Korn argues that this inequity, which depends on financial resources, should be rectified by making the alternatives of the rich available to the poor.

There should be little dispute that private industry (which is based on a profit motive) would be more efficient, thereby more effective in the correctional enterprises, than governmental bureaucracies (which are organized for self-perpetuation). Contractual arrangements with businesses would minimize the extent to which finances, buildings, personnel, purchasing, and in some cases the law inhibit the goals of penology.

Any administrator who works within a governmental structure is painfully aware of the vagaries of budget considerations that directly

---

[9] Richard Korn, remarks delivered before the Conference of Criminal Justice, Annapolis, Maryland, June 5, 1971.

affect the entire agency. He must make his pilgrimage annually to the mecca of money to beg for funding. Thus, to a large extent, programs and activities, for better or for worse, are contingent upon the whims of the legislators as well as superiors in the executive branch. As the Wizard of Id said, "He who has the gold makes the rule." To be sure, it would be necessary to maintain fiscal accountability even under a contractual system. However, establishing a flat daily rate for care and custody of wards for a period of five years, for example, would provide flexibility within that amount to expend funds without other approval from some bureaucrat.

If the contractor was unable to reduce recidivism or demonstrate some other tangible measure of improvement over the state-operated system, then the contract would not be renewed. Thus there would be a financial incentive to produce a better product—a condition that does not now exist in state systems. In fact, a reduction of the prison population is now antithetical to the objectives of state personnel. In effect, such a trend would threaten their employment, which depends on maintaining a large, incarcerated criminal population. The following examples are cases in point.

Because of a declining prison population, California corrections authorities planned to close a facility at Susanville, located in Lassen County, in 1973. Guards formed a "Save Our Center" citizens' committee to emphasize the economic loss to the community that would result from the institutional closing. In April of 1973, the corrections department, bowing to pressure, reversed the earlier decision and announced that the facility would become a prisoner vocational training facility. Jennie Kamps, a Lassen County employee, commented:

> *I personally think the vocational training center is a good thing. As a taxpayer I don't like seeing something become obsolete. Besides, Lassen County needs the revenue.*[10]

On the other side of the continent at about the same time, a similar activity was experienced in relation to juveniles:

> *In New York state, the legislature passed a law forbidding putting nondelinquent children in jail. The population of the jails dropped so drastically that 40 percent of the guards were found unneeded and were laid off.*

---

[10] *The Freeworld Times*, Minneapolis, Minnesota, June–July 1973, p. 9.

> *A delegation of guards went to Albany to protest. The legislature repealed the law. The kids were once again jailed and the guards all got their jobs back.* [11]

In July 1972, guards of the Brushy Mountain State Prison in Tennessee went on strike to protest the firing of a guard who had cursed the warden. Governor Winfield Dunn called in the state police to maintain security, fired the 170 striking guards, and transferred the 397 inmates to other state institutions. Thus began a lengthy controversy in Tennessee corrections.

The Republican governor had vowed to provide prison reform and had urged regionalization of institutions, building of newer, smaller facilities, and phasing out of the archaic institutions. The Brushy Mountain facility was built before the turn of the century on 4,900 acres for the purpose of using prisoners to mine coal. Governor Dunn contended that the institution was obsolete because inmates no longer mine coal, because the physical plant is archaic, and because it is located in a remote portion of the state.

Although three stabbings were attributed to overcrowding in other facilities that resulted from the forced transfer of the Brushy Mountain inmates, it has been demonstrated that the correctional system can get along quite well without the closed institution. Governor Dunn planned to channel operating funds from Brushy Mountain to two new regional centers that he proposed to build. However, pressure was brought to bear on the governor to reopen the Brushy Mountain institution. It was pointed out that the town of Petros consisted of only 1,000 inhabitants and was in danger of becoming a ghost town because the prison was its only industry. In addition to the $1.3 million direct annual payroll, townspeople also received money for produce, equipment, and supplies sold to the prison.

In response to the situation, Representative Thomas Burnett (who represented the district in which the prison was located) introduced legislation requiring the reopening of Brushy Mountain. The Democratic majority on the State Building Commission threatened to withhold approval of plans for the new regional facilities unless Brushy Mountain was reopened. Democrats in the legislature also threatened to block money for the proposed regional facilities.

On January 18, 1973, submitting to political pressure, Governor Dunn offered to reopen the prison and to rehire all but two of the

---

[11] From the August 1972 prison newspaper *Eye Opener*, Oklahoma State Penitentiary, MacAlester, as reported in *The Freeworld Times*, Minneapolis, Minnesota, September–October 1972, p. 2.

170 guards who went on strike. According to Dunn, "The Brushy Mountain institution can serve a useful, although not essential, function for a limited period of two years."[12]

A budget revision was necessary to raise the maintenance budget from $300,900 to a full operational budget of $2.5 million. The move might be "useful" in bargaining with the legislature for regional centers, but one wonders whether it is worth the cost of $6,250 per inmate per annum for this regression to the archaic facility.

Once again the proclivity is demonstrated for maintaining institutions *not* for the benefit of the inmates, but for the advantage of the staff who have a vested interest in continued incarceration of offenders and for the freeworld people who profit from the misery of their fellowman.

Changing the physical facilities represents one of the slowest processes in corrections because of the time it takes for an idea to go from conceptualization to fruition. All too often, once a need is presented to the legislature, debated, and finally approved, years have passed. Subsequent delays are a result of state architects imposing notions about construction that often are unenlightened and expensive.[13] In a private system, the administrator would have the flexibility of renting, leasing, buying, or building to provide the best facility at the earliest time for the intended programs.

In personnel selection, private industry is far more efficient than government agencies. In general, employment is contingent on producing a product that will increase the financial rewards to the organization. The civil service system that controls employment in most state agencies is probably the single greatest inhibitor of change. Although it was conceived of as a protection against political influence and a vehicle for proficiency, it has become what it sought to correct.

In the correctional field, most job descriptions assume a correlation between requisites and duties. Unfortunately, such correlations have never been demonstrated. Although certain tests do eliminate candidates with what is assumed to be obvious inferiorities, they may also remove from consideration those who might be most effective. Similarly, civil service is no guarantee that one cannot be removed arbitrarily. The end product is a system that fosters mediocrity and punishes innovation. What is being argued here is that a civil service

---

[12] *Chattanooga Daily Times*, Chattanooga, Tennessee, January 19, 1973.

[13] The initial construction phase of the Adult Conservation Camp in Alaska was built by staff and inmates for some $12,000 less than the state architecture fee alone would have been.

system cannot provide protection for the reformer, since he can be removed for political expediency. It does not assure that the "best" employees will be hired, and it is likely to entrench the incompetent. In a private system, on the other hand, there would be sufficient flexibility to hire and fire as the needs of the organization dictate.

State purchasing requirements have been designed to eliminate kickbacks, to obtain a high-quality product for the best price, and to enhance the free enterprise system through competitive bidding. However, the bidding procedure often is so slow and so cumbersome that needs must be predicted three to six months in advance. To anticipate what supplies will be needed in the future is not always possible when one is operating an institution with a fluctuating population. Also, the competitive bidding system does not remove the possibility of bidders collaborating to fix prices. Furthermore, my personal experience has been that items often cost more on bid than they do on open purchase. The private operator can make purchases as needed, take advantage of low prices by selective buying, and obtain the most suitable product.

There is more legal flexibility in the regulation of privately operated facilities than there is in their state counterparts. Since many offenders have an alcohol problem, some administrators have suggested that consumption of alcohol should be allowed on the premises of halfway houses, for example, so that the inmate could learn to deal responsibly with it. State-operated facilities, however, are prohibited from this option because laws forbid alcoholic consumption at state institutions. Similarly, other regulations promulgated by departments of correction are very restrictive and continue the adverse environment of the traditional institution. Restrictions against housing opposite sexes in the same facility, combining juveniles and adults, allowing conjugal visits, and lessening custodial considerations are common in state facilities but could largely be minimized in private operations.

Community control of the criminal offender by citizens is hardly new. As mentioned earlier, probation was first instituted under private supervision. In Scandinavian countries, probation and parole are largely the responsibility of private citizens. In London, law enforcement was a responsibility of the citizenry prior to the creation of the police force in 1829. In fact, there are more recent precedents. Litton Industries was awarded a contract for establishing regional centers in various parts of the United States in the mid-1960s for care and treatment of juvenile offenders. The project was something less than successful—not for lack of business management techniques but because the contractors patterned their treatment model after the official system to which they were supposed to create an alternative.[14]

Although a private correctional system should not be considered as a panacea for present ills, there is little question that its structure would provide great advantages for implementing innovative programs. It remains a debatable issue whether the programs, in fact, would be different or would take on the characteristics of existing models. Nonetheless, the idea seems to have merit, is within the realm of feasibility, and should be tried if for no other reason than it cannot possibly be worse than what now exists.

The Village

The model that I suggest for the principal institutional complex can best be described as a village. Whatever the final form of the village plan, whether it be based on the town square or some other concept, it would be a product of the design, concepts, and energies of those who would inhabit it—the inmates and staff within a secure perimeter.

Using the town square concept for purposes of discussion, the design would focus group activities in the center while reserving the periphery for residential and industrial activities (refer to the two diagrams). The town square would consist of a complex that would serve as courthouse, town meeting hall, and auditorium surrounded

THE VILLAGE SQUARE (SERVICE CENTER)

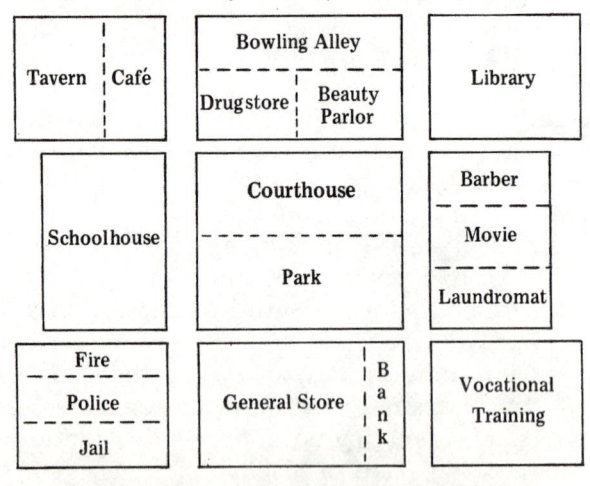

Tavern / Café	Bowling Alley / Drugstore / Beauty Parlor	Library
Schoolhouse	Courthouse / Park	Barber / Movie / Laundromat
Fire / Police / Jail	General Store / Bank	Vocational Training

[14] Minnesota provides for the commitment of offenders to the commissioner of corrections rather than to the department. This distinction enables the

by a park for less structured activities. Most of the group social activities would take place here.

Surrounding the square would be the central business district consisting of individual establishments providing the usual variety of goods and services. A medical clinic would provide services of doctors, dispense drugs from a drugstore or pharmacy, and possibly make referrals to the hospital. Other facilities might include a barber shop, beauty parlor, public library, laundromat, restaurant, cinema, bowling alley, and space for other recreational activities. A public safety complex housing police, fire, and sanitation personnel, a schoolhouse, and a general store would also be necessary. Vocational training programs would be housed in facilities located near the school facilities for easy access and support. Ideally, the majority of these enterprises would be operated by the inmates.

It would probably be necessary to construct a jail for temporary detention for those who pose a physical threat to the "free" prison community or who can be treated "locally" without referral to the institution's "prison."[15] However, alternatives to the bail system might be explored. In fact, alternatives to incarceration could be devised.

The next district would include prison industries housed separately according to their function. These industries would provide full employment at wages competitive with those in the freeworld. From his earnings, the inmate would be expected to contribute to his own support, self-improvement, support of any outside dependents, payment of fines imposed by the court, and restitution to the victim of his crime. The implications are obvious. An inmate would be rewarded financially for efforts that would reinforce the work-ethic value system for him when he returns to the freeworld.[16] Not only

---

administrator to contract with private groups for correctional services. However, the department has been reluctant to release control and through a variety of techniques has managed to retain sufficient managerial influence to obviate the advantages of a private, alternative system—in spite of the fact that the department is ostensibly committed to transferring state wards to private control.

[15] It is interesting to note that inmates sometimes refer to the "hole" as the "jail." The old isolation unit at the state prison at Lansing, Kansas, was a separate structure that looked like a jail and was thus known by both staff and inmates. It appears to be a social phenomenon for outcasts to form a new community that in turn creates an outgroup that may also in turn continue the deviant labeling and impose sanctions to set apart the "bad guys" from the "good guys."

[16] That is, being a productive, contributing member is equated with good citizenship in our society. Also, it is the only generally legitimate route to traditional goals of acquisition of material goods and upward mobility.

would he be reducing the costs of his incarceration, but he would also be compensating for his crime by making restitution to the victim and thus becoming involved psychologically in "undoing" the act.

THE VILLAGE COMMERCIAL AND RESIDENTIAL DISTRICTS

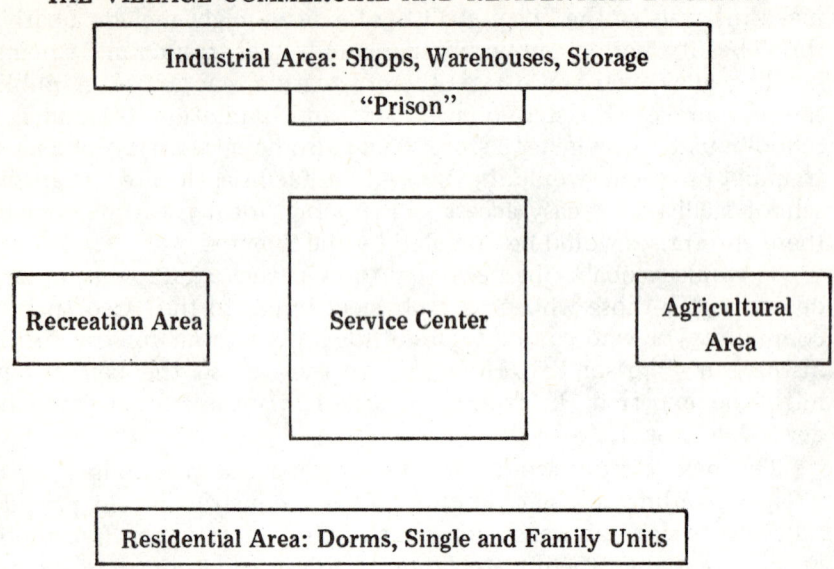

```
┌─────────────────────────────────────────────────┐
│    Industrial Area: Shops, Warehouses, Storage  │
└─────────────────────────────────────────────────┘
              ┌─────────────┐
              │  "Prison"   │
              └─────────────┘

┌──────────────┐   ┌──────────────┐   ┌──────────────┐
│              │   │              │   │              │
│  Recreation Area │   Service Center │   Agricultural│
│              │   │              │   │     Area     │
└──────────────┘   │              │   └──────────────┘
                   └──────────────┘

     ┌─────────────────────────────────────────────┐
     │ Residential Area: Dorms, Single and Family Units │
     └─────────────────────────────────────────────┘
```

The "suburbs" would be the residential areas where young and adult offenders would be housed separately (for the most part), but the sexes would be integrated in as many activities as possible both there and throughout the town.

Farther out might be minimum-custody facilities in the form of single-family housing units. These units would be desirable because at some point in the program it might be mutually beneficial for the inmate's family to join him. The inmate would be required to pay rent and utilities for this housing as well as to maintain the premises. The design and construction of new housing, as well as all other facilities within the complex, would be done jointly by inmates and staff.

It is probable that a certain percentage of the village community might pose a real physical threat to that community. In such a case, the traditional response is likely to arise in the form of demands for a "prison." Such a facility would be warranted for those who show high potential for escape or violence. This unit might be structured as a small maximum-custody facility

An Alternative Correctional Regime

wherein a variety of industrial and other activities would occupy the inmate. It would be interesting to speculate on the possibilities of developing new alternatives or techniques in reintegrating the "convict" back into the prison village.

An example of a village setting can be seen in Sweden, where prison officials acquired a lumberjack village as an experimental home for prisoners and their families in 1972. This "institution" is located in a forest 25 miles from the nearest town. The cost of the village, Gruvberget, was $100,000; another $100,000 was spent on refurnishing the homes. An additional $10,000 was used to clear away undergrowth to improve the aesthetic appearance of the site.

The focus of inmate rehabilitation is on his total family. Each family has its own fully equipped three-room house for use during the inmate's one-month stay in the village. Also provided are a grocery store, variety store, and library. Job training courses are provided during the mandatory three-hour morning study sessions.

According to Claes Amilon, an official of the Swedish National Correction Administration:

> *We believe in this idea of bringing the inmate, his wife and children together in something resembling normal everyday life.... While the inmate and his family live in Gruvberget the idea is that they will learn more about the way our society functions.* [17]

The program that opened in the spring of 1972 was designed to accommodate 20 inmates during the first year. Only inmates who have successfully returned from prison furloughs are eligible. "If the inmates—or guests as we might call them—want to leave the village for visits to the town nearby or something like that, the warden will give them permission unless there are very special reasons to deny it." [18]

New Delhi authorities report an even more innovative and extensive program for dealing with 200,000 prisoners in India. By mid-summer 1972, some 4,000 prisoners were reportedly housed in unwalled institutions. The largest one, Sitargani, contains 1,500 inmates on a 4,500-acre farm. At the other extreme, an unspecified number of inmates live and work "virtually without supervision" on ten acres of ground at Jaipur.

---

[17] "Sweden Tries Family Living for Prisoners," *Atlanta Journal and Constitution*, Atlanta, Georgia, April 2, 1972.

[18] *Ibid.*

An Alternative Correctional Regime

Prisoners are given a 15-day food ration and a portion of land when sent to the institution. Inmates can borrow money from a "prisoners' council" to meet farming expenses; the loan must be repaid after the harvest. Prisoners are allowed to market their produce in nearby villages and can sell their labor on other farms. The inmate's family is allowed to live with him on the farm and work in the fields if they choose.

Most of the inmates selected for this program (60 percent) are serving ten years or more, yet escapes have reportedly been very few from these open institutions. Only one out of four released prisoners gets into further difficulty with the law, a statistic considered lower than those released from the traditional prisons. Officials concede that the experiment has been conducted on "an unscientific basis" but observe that in addition to reduced escapes and less recidivism there is "an improvement in the health, work habits, and general behavior of the prisoners."[19]

In Illinois, the Vienna Correctional Center is a minimum-security institution that was designed on the village concept to foster "trust and responsibility."

> The hub of the Vienna complex of 19 buildings is the Town Square around which all the center's activities revolve. Surrounding the square are residential dormitories, the library, the dining hall, twin chapels, and a cluster of one-story buildings... which house the commissary, the barber shop, classrooms, and the music room.[20]

The Vienna institution was conceived as a maximum-custody facility. After one of seven housing units was built in 1966, Vernon Houseright, then associate warden, was able to stop further construction and obtain a commitment for creation of a "community prison." The philosophy of this institution is not the formation of a coalition between staff and inmates in a prison society, nor is it integration of inmates into the freeworld community through programs such as education, work release, or furloughs. Warden Houseright sees the function of the prison as a community center that can be used by freeworld people as well as corrections personnel. Thus he encourages freeworld people to attend church services along with the inmates in the prison chapels.

---

[19] "Open Jails Give Convicts Right Climate," *Los Angeles Times*, May 28, 1972.

[20] *Pontiac Flag News*, Illinois State Penitentiary, Pontiac, April 1974, p. 5.

The local junior college offers classes at the institution for inmate and freeworld students jointly. Inmates work with freeworld medical technicians in operating a rescue ambulance service. There is an umpire school at the institution that prepares inmates to provide services for Little League ball games.

Through joint participation, learning, and exchange of services, Warden Houseright hopes to break down barriers between the two groups, maximize the institution facilities, and develop responsibility on the part of the inmate by his contributing to others. As of May 15, 1974, the institution became coed, and this move should eventually make the Vienna facility an even more "normal" environment.

Construction costs for such facilities should be reduced considerably because of less reliance on concrete and steel to restrain the inmates.[21] Costs could be further reduced by allowing the inmates and staff to design and build as much as possible of the new complex.

Moreover, no new facilities would be required at all if an abandoned town could be acquired. Thus a new community could in fact be created. The town residents could conduct business, attempt to attract industry, and organize the prison community as a functional unit of the free society. This type of physical setting would probably be more conducive to family habitation than facilities artificially designed for that purpose. There would be minimal need for helping inmates make the transition to the community because they will have been living in a similar community, from an organizational standpoint, throughout their period of "incarceration."

Patterning an institution after the design and operation of a corresponding freeworld community is not a particularly new idea. The Bolshevo Colony in Russia, Las Islas Marias in Mexico, and the Davao Penal Colony in the Philippine Islands are institutions that purportedly approximate the freeworld in these respective societies. Professor Howard Gill speaks of such a prison community existing in China 3,000 years ago.

The ways in which people would be "committed" to prison communities modeled on freeworld communities could also differ from current methods. Voluntary commitment is also a possibility. For example, if a parolee felt the need for support or closer supervision, he could simply drive to the "town" and establish residence. In some ways, such a town could be a "City

---

[21] However, it cost $24,000 per man to construct the 20 buildings at Vienna to house and serve a population of 500.

of Refuge" where the criminal offender could withdraw from society temporarily until he is ready to cope with the free world once again without suffering the negative effects of criminal sanctions.

An illustration of how such a concept works in the animal world underscores the advantages that are inherent in such communities. An 1,800-acre wild animal park, an extension of the San Diego Zoo, was opened in May 1972. In this "institution," the animals run free in a habitat approximating their natural environment while the staff and visitors are confined to a small train that meanders through the park. Perimeter security consists of natural barriers that prevent the escape of the "inmates." Interactions between individual animals as well as between different species occasionally result in conflict—just as they do in the freeworld. Equilibrium in this synthetic world is established when the balance of nature is maintained through the law of survival. Because of adequate territorial space, however, the wild animals are able to maintain a "flight distance" or safe space separating them from their potential enemies. According to park officials:

> *In the conventional zoo, with limited space, caged animals cannot respond to this basic instinct and are thus forced to live a pathologically disoriented existence.*[22]

The vigor of the animals, the healthy adaptation to this artificial community, and the benefits of psychological freedom have all contributed to lessened violence and minimal pathology. If these animals or their descendents are ever returned to the African jungle and plain, there will be no need for a "halfway house" to help them make the transition from the institution to the freeworld.

The reproduction of nine endangered species for the first time in captivity attests to the value of this innovation in contrast with the conventional zoo (prison) where the animals (inmates) are confined in cages (cells). Animal husbandrymen long ago discovered that chickens become cannibalistic when confined in limited space. Psychologists have demonstrated the fatal aggressive behavior resulting from the overcrowding of mice. Zoo keepers have now rejected the existing, traditional model, have substituted a revolutionary (yet logical) concept, and have

---

[22] Edward Jay Epstein, "San Diego's Wild Animal Suburb," *Travel & Leisure*, American Express Publishing Corp., New York, October–November 1973, p. 66.

demonstrated that "it works." Perhaps it is time for the human sciences to rise to the level of the animal sciences. If the lot of the roosters, rats, and rhinos can be improved through logical application of research findings to the real world, why not, then, the plight of man?

It is conceivable that a system which used probation, community sanctions, and suspension of privileges would be highly practical. Perhaps suspension from work status (and thereby pay status) would provide economic sanctions not unlike those in the freeworld. But regardless of the "solution" to criminality within the village, the important thing is that the community would be forced to deal with it internally because the possibility of exile from the prison community would be limited by law.

As in society in general, it can be anticipated that deviance will result from the different value systems of both staff and inmate members in the new prison community. Not everything will run smoothly. One can expect some perversions in forms of violence, gambling, and abuse of sex and alcohol. Also, corruption of the town council is probably inevitable if the inmates are really allowed to govern themselves. But that may provide them with practical experience and more realistic assumptions about governmental frailties in the freeworld.[23]

Programs

The key to operating this community successfully would be to eliminate the traditional "we–they" syndrome common to existing institutions. And this, in turn, would require the maximum involvement of inmates in the process of community management. Initially, at least, the officials would want to be able to override the authority vested in a town council as a check on inmate control. But inmates should be on the town council and operate the facilities, including such services as the police department.[24]

---

[23] The probable inevitability of corruption of the town council would provide an opportunity to observe deviance in a new (to the inmate) form and, it is to be hoped, deal with it responsibly.

[24] We know from the Arkansas, Louisiana, and Mississippi prisons that inmates are capable of exercising far more responsibility than is generally acknowledged. The inmate sheriff and tower guards seem to function quite efficiently and more effectively than freeworld guard personnel. As noted earlier, both Gill and Maconochie also had inmates serving as a police force with no reported negative effects. However, one should not infer an endorsement of a system of inmate guards that creates other extremely negative side effects.

Those who deviate from the rules established for the prison community by its citizens would probably be dealt with in the usual fashion: a complaint filed with a "magistrate" alleging an offense, arrest by the inmate police force, and determination of guilt or innocence before a staff-inmate tribunal. It is hoped that new approaches to dealing with criminality would occur.[25]

In a village, the inmate would live in a residential area, go to other areas for school, vocational training, recreation, and work during the day, and return to the residential area in the evening. For special evening or weekend events, public forums, movies, and other activities, the inmate would go to the village center. Such a plan would provide the inmate with some sense of territorial rights as well as freedom of movement. The process would approximate the freeworld situation and give the inmate a feeling of choice, mobility, and experience in decision making.[26]

Reception and release facilities would not have to be provided for if the programs of the village functioned as designed. Perhaps the Welcome Wagon could be substituted for the formal orientation procedures that are customary in the traditional prison. Nonetheless, it might be advisable to provide additional testing and evaluation as a precondition for association in the freeworld. It is envisioned that inmates might enter and leave the village at different geographical and program points and move

---

[25] And then again, the elite might revert to traditional concepts of power utilization experienced in the freeworld and respond from that traditional role—thus visiting the same kinds of degradation on their fellow convicts as was done by the criminal justice system. See: George Orwell, *Animal Farm*, (New York: Harcourt, Brace, 1954).

If this were to occur in the context of "Friendly Village," the traditionalists would probably be justified in referring to the true reformer as the "Village Idiot."

[26] A limitation on the model being suggested is the quite obvious fact that the inmates will not be returning to a small, country "friendly village" on release. Many will return to an urban area, some to the ghetto. Nonetheless, the village would provide some experiences that could be transferred to a larger community, although it is recognized that the impact on the individual would be lessened. And, while it could be argued that such training and subsequent return to the ghetto existence would be dysfunctional and frustrating to the offender, this factor could be averted, perhaps, either by other societal efforts to remove the necessity of his returning to the negative environment or by change of that environment.

Often those in power excuse their failure to exercise their inaction by arguing that their efforts may well be neutralized by those with greater power, or by their successors in office. This argument is like suggesting that the physician quit wasting his efforts on healing because man is destined to die eventually anyway.

through the experience with varying degrees of rapidity.[27] Evaluation of inmate progress, promotion, and eligibility for release would be made primarily by inmates, with staff playing a supportive role. Some offenders would be asked to remain at the village as paid staff after discharge.

Prior to discharge from the village, and in preparation for this release, the inmate might be given the opportunity to become involved in the freeworld activities such as home furloughs, advanced schooling, medical treatment, and job seeking. Though this opportunity would be an integral part of the overall program, it would only be used where individually applicable and feasible.

Both male and female officers would work with inmates of the opposite sex as would be customary in a nonprison setting. No unnecessary distinction would be made based on sex or age in either institutional or noninstitutional treatment of the offender, except as mentioned earlier, in housing assignments. Legal prohibitions against mixing juveniles with adults might also limit their general integration in the institutional setting.

The judicious use of money, free time, and personal resources would be monitored by indigenous legal authority comparable to that in the free society. Varying degrees of responsibility would be granted as the offender is able to deal with it.

Freeworld staff would wear civilian clothing appropriate to their assignment in the prison community. They would be indistinguishable, by dress, from the inmates. Obvious exceptions might be medical staff, police, and firemen. As the inmate population becomes more confident, however, it is hoped that the traditional attitudes toward the necessity of uniforms would disappear.

How the community might evolve in attitudes, policies, and activities must remain speculative because the possibilities are almost limitless and probably unpredictable. More productive than such speculation is the recognition that the *village* is the treatment program. It constitutes the milieu within which the needs of both staff and inmates can be met through a variety of methods. It is the village as a total concept that fosters whatever change takes place within the individual. All other "programs" are peripheral to the bed-

---

[27] For example, the accidental offender, the white collar criminal, and the draft resister, in general, pose no threat of escape or violence and could be assigned immediately on incarceration to minimum-custody facilities—if, in fact, they should be institutionalized at all. Similarly, the educated or trained prisoner could benefit little from the educational programs and could therefore direct his efforts toward other interests.

rock of the new community's design and organization, and it is only in such a context that correctional energies will no longer be dissipated on fruitless efforts to reform part of the organism, part of the time, in part of the institution.

11

Reformation or Revolution?

MURTON: ... it's a *beachhead* here.

HALEY: The whole state's a beachhead, Tom. This state was rotten to the core for twelve years. It grew that way through sheer stagnation. I don't care who would have been the governor. I mean Orval Faubus may—if he were a knight in shining armor, after twelve years with the same administration, you're going to have stagnation through every department. That's what you've got.

If there's any beachhead, it's in the Governor's Office and we're part of a team and we've got to fight that way and you're not doing it if your whole microcosmic existence is Tom Murton and Penal Reform without regard to the consequences of your actions toward the total beachhead, which is Arkansas and the overall political reform. That gets down to the point of the matter. This is the thing that is of such urgency right now. It's not just penal reform.

MURTON: You're saying that penal reform as it is now being constituted is antithetical to the goals and aspirations of other reforms in the state?

HALEY: It is, as operated. That's the problem; that *penal reform, as operated, is antithetical to penal reform.* Now, try that one out for size.[1]

It would appear safe to argue that American society acknowledges that corrections have not corrected. Creating awareness of a problem is not particularly difficult; diverting social reformers from self-defeating "solutions" may not be so easy. An effort has been made in the foregoing chapters to focus on the real problems of prison reform and to offer some alternative ways of perceiving both the problems and their solutions.

---

[1] Extract from the transcript of an executive session of the Arkansas Board of Correction at Cummins Prison Farm, Grady, Arkansas, March 6, 1968, pp. 56–57. The dialogue was between Board Chairman John Haley and myself as prison superintendent.

The simplistic approach to reform is to rely on the penologists, the professional associations, the scholars, or the courts (in that order) to provide the answers. There is some comfort in the belief that the key to reform has been temporarily mislaid, or as yet is undiscovered, and that application of traditional, but more effective, techniques will somehow unlock the door to reform. Relying on these customary resources to lead us out of the penological wilderness has resulted in some catastrophic failures, and those who are sincerely interested in reforming the penal system should know about them. Although the following discussion based on specific examples cannot be generalized to *all* penologists, associations, scholars, or judges, it should cause reformers to pause and reflect on the merits of committing resources and efforts in a traditional manner.

The Penologists

Penologists generally recognize that many prison systems are deficient and that there is a corresponding need for reform. But very little has come out of this recognition in terms of real reform.

It may be that when a prison system is rather low on the evolutionary scale, the problems are simply due to an absence of reform efforts. Such systems are simplistic and relatively unaffected by efforts to change them. In the more sophisticated systems, once-attempted reform may have resulted in the facade of reform that masks the need for real reform. It is possible that many members of the system (excluding the inmates) may believe that reform actually has been achieved. It is generally assumed, erroneously, that *change* is synonymous with *reform*.

Errors in judgment occur as a result of conscientious, but unenlightened, reform efforts that do not result in real reform; and they, too, cloud the real issue. Then, of course, there exists the impact of the traditional obstacles to reform of any kind—public ignorance or apathy, legislative indifference, timid administrators, and a host of factors that tend to relegate prison reform to the last priority of concern.

All these factors contribute to, and offer an explanation for, the lack of prison reform. But there is a more insidious and less recognizable inhibitor of true reform—one that is the most difficult, if not impossible, to overcome. It is the "Art of Nonreform" as practiced by penologists.

> *Nonreform is an overt action taken by the official reformer to eliminate real reform.*

The official reformer uses this technique when all else fails to inhibit reform measures that threaten his desired image. It goes beyond mere mistakes, ignorance, or the simple lack of reform. It is an art practiced most skillfully and effectively by the decision makers ostensibly commissioned to provide the very reform they stifle. Those people, assigned by society the responsibility to "rehabilitate" the criminal offender, are the very ones who deliver the ultimate death blow to real prison reform.

In analyzing the situation in Arkansas, the art of nonreform resulted in the elimination of those elements that were essential ingredients of the reform movement: the removal of the reform staff; elimination of the prison dances; abolition of the Tucker inmate panel; discontinuation of the Tucker inmate newspaper; elimination of the school program; abolition of the inmate self-government; removal of the baby from the Women's Reformatory; and suppression of the truth relative to the murdered inmates buried at Cummins.

Taking another example from Alaska corrections, one could point to the firing of reform staff; appointment of top administrators who would assure the status quo; elimination of the forestry camp; the action of the commissioner to prevent completion of the adult camp; and construction of a prison.

The 7th Step Foundation[2] is purportedly four times more effective than the California State parole agents in reducing recidivism. Members have successfully, thus far, resisted efforts by the California Department of Corrections to take over its program. Although it's probably not how corrections personnel see it, if the 7th Step program were clasped to the bosom of the department, it would only assure its annihilation. Institutionalization would squeeze the last vestige of life from it. Because the inmate members refused to be co-opted, the department officials did the next best thing; they excluded the program from the institutions because of its phenomenal success. In so doing, they removed the embarrassment not only of the nonprofessional but also of the convict—the ignominy of the patient curing himself in spite of the physician!

The warden's self-perception as a caretaker is a philosophical frame of reference that not only fails to foster change but also assures that reform will *not* occur. This is so despite the fact that few people dispute that the prison inmate is denied most of his civil rights while incarcerated. Recent court decisions foretell of a time in

---

[2] This organization was founded by the late Bill Sands and consists of a coalition between ex-inmates and 7th Step Chapters of inmates in prison. The purpose is to help inmates deal realistically with themselves and provide assistance to the prisoner on release.

the not-too-distant future when those basic civil rights provided to the criminal offender in arrest and pretrial proceedings will be extended to the prisoner behind the walls.

> **REFORMER AWARD**
>
> TO: President Richard M. Nixon for his understanding and compassionate approach to crime in America. Requesting Congress to reinstate capital punishment for certain federal crimes and suggesting stiffer penalties for various other offenses, President Nixon demonstrated his concern for the offender in saying, "The only way to attack crime in America is the way crime attacks our people—without pity." [*The Freeworld Times*, March 1973]

The time may be at hand when guarantees of the United States Constitution, the dictates of humanity, and the reflection of a new era will provide the impetus from outside the system to force the granting, or at least the recognition, of basic human rights for prisoners. These rights will be granted by farsighted administrators, will be imposed by the courts, or will be taken by the inmates. As the following section demonstrates, it is unlikely that the professionals will ever rise to the challenge of doing the job themselves.

The Professionals

A cardinal rule of the penologist is never to expose a system to public examination because to do so might be embarrassing to his employers. While the Arkansas Cummins Prison Farm was in a state of upheaval during 1967, a consultant from the United States Bureau of Prisons had occasion to visit the prison. At the time of his visit, the Cummins kitchen had been condemned by the health department. It was filthy, food was being illegally sold to starving inmates, home brew was being made, and there was no aspect of the food service operation that could not have been improved.

It was in this context that the federal consultant recommended to the superintendent that the black-eyed peas be served at the beginning of the food line instead of at the end. He noted that under the method being used the lettuce was put on the trays first and the peas, served later, were spilling over onto the lettuce. His point was that food, to be made more palatable, should be separated so that hot foods cannot contaminate cool foods. That piece of advice was about as useful to the warden in correcting the primary problems of the prison as recommending to a fire chief that the fire truck should be polished while the station house is being consumed by flames.

Correctional prostitution can probably take other forms, but it appears to be most common in the area of consultation. The following incident is not atypical of prison depravations throughout the country. It is recited not as another case of prison brutality but to focus attention on efforts to correct the situation.

In June 1969 inmates of the Missouri State Penitentiary for Men were put into segregation cells at the main institution at Jefferson City. Some continued to make noise and were placed in two isolation cells; eight inmates in one, six in the other. The cells were stripped, and the inmates wore only shorts.

After three weeks these inmates continued to make noise, and the prison officials later testified that they were afraid the disorder would spread throughout the institution. Instead of shutting the outside solid door to the unit, which would be logical to reduce the noise level, the guards instead proceeded to Mace the inmates and spray them with a fire hose. These actions were taken to "punish them for making noise."

A four-inch curb outside the cells prevented the water from draining away. The inmates who remained conscious held those up who passed out to keep them from drowning. They were forced to stand or sit in four inches of muck including excrement, urine, vomit, and Mace residue. Then the outside door was shut, preventing any ventilation of the cells.

Warden Harold Swenson and Commissioner of Corrections Fred Wilkinson (both former federal prison wardens) contended in court that such practices were not only routine in prisons but were condoned by the Bureau of Prisons and the American Correctional Association. In fact, the *Manual of Correctional Standards*, published by the ACA, was cited as specifically approving the hosing of inmates for disciplinary purposes.[3]

Court action grew out of a petition by the inmates involved in the incident. Attorneys were appointed to represent them. The next step was to obtain expert testimony to refute the contentions of the prison officials. Gerald Walsh, an attorney for the inmate plaintiffs,

---

[3] But the testimony is in conflict with the manual. "Corporal punishment should never be used under any circumstances. This includes such practices as ... spraying with a stream of water...." See the *Manual of Correctional Standards*, American Correctional Association, Washington, D.C., 1959, p. 417.

contacted Myrl Alexander at Southern Illinois University, where he was then on the faculty. Alexander was the most recently retired director of the United States Bureau of Prisons, past president of the American Correctional Association, an international consultant in penology, and author of a book on jail administration. Walsh commented about Alexander:

> On his walls hung photographs of U.S. Attorney Generals since and including Robert Kennedy. Also hanging was a photo of James V. Bennett. Alexander generally disapproved the Jefferson City events, while at the same time, remaining reserved. . . . I asked him to come and testify on behalf of the plaintiffs. . . .
> He then went into how he had known Fred Wilkinson for 20 years. . . . I thought, and still think, he would not come because of his friendship with Wilkinson and because he could not testify against him.[4]

The next attempt to secure expert testimony was a contact with James V. Bennett, retired director of the United States Bureau of Prisons, past president of the American Correctional Association, and international consultant in penology. Another court-appointed attorney, William Morgan, reported:

> I phoned James V. Bennett on two different occasions in early and late March of this year concerning the case. . . . He did express some disbelief that the matters that I described had in fact occurred.
> I called Mr. Bennett again after I had taken the deposition of Warden Swenson and repeated the facts as they had been testified to by Warden Swenson at the time of deposition. Mr. Bennett indicated that he would be unable to come to testify for us concerning the event, but stated that he did feel that hosing men in cells and macing them while they are in their cells unless they are offering violence to each other or to guards would not be good prison practice. . . . [He] indicated that he could not take sides as would appear to be the case from his testifying as a witness called by us.[5]

---

[4] Letter from Gerald Walsh to Tom Murton, Kansas City, Missouri, September 20, 1971, pp. 1 and 2.

[5] Letter from William Morgan to Tom Murton, Kansas City, Missouri, October 4, 1971, pp. 1 and 2.

The attorneys also experienced some difficulty in obtaining psychiatric testimony. At one time, they believed they would be able to obtain Dr. Karl Menninger to testify in court, but he later declined. Walsh stated:

> I had a number of telephone conversations with him and generally he was most helpful. His office did inform me that he was quite friendly with Dr. George Beto, who was called as a witness by the officials at the penitentiary, and was also a great supporter of Attorney General John Danforth of Missouri. While these factors may have affected his decision not to appear, I realize that he is an extremely busy man and is of advanced age.[6]
>
> I went to the Menninger Clinic in Topeka on two occasions (because) I was primarily interested in finding some psychiatric testimony.... I was referred to Dr. Russ Settle, former warden at the Federal Pen. in Springfield, Missouri. He ... declined to testify at the trial because he said he could not stand to be cross-examined. He had known Wilkinson for a number of years.[7]

Maurice Sigler, then-commissioner of corrections in Nebraska and president of the Wardens' Association of America, testified that he saw nothing wrong with keeping men in isolation for two years. He stated that he had had a man in the "hole" for over eight years at that time.[8]

Dr. George Beto, then-director of corrections for Texas, past president of the American Correctional Association, and national consultant in penology, testified that he did not approve of the manner in which the prisoners were Maced by Warden Swenson. Beto stated that he would have Maced them three weeks *sooner* than the warden had. According to Walsh:

> After Beto testified, I caught him in the corridor outside the courtroom. I asked him if he wouldn't have shut the wooden door first. He said it wouldn't have done any good and he would have taken measures to silence the inmates earlier. He then told me about an incident in Texas.
>
> ... The inmates on one of his farms ... refused to go to work ... until Beto personally arrived and spoke with them

---

[6] Walsh, p. 3.

[7] Ibid., p. 1.

[8] Sigler served as president of the American Correctional Association in 1971 and subsequently was appointed to the United States Parole Board.

concerning their grievances. . . . Beto told the warden to . . . separate the men into . . . those willing to work [and] those unwilling. . . . After polling the inmates, approximately 30 refused to work.

Beto had given the warden the following orders. If anyone refused to work, have him sit on the ground together with the others who refused. The guards were instructed to get horses and wet ropes. Next the inmates were to be ordered back to work and, if they refused, the guards on horseback were ordered to ride through these men and force them to work.

The story ended with Beto laughingly saying that the 30 inmates who refused to work when confronted with his horsemen "went to work right quick."[9]

No reasonably prudent man (at least a humane one) ignorant of penology could be expected to advocate what the leaders of corrections did in this instance. It is obvious that such activities violate the United States Constitution, and if, in fact, these conditions are tolerated throughout the nation, then this revelation must remain an indictment of the prison systems and those who are responsible for them.

These men sealed their lips to protect a colleague, secure in the knowledge that if there comes a time when one of them is called to court to justify or explain his actions, he will be able to rely on his compatriots to bail him out, or not to testify, as the case may be. The relationship may be more of a kinship one than conspiratorial, but the result is the same. Those who know better bring to bear the power of their office to thwart prison reform.

Austin MacCormick[10] professes to have been a consultant in prison matters in 49 of the 50 states, and yet he refuses to expose prison conditions because he states that to do so would prevent him from having access to other institutions in the future. He argues that if he does not have entry to the prisons, he cannot then reform them. The inference is that if one is admitted to a prison, he will then in fact reform it. Although the reverse argument (that if he is denied access he will not reform it) has some defects, it is worthy to observe that MacCormick investigated the Arkansas prison system in 1927 and very adequately documented the deficiencies of that system. He

---

[9] Walsh, pp. 2 and 3.

[10] Austin MacCormick is executive director of the Osborne Association, a nonprofit New York corporation committed to prison reform. He has been an active penologist for more than half a century.

was to return nearly 40 years later in 1967 to repeat the task because his recommendations were never implemented and he had declined to release them to the public.

"He says he's writing a book exposing the prison reformers."

Reprinted with permission from John Howard Association *Newsletter*, Honolulu, Hawaii, December 1974.

In speaking of impact, one ponders how many inmates died in the Arkansas prisons during the four-decade interim between MacCormick's two reports. According to Rubin Johnson, the coffin maker, and other inmates, as many as several hundred prisoners had been murdered by trusty guards and prison officials over the years. Based on prison records of "escapes," the superintendent estimated

Reformation or Revolution?

that 213 inmates probably had been exterminated within the prison and were buried under the sod. On July 26, 1970, prison board chairman John Haley reported that the prison computer revealed that: "Between 1916 and 1950 there were 110 Negroes and 107 whites who were listed as escapees and never recaptured." Haley said he believes "a lot of them are buried out there in the field of Cummins Prison Farm and were conveniently listed as having escaped."[11]

According to the Talmud, "He who can protest and does not, is an accomplice to the act."[12]

It requires little persuasion for the student of penology eventually to become discouraged and, in despair, agree with the Prophet who concludes:

> *The greatest obstacles to real prison reform are those individuals ostensibly committed to bringing about real prison reform.*

The Professional Association

The American Correctional Association (ACA), founded originally as the National Prison Association in 1870, is the professional organization that encompasses all aspects of the field of penology. It includes the practitioner, educator, therapist, and volunteer under the umbrella of commitment to professionalizing the discipline of penology.

The association, consisting of an estimated 12,000 members, has not survived by accident. By exercising tight control over its proceedings, adhering to a philosophy of nonintervention in other jurisdictions, being cautious in who it canonizes by elevation to the priesthood, serving as a clearinghouse for correctional appointments, choosing those who will become consultants, purging itself of reform prophets from time to time, and ignoring fundamental issues in penology, the association has assured its position of authority in the field of corrections.

In 1969, some difficulties were experienced in the Alabama prison system. One warden was fired for using prison labor and materials for his personal benefit. Another warden resigned under threat of dismissal because of an altercation in a night club.

---

[11] *Arkansas Democrat*, Little Rock, July 26, 1970. See further: Tom Murton and Joe Hyams, *Accomplices to the Crime: The Arkansas Prison Scandal* (New York: Grove Press, 1969).

[12] Talmud, Sabbath, 54.

Commissioner of Corrections A. Frank Lee resigned at the request of the governor after an investigation by the state police into a mismanaged drug-testing program at the prison and other deficiencies.

At that time, Lee was president-elect of the American Correctional Association, which had planned for the previous five years to hold the annual convention in Montgomery in August 1969. Because of Lee's firing, the ACA canceled the convention at that site and moved it to another state. It was several months before a replacement for Lee could be found because the Alabama Board of Corrections was "getting no cooperation at all from the prison officials of the nation.... The national association will not recommend the Alabama prison commissioner's job to any of its members."[13]

The 1970 Annual Congress was held in Cincinnati in celebration of "one century of progress." Proceedings at that meeting[14] reveal to some extent the level of professionalism within the organization. President George Beto of Texas observed that the problems of corrections "are attributable to critics who say that the correctional administrators are wasting funds. The critics who should be silenced are those who speak before U.S. Senate Committees; those who voiced criticism of the system in Maryland...."

Other conferees, speaking from the floor, expressed different reasons for correctional problems:

> *Corrections is a game that is exploitive and egocentric. The ACA is devoid of accomplishment and is but another establishment. We need the religious approach to crime. Programs are shallow, and rehabilitation plans are phony because they treat symptoms instead of causes.*

Warden Winston Moore of Chicago agreed: "This Congress will not discuss real problems." One spokesman stated that "homosexuality involves at least 50 percent of my clinical staff. We should quit using this conference to meet old friends; we need workshops to deal with real problems."

An Indiana warden said, "Officers are bringing narcotics into my institution. It appears that we have to seek out information at lunch or informal meetings because it is not provided at the conference.

---

[13] *Atlanta Journal-Constitution*, Atlanta, Georgia, December 21, 1969.

[14] Unless otherwise noted, all the quotations in this section are taken from an unpublished report by Tom Murton: "The American Correctional Association Congress of 1970," October 1970, Minneapolis, Minnesota.

Reformation or Revolution?

There is a need for exchange of information. The police are able to get helicopters and tanks, yet we can't."

The keynote address to the wardens' session was delivered by James Gaffney, a retired warden of the St. Cloud Reformatory in Minnesota. Several hundred slides of ancient practices depicting conditions in the Colorado state prison in the "good old days" were reviewed to accompanying sighs of nostalgia. Torture devices were demonstrated and a round of hearty laughter and applause was evoked by a demonstration of the "Old Grey Mare," a device to which an inmate was strapped in a standing position bent double from the waist. While in this position, an officer provided "rehabilitation" by wielding a wooden paddle resembling a ball bat on the posterior of the offender in full view of the massed inmates who formed the traditional square in the courtyard.

Photos were also shown of bloodhounds, inmates who had been shot to death or beaten up in the process of recapture, and the "vocational training program" in the rock quarry. After the slides, Gaffney delivered his remarks to the assembled group of wardens. If audience response was a valid indicator, the speech represented a consensus of approval.

> *The do-gooders have had their day. We have gone through all this nonsense of rehabilitation, therapy, and the like, which has not worked. Now, praise God, the pendulum is swinging back to discipline, control and custody! [cheers]*
>
> *We are seeing a new age where the social workers and their like will be excluded from the prison. [more cheers] Who is to say that some of the methods that were used in the good old days were not effective? Who says prisons fail? What we need is more experience to again demonstrate that discipline can be effective.*

At another session of the Wardens' Association, Warden Leonard Meacham of Wyoming described one of his treatment programs:

> *We got some alcoholic inmates drunk to see what their real problems were. Some have a sex problem masked by the drinking problem. We hope nobody finds out about this program. We also use family counseling with the inmate.*

An unidentified assistant superintendent from Maryland contended that "treatment may be hitting an inmate on the head."

Warden W. J. Estelle of Montana, now director of corrections in Texas, declared that "it is not important that we understand the crime, the criminal, or society. What we really need is to become benevolent and reasonable autocrats."

Warden Estelle looked forward to the future when "we will have preventive detention and genetic control." In one of his better moments, Estelle unintentionally rendered the most pathetic and yet hilarious anecdote of the conference:

> *There was an outside group who got excited about the fact that one cell block had no plumbing. This was about three years ago. Ever since then, they have been screaming about the plumbing for the inmates, but nobody has said anything about the lack of plumbing in three of my towers.*
>
> *The officers used to climb the tower each day with a bucket of drinking water in one hand and a bucket for urine in the other. The buckets were labeled, but sometimes an illiterate guard would get confused and put his drinking water in his pot. So, I had to mark the pot with a red "X" so he could tell the difference.*
>
> *Yet, nobody was concerned with the poor officer. So, I put plumbing in the guard towers but did not in the cell block. Now this is not cheating the inmates because providing the staff with plumbing provides him [sic] with a staff of higher morale and efficiency; so really we are doing the inmate a favor.*

A final comment by a moderator of one of the warden's sessions seemed to summarize the feelings of the group: "We're doing a good job. We feed the inmates; we get them to work on time; and we get them to the showers on time. *That* is good administration."

I introduced a resolution asking the association to condemn the murder of prison inmates. It was the only resolution to fail. Among those speaking in opposition to it were James V. Bennett and Austin MacCormick. It was defeated by the wardens and directors of corrections of America.

The following August (1971), ACA members made their annual prilgrimage to the mecca of reform: the Annual Correctional Congress, held this time in Miami, Florida. In contrast with the colorful conference of the previous year, this one was rather pedestrian. The major "problem" facing wardens was again defined as outside agitators. Warden Raymond Gaffney of Kansas argued, "If

The Prison Reform Scoreboard

The American Correctional Association met in Cincinnati in 1970 to celebrate the founding of this professional organization of penologists and to inaugurate the second century of prison reform. Members of the association again met in Miami in 1971. The complete list of resolutions submitted and action taken are reported below.

1970 Congress

Resolutions	Sponsor	Resolutions Committee Recommendations	Action
1. Commending the Centennial Commission for a job well done in creating a "meaningful" Congress.	Resolutions Committee	Approval	Adopted
2. Commending the Ohio Host Committee for work well done in contributing to the conference.	Resolutions Committee	Approval	Adopted
3. Commending President George Beto for his able, competent leadership in advertising the Centennial Congress.	Resolutions Committee	Approval	Adopted
4. Commending Past Presidents for their continuing contributions in program developments.	Resolutions Committee	Approval	Adopted
5. Commending the Chaplain who has delivered the prayer at the annual prayer breakfast for "praying real good." Amended by Austin MacMormack to include other chaplains who also have said good prayers.	Resolutions Committee Austin MacMormack	Approval	Adopted
6. Commending the Citizens' Committee for Ohio Night for providing a "night of revelry."	Resolutions Committee	Approval	Adopted
7. Commending the Self-Evaluation Committee because a true profession has self-evaluation.	Resolutions Committee	Approval	Adopted
8. Commending the Committee on 1970 Principles for providing a "beacon to guide a nation in troubled times" into a "new era of corrections."	Resolutions Committee	Approval	Adopted
9. Commending the Committee on Riots and Disturbances for publishing a pamphlet entitled "Riots and Disturbances."	Resolutions Committee	Approval	Adopted
10. Commending the U. S. Junior Chamber of Commerce for providing leadership in public relations and corrections through 100 chapters in the U. S.	Resolutions Committee	Approval	Adopted
11. Urging grants for institutional construction be preceded by planning.	John Howard Association	Rejection	Adopted

Reformation or Revolution?

12. Asking the U. S. Congress to stop all traffic in obscenity and pornography because it is a menace and results in prison trouble.	Unknown	Rejection	No motion to adopt
13. Commending the Ohio prison staff for bringing inmate art to the conference.	Unknown	Approval	Adopted
14. Memorial commending Charles McKendrick, deceased, for his outstanding work.	Parker Hancock	Approval	Adopted
15. Condemning the killing of prison inmates and urging officials to render complete investigations.	Tom Murton	Rejection	Failed

1971 Congress

1. Commending President Louis Wainwright for an outstanding job.	Resolutions Committee	Approval	Adopted
2. Commending chaplains for having met the spiritual needs of conferees at the ACA Congress.	Resolutions Committee	Approval	Adopted
3. Commending the Florida officials for providing adequate facilities for the convention.	Resolutions Committee	Approval	Adopted
4. Commending Lawrence Carpenter for his work with LEAA.	ACA Board of Directors	Approval	Adopted
5. Memorial commending Chaplain William C. Jones, deceased, for sponsoring the annual prayer breakfast.	American Protestant Chaplains' Ass'n.	Approval	Adopted
6. Commending the South Carolina Department of Corrections for the proposed inmate art show to be held in the spring of 1972.	South Carolina Department of Corrections	Approval	Adopted
7. To endorse elimination of job discrimination against ex-offenders through legislation.	James Meeker, US Senate Sub-Comm. on Prisons	Approval	Adopted
8. To authorize the President to appoint committees to advise in new college criminology curricula.	Anderson College	Approval	Adopted
9. To appoint a committee to assess LEAA loans for training and establishment of a revolving fund.	Correctional Industries	Approval	Adopted
10. To encourage new membership in the ACA.	John Glover	Referral	Referred
11. To admit ex-offenders to membership in the ACA.	John Glover	None	Adopted
12. Condemning the killing of prison inmates and urging officials to render complete investigations.	Murton Foundation for Criminal Justice, Inc.	Rejection	Failed

Reformation or Revolution?

Playboy and Murton would stick to pornography instead of prison reform, we'd all be better off."[15]

The "murder" resolution was again introduced. The resolution was read to the assembly by Acting Chairman of the Resolutions Committee Walter Dunbar,[16] who announced that the committee recommended rejection because:

> *The allegations deal with a subject that properly belongs with the law enforcement authorities. The American Correctional Association for 100 years has enunciated principles of humane treatment.*[17]

Two weeks later, Dunbar was to announce the "throat-cutting" and "castration" myths to newsmen taken on tour after the Attica attack.

Austin MacCormick spoke against the resolution, saying, in part:

> *I know as much about Arkansas as anyone, and about the atrocities in the Arkansas system. . . . Tom [Murton] opened the graves. He knew it was illegal, one of the worst felony offenses, but he didn't get a court order, or have police standing by. This was a prison graveyard. But on the strength of one senile old convict Tom said the exhumed bodies had been murdered. I think many prisoners were murdered, although I've never said this publicly before.*
>
> *Arkansas was as mad as could be. We came within an ace of not getting our bills through [the legislature]. I'm unable to analyze his megalomania. Last year a lot of ACA members voted to sustain his motion because they're against murdering prisoners. The state police investigated the cases of 200 missing prisoners—some of those were killed, maybe, but the motion shouldn't be passed because it has no basis in truth.*[18]

---

[15] Gaffney resigned under fire on July 30, 1973, as a result of a confession by a former policeman that he had procured a prostitute for him. "I committed a sin maybe but I didn't violate the law," Gaffney said.

[16] Dunbar is a former deputy director of corrections in California, past president of the ACA, past member of the United States Parole Board, and currently director of the New York State Division of Probation.

[17] Transcript of remarks before the annual business meeting of the American Correctional Association at Miami, Florida, August 19, 1971. Extract prepared by Jessica Mitford, p. 1.

[18] *Ibid.*, p. 2.

The murder resolution was proposed a third consecutive year at the Annual Congress of the ACA at Pittsburgh in 1972. After amendments eliminated or seriously impaired all but the final paragraph, the motion for adoption was tabled for one year (by a vote of 51 to 18)[19] so that the resolution could be "studied in depth."

The 103rd Annual Congress of the ACA met in Seattle in mid-August of 1973 and, not unexpectedly, provided more grist for the mill of incredibility. The faithful (and the hopeful) gathered to give or listen to speeches, offer or seek employment, and, most importantly, to pay homage to the patron saints of penology.

The ACA reached for the apex of absurdity at the annual banquet when the E. R. Cass Award was bestowed upon Russell G. Oswald of New York. The text of the eulogy reads as follows:

As one who has devoted a life-long career dedicated to the benefits of those less fortunate, Russell G. Oswald has manifested those traits of humanitarianism, compassion and integrity so necessary in correctional administration.

A native of Wisconsin, he received his formal education at the University of Wisconsin and Marquette University Law School, and was awarded his graduate degree in his chosen profession from the Loyola University School of Social Work.

Committed to devoting his life to the principle that others might be the beneficiaries of his dedication, Russell Oswald progressed through various supervisory levels in local and state departments of public welfare, including the directorship of probation and parole in Wisconsin, and later as director of his state's division of correction.

With early recognition of his talent and ability in the highly specialized and sensitive field of correctional administration, Russell Oswald was appointed the Commonwealth of Massachusetts Commissioner of Correction in 1955 by the late and distinguished Governor Christian Herter.

In 1957, Governor Averell Harriman of New York recognized his achievements and named him as a member of the New York State Board of Parole and one year later as chairman of the board.

---

[19] Of the estimated 12,000 members of the ACA, a little more than 2,000 attended the congress, but only about 75 remained for the final business meeting. Thus a decision affecting, and presumably representing, the professional field of corrections was accomplished by only 51 members.

Under his energetic and dynamic leadership, Commissioner Oswald brought New York's parole system to its point of recognition as one of the nation's outstanding post-release programs.

In 1970, his elevation to the post of Commissioner of the expanded New York State Department of Correctional Services, embodying for the first time combined institutional and post-release services, was announced by Governor Nelson D. Rockefeller.

Molding one of the nation's largest and most complex correctional systems into an integrated and progressive program of service to prisoners and parolees, the Governor in mid-1973 appointed him to membership on the nation's first State Crime Victims Compensation Board.

A former president of the Association of Paroling Authorities and a member of the Board of Trustees of the National Council on Crime and Delinquency, Commissioner Oswald currently serves as First Vice-President of the American Correctional Association. An author and lecturer of note, and a member of the Alpha Sigma Nu, the prestigious national honorary fraternity, he served with great distinction in the United States Navy during World War II.

As an active participant in the affairs of the American Correctional Association since 1950, Russell G. Oswald is hereby recognized by its membership as a dedicated public servant in the field of correctional administration and as a true gentleman and statesman, deserving and worthy of the high honor embodied in this E. R. Cass Correctional Achievement Award.

Even the casual reader will note an omission in the chronology: *no* reference is made to the Attica riot where 43 men died. Nonetheless, without contemporary precedent, the "professional" association for prison workers has bestowed its highest award upon the man who presided over the greatest massacre in American prison history.

As Christ once observed, "By their deeds shall ye know them."

The Scholars

In Chapter 6, one of the characterizations in the penological cast of characters was the Oracle. The conclusion reached in that chapter was that "armchair penologists" often obscure, rather than enlighten, the foggy arena of corrections. The proposals of the following three scholars highlight one of the major reasons why real reform cannot rely on the academic world to offer the guidance needed.

Harvard law professor Ralph K. Schwitzgebel has proposed a method to reduce prison populations that he describes as "an electronic rehabilitation system [that] might be particularly helpful in working with chronic recidivists."[20] This technique is feasible for the first time in history, he contends, because "it is now possible ... to maintain a relationship 24 hours a day and beyond the usual geographic barriers."[21]

> A parolee ... would probably be less likely than usual to commit offenses if a record of his location were kept at the base station. If two-way tone communications with the parolee were included in this system, a therapeutic relationship might be established in which the parolee could be rewarded, warned or otherwise signaled in accordance with the plan for therapy.[22]

Describing a "crude prototype" constructed in 1969, Professor Schwitzgebel observed that the participant "wears two small units approximately six inches by three inches by one inch in size, weighing together about two pounds."[23] To prevent tampering and efforts to remove the devices, Schwitzgebel quotes a plan by D. N. Michael:

> [P]arolees will check in and be monitored by transmitters embedded in their flesh, reporting their whereabouts in code and automatically as they pass receiving stations (perhaps like fireboxes) systematically deployed over the country as part of one computer-monitored network... I am not prepared to speculate whether such a situation would increase or decrease the personal freedom of the emotionally ill person.[24]

But Schwitzgebel dispenses with the civil rights issues by proposing that monitoring systems be used only "with volunteering participants (such as inmates seeking release from an institution)."[25]

---

[20] Ralph K. Schwitzgebel, "Issues in the Use of an Electronic Rehabilitation System with Chronic Recidivists," *Law and Society Review*, vol. III, no. 4 (1969): 600.

[21] *Ibid.*, p. 605.

[22] *Ibid.*, p. 598.

[23] *Ibid.*, p. 599.

[24] *Ibid.*, pp. 607, 608.

[25] *Ibid.*, p. 608.

> Given the choice between "harassed freedom" in the community and tranquil deprivation in prison, inmates are likely to choose freedom. They should at least be given the choice.... If they did find the conditions of the electronic system too burdensome, they could choose to return to prison.... That an offender is unlikely to elect this option suggests that, in general, the system extends rather than curtails his rights within present correctional practice.[26]

Schwitzgebel assumes that the prisoner is, in fact, free to make a rational choice and that substituting one form of oppression for another somehow is an improvement in treatment programs. Most inmates would probably not agree with his conclusion that the more sophisticated surveillance system extends their individual rights to privacy.

Schwitzgebel does not rely solely on the advantages of control in his proposal but emphasizes the rehabilitative aspects of the treatment component wherein "the therapist [could] send the parolee signals indicating his general interest and support and thus perhaps enhance standard therapeutic effects."[27] Perhaps.

> With an electronic rehabilitation system, a parole officer could easily send a tone signal to the parolee asking him to call in. Tone signals would also be used to reward or warn the parolee regarding certain behavior. Thus, for example, if a parolee who had previously been very inconsistent in his work patterns was at work on time he might be sent a signal from the parole officer that meant, "You're doing well," or that he would receive a bonus.
>
> On the other hand, if it appeared that the parolee was in a high crime-rate area at 2 o'clock in the morning, he might be sent a signal reminding him to return home.
>
> The proposed system provides the possibility of rapid and strategic intervention within the parolee's natural environment... a procedure not previously possible but vitally important in the application of many learning theory and community health principles.[28]

He contends that a trusting relationship between the treater and treatee prior to the "therapy" is unimportant. According to

---

[26] *Ibid.*, p. 606.
[27] *Ibid.*, pp. 604, 605.
[28] *Ibid.*, p. 603.

Schwitzgebel, "Trust, in gradually increasing degrees, may be considered the result of treatment rather than its precondition."[29]

More recently (1972), sociologist Gerald W. Smith of Utah has proposed attaching an electronic device to prison parolees so that authorities could monitor them 24 hours a day. He stated that this would be done only with the consent of the convicts with just "a mild form of persuasion."[30] Those who agreed to participate would get out of prison early; those who did not would remain in prison.

Professor Smith explains that the device would help reduce the high rate of return to prison by channeling habitually deviant behavior into socially acceptable avenues. If the gadget were removed, a fail-safe mechanism would warn the monitors. To avoid tampering, the electronic bug could be implanted, according to Smith, like heart pacemakers into every American, and the police would have less difficulty in keeping everyone under control.

For the system to work, Smith warned that people would have to get over their "1984 fear that Big Brother is watching."[31] That "neurosis" could be overcome, Smith contends, by inserting the device at birth. By the time the potential criminal grew up, he would "regard his built-in transistor with affection—something akin to his security blanket."[32]

In 1973, Dr. Barton Ingraham, professor of criminology at the University of Maryland, announced to a symposium for the State Probation and Parole Officers that he had devised a method of eliminating prisons in this century. Ingraham's plan is to implant tiny sensors in the bodies of convicts that would "transmit brain-wave patterns, blood pressure, respiration rate, amount of adrenalin, heart rate and muscle tension."[33] Under Ingraham's proposal:

> *The sensors would be hooked up to a computer which would monitor the results. Then, if either a convict's location or his bodily functions indicated that he might be bordering on criminal activity, an electrical signal could be transmitted which would block further action by the subject.*

---

[29] *Ibid.*, p. 604.

[30] *The Freeworld Times*, "Crime Prevention Plan Proposed," April–May 1972, p. 5.

[31] *Ibid.*

[32] *Ibid.*

[33] *Rochester Times-Union*, "Prof's Vision: 'Bugs' Instead of Bars," Rochester, New York, October 19, 1973.

> *Put simply, the person would forget what he was preparing to do and abandon the act.*[34]

Ingraham fears that his proposal may never be implemented because people are afraid of science tampering with the human psyche.

> *People just don't understand modern science. They read books like "1984," "Clockwork Orange," and "The Terminal Man" and they have a Buck Rogers idea of what is possible. And they're worried it might fall into the wrong hands. But that's possible with any new development.*[35]

This line of reasoning calls to mind an admonition in the Scriptures: "Physician, heal thyself!" Or, as Mark Twain observed, "Oft times it does seem a pity that Noah and his party did not miss the boat."

The Courts

If the administrator would take the time to interpret the handwriting on the wall of prisoner rights and act accordingly, he could obviate the necessity for "interference" by the courts or a revolt by the slaves. But, unfortunately, myopic vision appears to be a genetic defect resulting from the inbreeding of prison officials. Thus it seems that court-ordered reform is a necessity. If the Daniel has been driven from the king's chamber into exile, the administrator will be forced to await interpretation (and perhaps implementation) by decree of a high tribunal. If he devotes his energies to circumventing the court's orders and fails to meet the needs of his subjects, he may be swallowed by the revolution. It is probable that neither his dynasty nor the kingdom itself will survive.

The courts have indicated a reluctance to become involved in prison management, but they have been forced into this role by default of prison officials. Attorneys recently have "discovered" the prisons, and, as a result of current popular aspects of prison reform, have directed their energies toward challenging some of the practices within the institutions. Class actions on behalf of prisoners have been filed throughout the country.

---

[34] *Ibid.*
[35] *Ibid.*

> **REFORM RHETORIC**
>
> "I haven't been to that prison in 30 years. It might be helpful if I went out and looked at it."
>
> *United States District Judge L. Clure Morton's statement during a hearing on a petition filed by inmates alleging that the Tennessee state prison subjects inmates to cruel and unusual punishment. [The Freeworld Times]*

The most far-reaching decision originated in the federal court in Arkansas when it declared the entire prison unconstitutional and threatened to close it. This ruling was later upheld by the Eighth Circuit Court on May 5, 1971. Arkansas officials declined to appeal to the United States Supreme Court because they anticipated adverse publicity if the prison's defects were paraded before a national forum. Had it been appealed and affirmed, there could have been a positive effect on prison systems outside the Eighth Circuit, such as in Mississippi.

Court intervention in some cases is welcomed by the progressive prison administrator who has long recognized the need for change but has lacked the courage to prod legislatures and other officials to do their duty. Unfortunately, however, the courts may not always be patient and thus not allow adequate time to implement radical change of the prison. Instantaneous racial integration of a prison could result in a disaster because such a basic change requires education, cooperation, understanding, and acceptance by the inmates. The warden cannot impose (without incident) racial integration; he can only provide that "unstructured" structure which will encourage the inmates to integrate the prison. The courts may thus impose liberal rules on the prison, but the implementation of the rules conflicts with judicial intent.

There is another danger. Jurists are not penologists, and the expert testimony espoused in the courtroom frequently does not provide the requisite knowledge to understand the basic evil of the prison. This understanding is essential in order to diagnose the prison illness and provide a remedy that will not kill the patient.

The impact of the court on school segregation is a case in point; that impact has been comprehensive, but a slow process nonetheless. Because of the similar glacial progress provided by court action in relation to prisons, administrators have been quite successful so far in either ignoring the law or at least in neutralizing it. There is not a

"DAMN THE COURT ORDER. I KNOW HOW TO RUN A PRISON."

warden in the United States who cannot, if he chooses, circumvent the decree of any judge. If, for example, a court were to decree that all prisoners in isolation must be fed an 1,800-calorie minimum daily diet, the warden could comply by feeding each inmate one head of cabbage. If the judge counters by ordering smaller quantities of the regular food served to the majority of the population, the normally hot foods such as meat would be served frozen, and the usually cool foods such as salads would be served fried.

Reformation or Revolution?

If the judge clarifies his order by requiring that hot food be served hot and cool food served cool, the warden can order that the food be so prepared but combined into a single bowl; thus the chili, lettuce, coffee, and jello mixed together would constitute an unpalatable mess.

Federal Judge J. Smith Henley ruled in 1969 that the method of feeding men in isolation at the Cummins Prison Farm in Arkansas was unconstitutional and ordered a revision of the diet for all men in such status. Several months later, an investigator visited the isolation unit at Cummins and observed the following:

> [T]his inmate shoved his tray out of the cell door and says, "I want to show what they fed me this morning." His tray consisted of a piece of cardboard upon which were deposited about four or five different items of food, but it was ground up and in little piles, like cat dung, and it was pretty difficult to tell what it was.
>
> I asked him if he could identify the food items and he said "no." But he said this is the way he is fed.[36]

Such activity by prison officials seemed to be in direct defiance of the court prohibition. However, it was soon discovered that the roster of men in isolation had been "corrected" to reflect that all men in the "hole" were there for "protective custody." Since Judge Henley's order did not apply to this category, the prison officials were not violating the *letter* of the law.

A Texas prisoner describes an example of court orders being circumvented through the semantic game:

> One of the most oppressive penal systems in America is the Texas Department of Corrections where the ruling regimes use Building Tenders as "convict-guards." Several TDC prisoners who had been beaten up by the Building Tenders filed a class action suit in 1973 seeking an injunction against the TDC officials. When the TDC officials received a court injunction prohibiting the use of Building Tenders and the Texas Legislature in May 1973 made it unlawful to use Building Tenders, the TDC ruling regimes were not going to be changed by these means.
>
> The TDC officials simply renamed the Building Tenders after "firing" them in that capacity and then called them "Corridor Boys" and told them to go back to work doing the

---

[36] Tom Murton, "Report of Investigation: The Arkansas Department of Correction," October 11, 12, 1969, p. 26.

same "Building Tender" work and performing the same reactionary function.[37]

Attorneys, some reformers, and many laymen firmly believe that the only sure way to bring about prison reform is through court litigation. However, it does not take a very enlightened citizen to point out that murder has been prohibited by some form of penal code since Cain slew Abel, yet contemporary societies still are plagued with murder.

Although court-ordered reforms certainly contribute to a multifaceted attack on prison defects, alone they have little impact. The two primary reasons for this ineffectiveness are: (1) the judicial process is so slow that the complaining inmates are likely to expire of old age before the appellate procedure is completed, and (2) the substance of the court orders are so narrow that they are usually insignificant in curing the root problems of the prison.

The prisons have proved to be a bonanza for the legal profession. Suddenly the American Bar Association has found that there is a new field where lawyers can establish a reputation through case law, and that can also be lucrative. The legal crusaders have focused exclusively on making the existing prison "better."

An example is the Mississippi prison system, which in terms of notoriety is similar to the Arkansas system. Until recent times, inmates were whipped with a leather strap called "Black Annie," forced to work in the fields as slaves, and not infrequently have been murdered within the prison. Attorneys in Jackson filed action in federal court to correct the blatant deficiencies of that system in 1970. After one year's litigation, then-superintendent Tom Cook bowed to court pressure and agreed to increase the diet of inmates in the maximum-custody unit to "one eight-ounce glass of milk, two hot cakes four inches in diameter, two tablespoons of sorghum syrup, and a cup of sauerkraut" for breakfast.

The evening meal was even more appetizing. In addition to a beverage, the lucky inmate received "a cup of beans, a cup of sauerkraut, and one square of cornbread 3½ inches in diameter and at least 1½ inches thick."[38] Somehow I suspect that the inmates of the Mississippi prison perceived that prison reform would be more than "measuring the corn bread."

---

[37] George Knox, "Prison Violence," unpublished manuscript, Seagoville, Texas, 1974, pp. 253-254.

[38] *Delta Democrat-Times*, Greenville, Mississippi, April 13, 1971. Subsequently, an order by the federal court has resulted in the elimination of inmate guards and some impetus for change (but not reform) of the prison system.

As mentioned earlier, a similar court action took place in Arkansas with the now-famous decision in the *Holt v. Sarver* decision of February 1970. Even though the court has retained jurisdiction over the prison system for several years in an effort to eliminate the unconstitutional status of the prison, the judge himself expressed pessimism about the efficacy of court-ordered reforms.

> [T]here is actually very little that a federal court can do to protect individual inmates in penal institutions from mistreatment by individual guards or individual occasions whether those guards be trustee [sic] inmates or whether they be freeworld employees. About all that the courts can do is to try to get at and eliminate or alleviate underlying causes for prison practices where they give rise to federal constitutional problems.[39]

At the 1971 congress of the American Correctional Association at Miami, Florida, major discussions were directed toward the inequity of the government providing attorneys for inmates but not for the warden to defend himself against resulting law suits. The attorney general of Missouri talked specifically at the closing session about how (as in the Missouri case previously cited in this chapter) the technicalities of law were used to thwart resolution of the case in the inmates' favor.

Some wardens openly resist court "interference" in prison management. Warden Harold Cardwell, formerly of Ohio, was appointed to reform the notorious Arizona prison in 1973. In the spring of 1974, Cardwell called a news conference to discuss his management of the prison and was asked by a reporter his opinion of court orders affecting the prison. Cardwell labeled as "asinine" past judicial decisions giving the inmates the right to confront accusers and to question the charges made by prison staff against them. As Cardwell observed:

> What do they know? Hell, we gotta live around here after they come and stir things up. There was a time, you remember, when the warden ran the prison ... and you didn't see them confounded riots then. Why is it a man ain't king of his castle no more? You call this America?

Referring to himself, Cardwell added:

> Ol' Jimmy Joe Bob didn't come this far to be shot down by a

---

[39] *Pine Bluff Commercial,* Pine Bluff, Arkansas, November 15, 1971.

coupla sissy judges lookin' to make political hay. Well, I'll say this about that: Their ass is grass and I'm the lawnmower![40]

Those who rely on court remedies for reform of the prison must have a lot of patience, a great deal of faith, and a tremendous lack of insight into the prison reform movement.

Summary

The natives are getting restless and may choose not to wait any longer for their problems to be solved by the usual processes. The reason why disturbances do not always result in riots and that riots have not, thus far, resulted in revolution is primarily a function of the dynamics of the prison community. The prison autocracy pits one inmate against another, one staff member against another, and inmates against staff. As long as this condition prevails, a coalition will not form easily. Even though the inmates traditionally are in conflict with the staff, there is no real unanimity in the opposition. A full-scale war would at least provide the cohesion necessary to sustain a long-term revolt.

BY MIKE VINEYARD

So many days keep going by
Numbered like an hour glass
i know that soon i'll lie
In oneness with the grass

And would you come to mourn me
Between the ones who stare
And would i be set free
Or is hell really there

And is my death protection
From all my pain and strife
Or just a mere reflection
Of how I failed in life

[Reprinted from The Weekly Echo, *Medical Center for Federal Prisoners, Springfield, Missouri, February 9, 1973.*]

---

[40] *The Arizona Cilbuper*, Tucson, Arizona, March 27, 1974.

But, understandably, the inmates want out of prison and are hesitant to take any action which would jeopardize that objective. Release, not prison reform, would seem to be the first priority for the inmate. There is always a great number of inmates who are about to be released conditionally at the expiration of sentence; to be granted parole; to be considered for a promotional assignment or transfer to a paying job in the institution; to be assigned to a lower-custody status with more privileges; or who anticipate other changes in status that will reflect a chance to do easier time. The risks of revolt are real. The system has an arsenal of tools of repression, and the sacrificing of short-range objectives (for the inmate) for anticipated long-range gains (for the prison) does not appear rational to the inmate.

In view of the depths of depravity evidenced in the Arkansas prison system over the past 100 years, one can only speculate on the *degree* of degradation required to ignite a penal slave revolt. If systematized brutality, torture, and murder of inmates is not sufficient to bring on revolution, it is difficult to envision what would be.

Perhaps the elements for violent change are embodied in a new dimension that has been added to the prison experience during the past few years. Whereas the average prisoner has been one with a junior high school education, and from the poor and powerless groups, these characteristics are not true for the so-called "political prisoner." We know that college students, some with financial means, have been sent to prison for burning draft cards, opposing the Selective Service System, refusing to submit to the draft, or for other acts of civil disobedience. For the most part, these appear to be sincere acts of commitment in opposition to what are defined, by them, as serious defects in the American way of government.

The activist who goes to prison may be of high intellect, an academician, and something of a philosopher. He enters the prison because of deep concern for the alienation, frustration, and lack of power felt by the masses on the street. But if he felt disadvantaged on the street, the activist is in for a rude awakening when he is subjected to the degradation and arbitrary imposition of control that permeate the prison community. If his commitment was "for real" on the street and not merely a popular intellectual exercise, it is probable that he will turn his efforts to reforming the prison society.

In general, the activist is not hampered by lack of education or the inability to communicate. He is able to articulate the depravity in analytical terms and is trained in leadership. He brings to the prison the skills of organization, slow play, sabotage, interruption, and defiance; thus he probably knows enough to bring the prison machine to a screeching halt.

It may be the activist who finally will be successful in interpreting to the inmates what Pogo meant when he said, "We have met the enemy and he is us." Inmates are beginning to realize that they are participating in their own degradation and many are refusing to perpetuate this destructive relationship.

> *A system of oppression can only exist with the tacit cooperation of the oppressed.*

As Martin Luther King, Jr., once observed, "Freedom is never willingly granted by the oppressor; it must be taken by the oppressed!" A historical evaluation of prisons certainly affirms the validity of the first statement. The characteristics of recent prison disturbances indicate the effectiveness of the second.

Arkansas inmate D. C. Bartlett made some observations on that infamous prison system, following the second court order declaring it unconstitutional. Bartlett's comments could well be considered the epitaph for contemporary prison reform efforts. Or are they a hint as to the future direction reform might take?

> *Penal reform is the topic of conversations, newspaper articles, political rallies, and numerous other communication devices throughout this country.... Literally millions are more than "just aware" of the dilemma.... Still there is nothing being done to change the "system" of corrections!! Why?*
>
> *To begin with, it means we must stop looking for help from areas where none will ever come. If you're expecting a politician to make a change here or there, forget it!!*
>
> *If your hopes lie with... a progressive type penologist who is waiting to introduce his ideas; without losing his job in the process, forget him!... if he has the intestinal fortitude to stand up to his beliefs, and attempt to initiate the programs that his theories require to become effective, he'll just end up like David. He might get a taste of the lions.*
>
> *The leaders in our government cannot afford to retain, in their administrations, any penologists who will "rock the boat." This system here at Cummins like all system[s] has not [sic] desire to commit suicide. Why shouldint [sic "should"] it allow programs to be implemented which would eventually lead to it's [sic] own demise?*

> *There is no hope within this system!!! [sic] here at Cummins, the Arkansas Department of Corrections. We must look to ourselves for the relief that is needed.*[41]

Once the activist comprehends that inmates run, directly or indirectly, all institutions and that the monster cannot function without the permission and assistance of the inmates, he may then conceptualize a plan for revolution. He can provide the charismatic leadership not heretofore generally available because the natural screening process of our criminal justice system has usually excluded the thinker from the prison. A combination of commitment, power, and expertise poses a formidable threat to any power structure.

Prison officials are not unaware of this potential. At the Wardens' Association of America meeting at Cincinnati in the fall of 1970, one of the priority items on the agenda of problems facing prison administrators was the dilemma of how to deal with the political activist. Wardens long ago learned to isolate those leaders who could foment disorder or trouble within the institution. Most wardens reported that they were keeping these prisoners segregated from the rest of the inmates by placing them in single cells. There is a fear that if they are allowed to work or associate with the general population they could "cause problems." The wardens are right!

But the activist, too, will one day be released from prison. Even though he may have been successfully incapacitated inside, he will be able to communicate his observations and critical analysis of the prison experience to the larger society after release. The dawning of a new age of reform may be sown in the very seeds of oppression by those who seek to eliminate opposition to the existing system.

Efforts to silence the activist by subjugating him within the prison may in fact provide the previously lacking information about the prison that, when coupled with personal outrage, may give enough people the impetus for the life-or-death commitment required to sustain a revolution. Inadvertently, the political process that puts some political activists in prison may be creating the very catalyst for the prison reform that has been so successfully avoided thus far.

And, if this proves to be so, it is altogether fitting and proper that real reform emerge from the ranks of the oppressed and not from the alleged reformers who deviate not from the script of historical reformations. It is apparent that killing a prophet does not ensure eradication of an idea. It is this residual idea (not the prophet)

---

[41] D. C. Bartlett, "Public Doesn't Care About the Prisons," *Pine Bluff Commercial*, Pine Bluff, Arkansas, October 15, 1974.

with which the pseudo-reformers one day may be confronted in the Armageddon of real prison reform.

There is no shape more terrible than this—
More tongued with censure of the world's blind greed—
More filled with signs and portents for the soul—
More fraught with menace to the universe.

* * *

Through this dread shape humanity betrayed,
Plundered, profaned and disinherited,
Cries protest to the Judges of the World,
A protest that is also a prophecy.

O masters, lords and rulers in all lands,
Is this the handiwork you give to God,
This monstrous thing distorted and soul-quenched?
How will you ever straighten up this shape;
Touch it again with immortality;
Give back the upward looking and the light;
Rebuild in it the music and the dream;
Make right the immemorial infamies,
Perfidious wrongs, immedicable woes?

O masters, lords and rulers in all lands,
How will the Future reckon with this Man?
How answer his brute question in that hour
When whirlwinds of rebellion shake the world?
How will it be with kingdoms and with kings—
When this dumb Terror shall reply to God,
After the silence of centuries?[42]

---

[42] Edwin Markham, "The Man With the Hoe," from *The Man with the Hoe and Other Poems*, (New York: McClure, Phillips and Co., 1902), pp. 2, 3.

Reformation or Revolution?

Epilogue

Reflections on Reform

After every "failure" of the reformer,
    There mysteriously materializes
The omnipresent truth-giver,
    Who meditates and analyzes.

With great ardor and enthusiasm
    He sets about his task;
How the reformer could have been saved,
    Had he but condescended to ask.

"It's not his goals nor objectives
    With which we take exception;
But, his unbending dedication
    Coupled with myopic perception."

"He never sees the Big Picture," is heard
    The cry from countenance grim,
"He is his own worst enemy,
    Alienating those who could help him."

The explanations and analyses
    Flow freely from the critic's pen
Who shirks not from his mission
    Of proclaiming "what might have been."

The wounded reformer rises
    From the field of battle,
To ward off assassination
    By the purveyors of prattle.

"Where were you when I needed you?"
    He cries aloud in vain
"When they took me to the Wall,
    For my ideas to be slain.

"Where are your wounds?
    Have you been to the Wall?
Have you known the loneliness
    Of answering the Call?

"Do you have the audacity to suggest,
    To both the masters and the slaves,
The 'folly' of probing the gruesome soil
    For inmates consigned to graves?

"Are you really suggesting
    From your 'knowledge' and 'wisdom'
That you can pose a solution
    Without understanding the problem?

"I shall believe your truth
    Does not foretell disaster
In that illusory day when the
    Slave embraces his Master.

> "When you show me your
> Wounds from battle fresh
> Then shall you have the right
> To attack my flesh.
>
> "If you would speak with authority
> To convince those behind bars,
> Then you must display your credentials—
> You must show them your scars."[1]

As Joe Lohman contended, the efficacy of a solution is predetermined by the decision maker's perception of the problem. When natural catastrophes were attributed to the displeasure of deities, human sacrifice for appeasement of the gods was the solution. When human illness was diagnosed as a case of "bad blood," the physician applied leeches to drain the plasma from the patient. When criminal behavior was seen as a result of slothfulness, training in good work habits was the remedy.

If one accepts certain premises, then the conclusions logically follow. And therein lies a major difficulty with social reform. Everything appears logical as long as one never questions the original hypotheses. However, those people willing to risk ostracism can succinctly set forth the unhappy consequences of traditional courses of action while suggesting more viable perceptions of the problem.

It is not particularly difficult to see that problems exist in every area of society, including the penal system. But the real causes of the problems must be rooted out before it is possible to develop a strategy of intervention that has the greatest prognosis for success and before resources can be mobilized to implement the necessary remedy. The major difficulty confronting the social reformer is not conceptualization of the problems; it lies in the dilemmas that emerge as a result of conflicting interests involved in resolving those problems. Unfortunately, the dilemmas are masked by the hidden agenda of reform movements. Those reform "actors" with low perception levels can be deluded by the facade of reform, co-opted by the gradualism theory of change, and deceived by the myths of rehabilitation. They can be diverted by the art of nonreform, seduced by the Clark Kent syndrome, or neutralized by accepting the dogmas of penology. Those reformers who successfully navigate the maze of rhetoric find themselves, not in the promised land, but in a state of confusion. The real reformers who survive the selection process and who perceive both the basic problem and the probable solution find themselves in the midst of the quandary.

---

[1] Tom Murton, "Show Me Your Scars," *The Freeworld Times*.

Although it has been demonstrated that incremental changes do not result in real reform, "radical" innovations instituted rapidly do not have longevity. Thus it appears impossible to assess the value of one method over the other. The level to which thwarted radical reform efforts regress may not seem significantly above the level achieved by the gradualism theory; therefore, is the trauma of the former approach warranted?

The would-be reformer quickly learns that it is necessary to possess power to effect change. Yet how does one achieve power in a corrupt system without becoming corrupt? The trap of the Clark Kent syndrome is obviously self-defeating. But if one maintains his integrity, it is equally obvious that he will be neutralized by transfer, promotion, or expulsion from the system, and his effective power is therefore lost.

Realizing that if he is not in the system he has little potential for changing it, the reformer may be duped into a false assumption that if he compromises his integrity sufficiently to survive professionally, then he will be able to bring about the desired change. Confusion often arises over the fuzzy distinction between compromise of strategy and compromise of integrity. Integrity, which is more easily recognized than defined, is an elusive trait that means different things to different people. The difficulty is in choosing the right time and place to draw the line of no compromise. Different actors will draw the line at different points that will be most functional for them and the movement at that time. Critical examination is required to assure that the line is not drawn arbitrarily, prematurely, or over a nonessential element of the reform movement.

It must be recognized that systems are designed for stability, order, and control and not for change, flexibility, or self-improvement. The managers of the existing systems are not "evil" men; they are weak. They are not willing to risk failure to achieve success. Therefore it is not the agents of the organism, per se, that must be attacked, but the organism itself. Although the organism is constituted by the collective individuals who keep the machine operating, it is not the *individuals* who are the real enemies of reform but the collective organizational mind that directs, coordinates, and sustains the status quo.

The reformer is aware that the prison does not exist in a vacuum but is part of a larger criminal justice system that maintains equilibrium through functional (if undesirable) trade-offs among the component parts. Furthermore, a real modification of the criminal justice system cannot be accomplished outside the awareness that it too is only part of the larger society. The reformer who is not overwhelmed by the enormity of total reorganization of the entire society will come full cycle and restrict his efforts to a specific problem area within which he has both the power and expertise to exercise his potential for change.

Once he has experienced a serious effort to change the system, the reformer is faced with the consequences of aborted reform efforts. He may correctly conclude that his efforts have been antithetical to future and present reform efforts. The reformer suffers personal agony resulting from the knowledge that he contributed to the abortion of reform. While preparing himself to go forth in search of other dragons to slay, he may ponder the virtue of having lighted the candle of hope for the inmates with the foreknowledge that it would inevitably be blown out.

The slave once temporarily freed is never thereafter content to remain shackled. Had the reformer not offered hope, the inmate would not have known the taste of freedom, and thus he could have served out his time without becoming frustrated over "what might have been." The real reformer accepts as an article of faith that it is often necessary for a few to suffer temporarily in order that the greater number may gain in the long run. He is compelled to fulfill his mission irrespective of the knowledge that the opponents of real reform also will fulfill their mission with equal vigor.

The prison physician finds some comfort in this rationale as he fulfills his obligations by healing the condemned prisoner. Others perform their functions by executing the healed prisoner. Each may one day be held accountable for his actions.

One cannot justify personal inaction by arguing that others also fail to perform or that they will neutralize his efforts. Achievements are brought about by those who dare to ask "Why not?"

One difficulty in assessing real reform efforts may be because the inmate, the officer, and the system all possess only an abstract idea of what justice, equity, dignity, and integrity are all about. Reform efforts may not bear fruit immediately because they simply have sown the seeds of change in the fallow field of penology. They may lie dormant until their time has come to germinate, and in that day some may reap what others have sown. Thus those who would change the system must not lose heart because of the paucity of immediate gains. Judgment should be reserved until all the evidence is presented and a long-range assessment is possible from a historical perspective.

The dilemmas of prison reform are not easily resolved individually or collectively. At best, each of us must decide for himself what is the right approach to achieve what he thinks needs to be done to change the society. The only thing that will cause a reform movement to "fail" is underestimating the reformer's ability to "succeed."

> *The possibilities of human achievement are limited primarily by the arbitrary boundaries we ourselves place on our own imagination.*

As the Scriptures tell us, the dictum that there is "a time to be born and a time to die"[1] applies universally to all mankind. The uncertainty lies in the different time span for each individual between those two events. Each person is alloted a specific, but unknown, number of hours, days, and years of existence on this Planet Earth. No one can foretell his birth; only a few, by their own hands, can predict their deaths.

The crucial consideration, then, is not how long the journey is for each of us between the Womb and the Tomb. The significant criteria for evaluating our effectiveness will be how we dealt with our fellow wayfarers, how we faced adversity, and whether we used our talents honorably. As we approach the Tomb and cast one last glance over our shoulder at the trail we have traversed, will we be able to say with the apostle Paul, "I have fought a good fight, I have finished my course, I have kept the faith"?[2]

Life is not *given* to each mortal soul; neither is it earned. Life is entrusted to us on loan for an undetermined period of time. Interest on that debt begins at birth and continues to death, and payment in talents is demanded from time to time along the journey. For those who are given many talents, the interest payment is proportionately higher.

As we enter the world from the Womb owning nothing, so we must enter the Tomb owing nothing. To do less means we have failed to pay our dues for the privilege of life. Since we do not know our day of reckoning, the ledger must be balanced daily so that there will be no outstanding indebtedness when the book of life is closed. Responsibility requires no more; integrity demands no less.

---

[1] Eccles. 3:2.
[2] 2 Tim. 4:7.

Epilogue